D0176369

THE Rebel Rules

DARING TO BE YOURSELF IN BUSINESS

Chip Conley

A Fireside Book
Published by Simon & Schuster
New York London Toronto Sydney Singapore

FIRESIDE
Rockefeller Center
1230 Avenue of the Americas
New York, NY 10020

Designed by William P. Ruoto

Manufactured in the United States of America

10 9 8 7 6 5 4 3 2 1

Library of Congress Cataloging-in-Publication Data
Conley, Chip
The rebel rules : daring to be yourself in business/Chip Conley.
p. cm.
"A Fireside book."
Includes index.
1. Success in business. 2. Creative ability in business.
3. Entrepreneurship. I. Title.

HF5386.C746 2001
658.4'09—dc21 00-059600

ISBN 0-684-86516-5

Acknowledgments

I must be insane. How did I think I could run a fast-growing company and pen a manifesto at the same time? This past year and a half is full of stretch marks. Yet, there's absolutely no way I could have birthed this rebel handbook without the help of a remarkable support network.

There's the vision team that kept me focused on the big picture. Seth Godin, Barb Waugh, and Rob Delamater helped keep my mind open, even in the midst of writer's block. And Anthony Laurino, Joie de Vivre's graphics guru, took my vision and put it into pictures. The passion team kept me fueled up with encouragement. Samantha Bryer, Pamela Adams, and my sister Anne helped edit, research, and pump me up when my spirits would flag. My cousin Ed Stackler, editor extraordinaire, led the instinct team—the folks who corrected my syntax and refocused me when I was hopelessly out on a limb. Finally, thanks to the folks who kept me agile—Jack Kenny and the Joie de Vivre management team—by helping steer the company while I suffered through months of my red-eyed distractions.

Thank you to the dozens of rebels who lent me their expertise and wisdom. *The Rebel Rules* is the manifestation of a movement of courageous and authentic business superstars who are truly changing the way we work. My list wouldn't be complete without my friends from the literary world. My agent, Amy Rennert, pushed me out to the end of the diving board and told me to jump. And my editors at Simon & Schuster, Airie Dekidjiev and Doris Cooper, taught me how to swim.

Finally, just a few random thank-yous. To Oren Bronstein, for the remarkable partnership, the never-ending support, and the truly incomparable design talent. I couldn't have done it all without you. To Larry Broughton, for helping breast-feed Joie de Vivre in its early years. To Steve and Fran Conley, for always believing in me. To the late Glenn Wilbur and the late Debra Pultz, who were part of the fearsome foursome JdV brain trust in our formative years. To Shawn Hall and Jann Eyrich, who designed and renovated our first couple of ventures. To Dick Bernstein and Jay B. Hunt, who always had more than a little wisdom to offer me. To Bill Kimpton, for his inspiration and support. To April Murphy and Scott DeGuzman, for connecting me with Richard. To Cecil Williams, Janice Mirikitani, and Douglas Fitch, for providing me a spiritual rebel role model of courage of authenticity. To David Sibbet and the Grove Consultants, for making my vision visual. To Diana Arsenian, for her spirit and infectious optimism. To Kathy McKenzie, for supplying me with the beachside writing cottage I'd always imagined. And last but not least, an enormous thank-you to my associates at Joie de Vivre. On a daily basis, these people make these rebel practices a reality. As a team, we don't always get it right, but the *joie de vivre* spirit that exists in our people is the most valuable asset of this rebel company.

Contents

THE Rebel Rules

Foreword

Richard Branson, Founder and Chairman, Virgin Group of Companies

I've spent a lifetime thriving on opportunism and adventure. If business weren't so much damn fun, I wouldn't be doing it. Sometimes people ask me what's my secret to success. There is no secret. There is no formula. While it is impossible to distill the essence of a business philosophy into an easy-to-use recipe, Chip Conley has done a remarkable job outlining some of the common principles that define successful entrepreneurs and innovative companies.

For the longest time, I felt like a walking oxymoron: the rebel businessman. I was a black sheep among sacred white cows. But during the past decade, I haven't felt quite so lonely. The rebel insurgents are gaining a stronger foothold in the starched corporate boardroom. Steve Jobs, Anita Roddick, Herb Kelleher, Jeff Bezos: the youth movement of the sixties has merged with the practicalities of the digital nineties. The result, as Chip Conley so aptly puts it in this book, is a rebel revolution of the Woodstock and Internet generations. For the first time in modern business, companies are actively recruiting rebels into their ranks to initiate innovation and change.

Of course, the Internet has accelerated this revolution. Built on an infrastructure of openness and free communication, the Internet is a democratic medium that gives power to the people. Internet companies play on a more level playing field, as the start-up costs are much more manageable—especially compared to airlines and cola companies. It is a business model that is ripe for the curious, the idealists, the adventurous—in other words, rebels. During the sixties and seventies, these folks devoted their rebel energies to saving the world. Now they've come to recognize that business can be the greatest vehicle for social change. This book serves as a handbook for people who want to make a difference. *The Rebel Rules* emphasizes four talents that define the business rebel: *vision*, *passion*, *instinct*, and *agility*.

Chip and I were rebels long before the current dot-com revolution. We found success as unyielding lunatics with a wacky idea. Some might call that being visionary. Others have called me delusional, wondering how the guy who brought you the Sex Pistols (with Virgin Records) could also offer you financial advice and a pension (with Virgin Direct). The fact is, "visionary" is a title we bestow on someone after they've proven that they were right. My vision has never been rigid. It's constantly changing, just like the company. Visionless companies are dead organisms. Yet, companies like Virgin are constantly mutating—organically synthesizing new ideas that help build the brand in both the heart and mind of our customers. Virgin enjoys being the underdog. Our goal is to be the consumer's champion, finding stodgy industries like air and train transport, financial services, and cola, and shaking them up. As someone once said, vision is all about seeing the invisible. I think it's also about imagining the unimaginable.

Once the vision is established, rebels need to engage their employees and customers with a passionate zeal that verges on the missionary. Virgin's brand identity has grown because we make each new business a crusade: an epic struggle to beat the big guys and deliver value to our customers. But without an ample dollop of fun and frivolity, this struggle wouldn't carry much momentum. Virgin has succeeded by connecting with the hearts of our employees, making them passionate entrepreneurs in their own right. I love the Joie de Vivre Heart icon that Chip uses to illustrate how a passionate corporate culture breeds happy employees, which leads to satisfied customers, which results in a profitable and sustainable business. For too many companies, the blood in this heart moves in the opposite direction.

Next there's gut instinct. People often ask me how I come up with new business ideas. The truth is that I just try satisfying myself and follow my instincts. For example, back in 1992 during the depths of the recession, I was trying to raise money to install individual seat-back video terminals in all our Virgin Atlantic aircraft. I was committed to Virgin's having the best in-flight entertainment, and I knew that I'd be a little more satisfied as a customer if my airline provided me this service. Even though my gut told me this was the right move, it was virtually impossible to finance this $10 million systemwide installation. But I persevered (ultimately calling the CEOs of Boeing and Airbus) and found that it was much easier financing the purchase of a $4 billion new fleet of planes with these video terminals than it was to get the $10 million credit for the video sets alone. Thus we were the first in the airline industry to offer this unique service, and as is typical for rebels, the big guys were copying us as soon as they could get their act together.

The final talent is agility, a quality that favors the little guy. Soon after I'd established Virgin as a mail-order record company in the early seventies, Britain experienced a six-month postal strike. You can imagine an undercapitalized twenty-year-old trying to survive when our method of distribution was eliminated overnight. Within days of the strike, I opened our first Virgin retail record store above a shoe shop. If we hadn't reinvented ourselves, Virgin would never have survived. This little record store and the ones we opened soon after taught me virtually everything I needed to know about retailing firsthand. I can see the seeds of this early learning in our current Virgin Megastores even though the scale is now much larger. As Virgin has grown, we've become a big brand made up of small companies. We can still identify opportunities and move quickly. It took us just five months to take Virgin Atlantic airborne after our first conversation about the airline, and almost the exact same amount of time to launch Virgin Direct, our financial services arm.

God bless the rebels. We'd live in an awfully boring world without these crazy fools. But just being crazy and adventurous isn't enough. That's why I enjoyed reading *The Rebel Rules.* It gave me some tools and strategies that can help any new business. I was impressed to find that Chip adheres to one of the same practices I follow when I launch a start-up: calling new customers. Each time Virgin Atlantic starts a new air route, I call about fifty customers per month to ask them about our service. This keeps me close to the customer and helps me understand the challenges our staff is facing. So being a rebel isn't all about courage, charisma, and creativity. It's a matter of creating personal habits that help me to serve my employees and customers.

How do you know if you're a rebel? Rebels live by this rule: "The more people say it can't be done, the more I want to do it." My headmaster told me during my teen years that I would either go to prison or become a millionaire. By the time you've finished this book, you'll recognize whether you've got a little rebel inside you. Whether you're a rebel or not, just make sure whatever you do, enjoy it to the fullest. Cheers!

I. INTRODUCTION

The New Rules of Business

With unsettling speed, two powerful forces are converging: a new generation of leaders is coming to power in the business world, and a group of "fast companies" is rewriting the rules of doing business around the world. The result: a revolution as far-reaching as the Industrial Revolution 100 years ago.

—*Fast Company* magazine

A generation ago, rebels staged sit-ins and set their bras aflame. Today rebels create start-ups and light their companies on fire. We live in a time of rapid change. Today's business leaders do not try to anticipate the future. They create it. The ones who build the right model become billionaires.

A changing world demands daring, break-all-the-rules leaders. The Industrial Revolution took nearly a half-century to mature and was based upon increasing "muscle power" by forty- or fiftyfold. Today's digital revolution is happening virtually overnight and in magnitudes of a millionfold. The effect of this change is pervasive. We're all touched by it.

Maybe that's why rebel entrepreneurs have become the world's business folk heroes: they are a barometer to our brighter future. Personified by pop icons like Richard Branson, today's business success stories are high-profile rebels, authentic and courageous initiators of change. Their companies are a direct extension of who they are. Ironically, these nonconformists provide us comfort and hope: be yourself and you'll be a success. Never before has the business world experienced such a universal quest for originality and such a disdain for the status quo. As *BOBOS in Paradise* author David Brooks writes, "It's Lucent Technologies that adopted the slogan 'Born to Be Wild.' It's Burger King that tells America, 'Sometimes You Gotta Break the Rules.'"

REBELS RULE WITH COURAGE AND AUTHENTICITY

The day I began writing this book, I found under my computer monitor an old postcard of James Dean, a forty-year-old poster child for disaffection, apathy, and danger. James Dean: the "rebel without a cause."

For me, though, the business rebel succeeds because of an obsession *with* a cause. While many shaggy new business leaders of this digital era may look like a James Dean character or sport a disaffected-youth image, their impatience and determination are fueled by a contrarian concept or cause—often a simple desire to beat the big guys.

While the money being made on stock options are the gravy, what inspires these rebels isn't usually money. It's the need to prove themselves, the sense of mission in their product or concept, the desire to experiment, and their love of the work itself. Today's Internet generation has learned that there is no better place to make an impact than in the business world.

Professor Frank Farley at Temple University calls these rebels the "Type-T Personality," those thrill-seekers who are willing to take risks to test their limits. They're drawn to challenges, paradoxes, and new ideas. They break rules, resist authority, and can't stand calm. They're some of our best-known entrepreneurs—and some of our most feared sociopaths. How can you tell the difference?

The litmus test for rebels is whether they are courageous and authentic, whether they stand their ground against the voice of conventional wisdom. Like Bob Pittman, president of America Online, who helped create MTV at a time when everyone said, "Music is meant to be heard, not seen." Or Steve Jobs and Steve Wozniak, who while barely of legal drinking age founded the modern version of the personal computer after the experts at Xerox said there wasn't a market for such a contraption. Like Anita Roddick of The Body Shop, rebels wear their values on their sleeves and use their companies as a vehicle for change.

Rebels stage revolutions, internally and externally. The greatest rebels are those who have completely changed their industry. They don't stop at challenging the status quo, they break the mold. Sam Walton did this in retail. Jeff Bezos did this with e-commerce. Martha Stewart's done it with brand identity.

The successful rebels are those who can capture the minds and spirits of their organization and leverage that "intellectual capital" into a sustainable force to be reckoned with. Rebel companies can't just be judged by their balance sheets. Today's new math requires that intangible assets, such as capacity for learning, networking prowess, and brand reputation be virtually as relevant as the warehouses and equipment. Competition today is about how much innovation an organization creates, not about how many factories it builds.

The old-school behemoth companies that have fallen asleep at the wheel (I call them "Rip van Rockefellers") enter the new millennium with RIP chiseled on their corporate forehead. Why didn't Maxwell House create Starbucks (as my friend Seth Godin ponders)? Or why did it take so long for Merrill Lynch and other traditional brokerage companies to jump on the online trading bandwagon (yet Charles Schwab was able to make the leap quite early)? Success handcuffs yesterday's champions as they tinker with yesterday's successful business model. Newcomers have an advantage in today's rebellious marketplace as they're willing to scrap the old model for something improved.

What makes this particular time unique is the confluence of factors that have thrust rebels into the limelight. The corporate reengineering and downsizing of the early 1990s forced middle managers to rethink their concept of job security. The net result: For every job wiped out at a major company in the mid-1990s, 1.5 jobs sprang up in its place, mostly in small firms. By 1995, only 10 percent of all American jobs existed in *Fortune* 500 companies, a group that accounted for 20 percent of all jobs thirty years earlier. And with the proliferation of personal computers and the emergence of the Internet, anyone with an extra bedroom can create their world headquarters at home. For the first time, the playing field had been leveled for David and Goliath.

I learned my own Rebel Rumba when I started my company at twenty-six. I broke the two cardinal rules for starting a business: pick something you know and think location, location, location. I had no experience in the hospitality industry, and my first two key decisions were picking an unpronounceable name (Joie de Vivre) and purchasing a bankrupt "no-tell motel" in the wrong part of town. My friends called me "Mr. Bad Ass-ets."

Joie de Vivre Hospitality has grown into one of the largest hospitality companies on the West Coast, with twenty-five businesses under its umbrella and annual sales exceeding $50 million. Fortunately, our mission ("creating opportunities to celebrate the joy of life") helped us find the enthusiasm to overcome many of the classic obstacles a young rebel entrepreneur encounters.

Francis Ford Coppola, filmmaker, winemaker, hotelier, and rebel through and through, said, "Everything I love has in one way or another become a business for me." This was a guiding inspiration for me as I grew a company that challenged the status quo. I followed my heart creating projects that hadn't been done before—hospitality businesses that would attract a guy like me as a customer. While my goal wasn't intentionally to shake up a stodgy industry, the result of my company's creative endeavors was to force my elder hotelier peers into a little professional soul-searching.

Joie de Vivre is a classic rebel company, an "incubator for entrepreneurs." My greatest challenge has been translating my passion for calculated risk-taking to the employees who operate our hotels, motels, resorts, campgrounds, restaurants, bars, and day spas. The common thread throughout is creating products and an atmosphere that foster *joie de vivre.*

Virgin has taken a similar eclectic approach globally—with airlines, colas, record stores, and even bridal shops—all with that quirky and fun sensibility that defines the brand. Fortunately, Joie de Vivre's odd business strategy has succeeded, as we were recently named San Francisco's "Emerging Growth Company of the Year"—no mean feat in a community brimming with prosperous Internet start-ups that could just have easily won the award.

The Rebel Rules is your wake-up call—a personal handbook to help transform you into a groundbreaking leader in whatever you do and to give you another way to look at the traditional business model—whether you're a young hipster in a start-up or a middle-aged manager in a multinational conglomerate. Those of us who continue to use the old rule book are going to be left behind. Though the world may seem increasingly out of control, *The Rebel Rules* focuses on what you *can* control: your own habits and aptitudes.

My purpose is to help you capitalize on your own natural talents by showing how other rebels have flourished using theirs. There is no right kind of rebel. Ross Perot has little in common with Master P other than the fact that they've both revolutionized their industries. It isn't enough to dare to be different. You need to dare to be yourself. Hopefully, *The Rebel Rules* will provide you the philosophy, attitude, and strategies you need to find your own path.

The entrepreneur starting a business will learn valuable lessons and hear straight talk from people who've learned from the school of hard knocks. The corporate manager will learn how America's largest companies have realized you have to "think small to grow big" and how they're dramatically altering their rules to encourage rebellious behavior because otherwise they'll be "Amazoned" or "eToyed" to death (challenged by an Internet start-up such as occurred to Barnes & Noble and Toys "R" Us).

The rebel working for a nonprofit or in the government will see why the principles in this book apply universally to anyone who wants to create a humane and empowered workplace. Today nearly every organization is becoming more rebellious, helping their people recycle themselves as entrepreneurs.

Being a rebel is like sipping from the fountain of youth—you're infused with irrepressible enthusiasm and boundless energy for your mission. Ideally, your chosen work is a natural extension of you. One of the best compliments I ever received was when someone told me they could see my "messy, unique fingerprints all over the product." Work should be like grown-up fingerpainting. *The Rebel Rules* will help turn your fingerpainting into a successful, unique business model. Your legacy isn't just the company you've built. It's the business model you've created and taught your people.

II. FEELING EIGHTEEN YEARS OLD AGAIN AND ACTING LIKE IT

1. Getting in Touch with Your "Inner Rebel"

What seems different in yourself; that's the rare thing you possess. The one thing that gives each of us his worth, and that's just what we try to suppress.

—André Gide

Most of us feel the pulse of our talent at a very young age. We know intuitively who we are and have a passion for discovery. Somehow though, as we grow older we fall into culturally proscribed patterns that create a wedge between our tightly scripted public image and our original private reality. The wider that wedge grows, the further we are from authenticity and happiness.

You can see the origins of many business rebels in their childhood. Most accomplished leaders and geniuses have managed to weave their childhood passions and aptitudes into their career. Richard Branson pieced together a couple of seemingly disparate businesses: breeding parrots and growing Christmas trees. Al Ramadan, founder of the innovative Internet media network Quokka Sports, was an antiestablishment Australian surfer and skateboarder dude when he was a teenager. Now, Al is changing the way the world experiences spectator sports by allowing people to follow adventurers on their climbs of Mount Everest or their solo sailing treks around the world. Bob Moog, founder of University Games (America's third-largest board game company), fell in love with games as a kid when he shared a room with his disabled younger brother. Creating new games comes naturally to Bob, even in his adult years.

This chapter is dedicated to helping you do your best at *what you do best*—in effect, to turn up the volume on your rebel amplifier. Unfortunately, most adults tend to get caught up in day-to-day, task-oriented achievements. Then one day we wake up and realize that we've become masters of meaningless tasks yet failed to accomplish anything that's truly satisfying. You've heard of having a midlife crisis: it's just another way of saying you've lost touch with your "inner rebel."

Becoming a business rebel is like turning back the clock. We all know that true rebels march to the beat of their own drummer, but quite often they are unaware of just how unusual they may appear, like the child banging a pot on his head or the kid making herself dizzy turning in circles. Such youthful zeal can be infectious. That's why many of us are strangely drawn to the rebel—one part envy and one part pure fascination.

Pablo Picasso said, "Every child is an artist . . . the problem is how to remain an artist once he grows up." How far have you strayed from your childhood rebel? Take this test to determine the current state of your rebel consciousness.

ARE YOU A REBEL?

1. How important are others' opinions to you when you're determining an important course of action?
   (a) Very
   (b) Somewhat
   (c) Not important

2. When you show up at a cocktail party, how often are you dressed in accordance with the official or unspoken dress code of the event?
   (a) Often
   (b) Sometimes
   (c) Almost never

3. How often do your activities provide you with that ecstasy that makes you completely lose track of time?

(a) *I don't know what you're talking about*
(b) *Relatively regularly*
(c) *Those are the only kind of experiences I'm aware of*

4. Is your career a direct reflection of who you are and a natural progression from your most innate childhood skills?
(a) *No*
(b) *Sort of*
(c) *Absolutely*

5. If you were to discover a list of your favorite future jobs that you created at age ten, fifteen, or twenty, how far from the top is your current job?
(a) *My current job wouldn't be on the list*
(b) *Probably about midway down the list*
(c) *Near the top*

6. What's the most accurate description of your teenage personality?
(a) *Straight-A student, big man/woman on campus, homecoming king/queen*
(b) *Jock, nerd, druggie*
(c) *Juvenile delinquent, naïve idealist, artist-freak*

7. If someone asked you "What would you attempt if you knew you could not fail?" how would you respond?
(a) *How could I be assured I wouldn't fail?*
(b) *I'd probably quit my job and follow my lifelong passion of . . .*
(c) *That's a stupid question!*

8. How quickly could you answer the question "In what field would you like to be the world's leading expert?"
(a) *Let me think about it and I'll get back to you*
(b) *Fifteen minutes*
(c) *I thought you already knew that I'm the world's leading expert in . . .*

9. Think back to age eighteen and the social or political causes that most stirred your passion. How do those causes compare with your current beliefs?

(a) My passions were much stronger then—my current beliefs aren't as clear since I'm not so blindly idealistic
(b) I think I'm almost as passionate, but my beliefs have changed some
(c) I'm more passionate about those causes today than I was at age twenty

10. When someone says "No" to you, what's your emotional reaction?
    (a) Dejection or acceptance
    (b) Disappointment or anger
    (c) I don't accept "No" for an answer

Now tally your answers, scoring each "a" answer with one point, each "b" answer wtih two points, and each "c" answer with three points. If you scored:

10–16 = Anti-Rebel: We've got lots of work to do in the next few chapters.
17–24 = Budding Rebel: You've got potential as long as you follow your passion.
25–30 = True Rebel: You should be writing this book!

FINDING YOUR GLASS SLIPPER

I wish someone had asked me, "What do you want to *be* when you grow up?" I was too focused on what I wanted to *do*. As with many of you, my growing-up experience taught me more about what I *don't* do well than what I *do* do well. Somehow modern culture forgot the important message of Cinderella's fairy tale—that there is a perfect-sized glass slipper out there for every child. Our work needs to fit our passions and aptitudes just like our shoes need to fit our feet. But most of us end up wearing an awfully uncomfortable pair of shoes.

Ironically, I became aware of my sore feet while attending perhaps the ultimate socializing institution—graduate business school. (My rebel-in-the-making classmate Bob Moog, mentioned earlier in this chapter, had dirty feet all through business school since he never wore shoes.) Surrounded by other competitive, people-pleasing Stanford M.B.A.'s, I became hyperaware of how I differed from my classmates. I'd spent high school and college wearing the slightly ill-fitting mask of superachiever, but underneath I feared being an outcast while longing to be a rebel. Following the lead of my competitive peers in business school, I initially tried to compete according to the traditional investment banker/management consultant rules. But, it wasn't working.

Almost without realizing it, I began to withdraw from the business school routine, strangely drawn to studio art classes instead. In the end, I took nearly a half-dozen studio art classes far away from my M.B.A. brethren. It was nearly graduation time when I remembered that the last time I'd taken an art class had been in the seventh grade with Mrs. Ada Wurst. Ironically, it wasn't until I surrounded myself with a group of M.B.A.'s, with whom I thought I had everything in common, that I learned how far I had strayed from my true path.

Although it took business school to stoke my rebel fire, there were many indications of it in my childhood. Until my teen years, when I blossomed into Mr. Popular, I was a loner who had a collection of imaginary friends. I kept notebooks of fantasy sport leagues I'd created. I pretended to make movies in the jungle of our backyard. And, as a precursor to what would come later, I even sketched a floor plan for a resort hotel and set up a restaurant in my mom's kitchen (we only served dessert, and this venture lasted less than a week). Fortunately, by my mid-twenties, I was able to realize that my creative abilities were an asset.

Most people never make this connection. They jump on society's bandwagon, averting the risk of repeating some painful childhood memory. They continue to fear and avoid dangers that, while once all too real, have no relevance in their lives today. Sometimes we even try to hide our youthful talents and gifts for fear that they're not acceptable. The net result is a disconnected life—one that is too familiar to many of us.

How do we break free from this cycle to connect with that youthful spirit? I'm reminded of Anaïs Nin's remark "Life shrinks or expands in proportion to one's courage." There was a time when we all moved from crawling to walking and from infatuation to love. It took a certain amount of fearlessness and some bruised knees and broken hearts to make these transitions. John F. Kennedy used to recount a story about a band of courageous boys he met in Ireland. The boys were afraid to climb a fence that stood virtually twice their height. So each boy threw his hat over the fence, which forced them to scale the awesome wall. What metaphorical hat can you throw over your fence?

Kirk Perron, founder of Jamba Juice, America's largest chain of juice and smoothie bars, threw his hat over the fence in high school. Kirk grew up in a family that never owned its own home. At age seventeen (after reading Robert Allen's landmark book *Nothing Down*), Kirk put a small apartment building into escrow without a clue as to how he could afford it. He put all of his savings ($2,000) in as a down payment along with $12,000 borrowed from his high school counselor, the school bus driver, and the school librarian. He got the owner to take back a second mortgage and the broker to take back a third. Kirk had an intense passion to prove that he could live the American Dream just like the families down the block. He was a landlord before he was an adult. And now, almost twenty years later as America's "Juice King," Kirk has built his mom her dream home.

This life ain't no dress rehearsal . . . no omnipotent butler will appear with a silver platter, announcing, "Your life is now served." It's up to *you* to make the shift from conformist to rebel. And you can start by going back to your roots.

★ ★ ★

BUSINESS REBEL HALL OF FAME PROFILE

Richard Branson (Founder and Chairman of the Virgin Group of Companies)

Perhaps no living businessperson personifies the Business Rebel better than Richard Branson. In his book *Losing My Virginity,* he recalls that his parents were always setting challenges for the kids. When he was eleven, his mother packed him some sandwiches and an apple and sent him off on his bike to Bournemouth, England, to visit relatives . . . more than fifty miles away.

Despite suffering from undiagnosed dyslexia that forced some overcompensating concentration, he started his first business, a magazine called *Student,* when he was sixteen. Four years later, Richard began Virgin as a mail-order record company. It has since expanded into more than one hundred businesses in areas as diverse as travel, entertainment, retailing, media, financial services, publishing, and even bridal services and soft drinks. Starting from scratch, Richard was able to build a net worth of nearly $300 million by age thirty-five and he sold his music company for nearly $1 billion at the age of forty-one.

Richard has been my inspiration because he taught me two fundamental rebel principles: (a) position yourself as the underdog and you will always find a receptive niche in the marketplace, and (b) create a product line that connects with people on an emotional level even if there's little rational connection among the products. The brand is the connection, not the products. That's rebel thinking!

THINKING OF YOUR LIFE AS A NOVEL

Getting in touch with our inner rebel requires that we reconnect with the mythology of our childhood (and, frankly, the myths we carry with us in our present-day lives too). As author Richard Stone suggests in *The Healing Art of Storytelling,* we live in a world addicted to speed and the bottom line. Few of us have the patience to listen to stories, much less explore their deeper relevance for our spiritual and emotional well-being.

Yet, as adults we allow ourselves to be ruled by the childhood conclusions we've reached regarding the meaning and relevance of our formative experiences. If we never revisit these conclusions, not only is our past frozen in time—a story with no room to breathe—our present and future may become extensions of this cold reality. The elixir of metaphor can help you to take that collection of joyful and painful childhood experiences and transform it into a story with meaning. By retelling the story, you are no longer the victim of circumstances beyond your control. You weave a persuasive tale; full of important themes that describes how you came to be who you are.

Andy Grove, former CEO of Intel and *Time*'s 1997 "Man of the Year," can point to his childhood poverty and escaping the Holocaust or his adult bout with prostate cancer. Faced with poor medical prospects, he worked with a dozen doctors to create his own successful treatment plan. Both of his stories helped his employees understand Andy's main theme that you can control your own destiny if you persevere.

If you've ever listened to a powerful CEO tell his or her story, you've witnessed the remarkable effect it can have—both in creating an intimate connection with an audience and in making sense of a life. We just may discover our own particular genius when we allow our personal saga to take shape.

Rebels need not overanalyze their past, but they do need to discover the seeds that make their life unique. Most of us are socialized into conformity during our younger years. Shoeless Bob Moog's parents sent him to St. Louis Country Day School at age ten to give him some discipline. He was forced to wear a tie and uniform daily. Beset by migraine headaches, little Bob ran away and vowed he'd never blindly submit to authority figures again. Today he's one of America's leading business rebels.

For most of us, our idiosyncrasies, rough edges, and quirky behavior become polished like a shiny apple on our teacher's desk, while innate talents and interests that could serve us well in today's business environment go by the wayside. Perhaps by re-creating your life story, you'll rediscover the origins of passions upon which you can build a career.

RECONNECTING WITH YOUR CHILDHOOD PASSIONS

Richard Stone, as well as Julia Cameron (in her book *The Artist's Way*), has created excellent exercises for getting in touch with that youthful spirit. I was inspired by these as I created some exercises that have worked for me. You may find these a little frivolous, but just relax. You're not going to show these to anyone. Let's search for some of your rebel roots.

IMAGINARY LIVES

If you had five other lives to lead, what would you do in each of them? What were your "dream careers" as a kid? Amazingly, I recently found an essay I wrote at age eight that suggested that my dreams included being a professional basketball player, a movie star, a teacher, and a "hotel man."

CHILDHOOD DETECTIVE WORK

Allow yourself to free-associate for a sentence or two to complete each of the following phrases:

- My favorite childhood toy was . . .
- My favorite childhood game was . . .
- The best movie I ever saw as a kid was . . .
- My three favorite traits/skills as a kid were . . .
- I'm most proud of the following achievements from childhood . . .
- In times of trouble, I would retreat to such familiar activities as . . .
- The habits that most upset my parents were . . .
- My favorite secret hiding place in the neighborhood was . . .
- I would completely lose track of time when I was . . .
- The best thing about my childhood room was . . . (sketch your room and house)
- The silliest thing I did as a child was . . .
- The most rebellious thing I did as a kid was . . .
- I don't do it much anymore, but I used to enjoy . . .

REBEL RECALL

Now we'll review your teen and college years—the last time many of us were inclined to rebel. If you come up with a memory or rebel role model that is particularly energizing, tape up a little reminder of this on your computer screen. You didn't lose your right to be a rebel when you became old enough to vote or drink.

- If I were twenty and had money . . . (list five adventures you'd seek out)
- If I could do it all over again and my parents had no influence over me, I would have pursued a career in . . .
- During high school, I felt the most unusual or successful when I was thinking or doing . . .
- My favorite rebel music when I was growing up was . . .
- I got my most creative ideas when I was . . . (showering, running, sleeping, making love, driving down the coast, etc.)

- During high school, I secretly admired ________ because he/she was different
- I most wanted to subvert authority on the following occasions: . . .
- My most influential rebel role model was . . .
- I can remember striking a "rebel pose" when I . . .
- My three greatest strengths in college were . . . (remember a situation that underlines each strength and create a three-to-five-sentence story for each)
- My great fears I had in high school or college that I overcame were . . . (list up to three and tell a story about the event or incident that helped you overcome each fear)
- A childhood fear I haven't overcome is . . . (how is it haunting you in your adult life?)

FINDING PASSION
This can be used for groups who need to recapture their childhood spirit. After doing some of the exercises listed in "Childhood Detective Work" and "Rebel Recall," each member of the group has one hour to go shopping for something that epitomizes their childhood passion. Then the group reconvenes for some show-and-tell, with each member telling a story about how this object evokes their childhood passion and how they can use it as a motivating influence in their adulthood.

HOW YOU BUCKED THE NORM: AN EXERCISE

Now that you've mined the depths of your past, what are the common themes? Are there parts of your life that feel like a tragedy but can be retold as a comedy, complete with a healthy sense of the lesson that was learned?

Write down three or four anecdotes that capture your formative years and have some relationship to the person you are today. Place a special focus on what made you a rebel in each instance—how you bucked the norm. Once you've gotten this minibiography on paper, try reading it out loud to yourself with a good sense of humor. Then start weaving these stories into your conversations with close friends. Don't brag. Don't focus on victimization. Don't overact. Just recount some specific unique childhood memories or pivotal life experiences that capture your nascent self.

As you gain confidence, feel free to share these stories with coworkers, and even consider using them as motivational tales for those you lead. Remember that the trick to compelling storytelling is *tension* and *discovery*. You'll probably find that as the stories become more familiar to you, they will strengthen your own rebel willpower.

This sort of storytelling has helped me to redefine my sense of success. For too long, my definition of success was prescribed by society: going to the right school, marrying the right mate, making the most amount of money, joining the right clubs. Getting in touch with my childhood path helped me to have the courage to redefine success as "that which brings me joy" (a perfect definition for a guy who founded a company with the name "Joy of Life"). I can control that which brings me joy even if I can't always control all other measurements of success. And I've been able to carry this message to my employees.

In fact, I've recounted one college story to many employees when they ask, "What got you into the hotel business?"

When I was studying in England, I traveled to Germany for a few weeks of hitchhiking. Somewhere near the Black Forest, I contracted a serious bug that had me rushing to the bushes by the autobahn every few minutes. Needless to say, I didn't get far with my hitchhiking. I ended up in a small town, feverishly sweating and carrying precious little money. Speaking no German, I was panicked. Somehow, I found an innkeeper named Maria who was willing to rent me a room in her bed-and-breakfast for half-price.

For the next two days, I suffered through this illness while Maria cooked me homemade chicken soup and concocted strange-smelling herbal potions. I was feverish and worried, yet somehow I felt safe in Maria's home even though she didn't speak a word of English. Once I started recovering, I noticed that Maria had placed a bouquet of flowers next to my bed to cheer me up and left me three days' worth of *International Herald Tribunes*. Finally, I felt strong enough to walk and we spent a lovely afternoon together, with Maria showing me all of her favorite shops and streets in the village. I left the next day, feeling like I'd spent a long weekend with a long-lost friend.

I tell this story because it demonstrates the nobility of the hospitality industry. Many of our new employees have jobs that some would find demeaning—dishwashers, room cleaners, bellmen, night auditors. Without a sense of purpose, these jobs can be mere drudgery. But our mission statement, "creating opportunities to celebrate the joy of life," reminds us that our actions make other people feel good. Just like Maria, our employees can make travelers feel at home even when they're from halfway around the world.

Stories help give your employees a clear picture of what their lives will be like if they carry out their responsibilities properly. A good storyteller can paint a compelling future that employees find motivating. When this works, you can hear your people saying, "How can I help to get us there?" Your personal story also gives you and your employees momentum. With a little attitude adjustment, you can develop a powerful sense of purpose that will help jump-start your career and make you a role model for your staff.

HOW TO CREATE YOUR OWN PERSONAL MISSION STATEMENT

Corporate mission statements can be like dusty trophies on a mantel. Or worse, they can be the subject of derision by employees if management isn't "walking the talk."

Your personal mission statement doesn't have to appear on any wall or mantel. It just needs to be engraved on your heart and mind (our employees created T-shirts with their personal statements, such as "Play life like it's the bottom of the ninth" or "Be the ultimate boss I always wanted: listen, acknowledge, lead with confidence"). The purpose of creating one is to remind you why you're here on earth and to compel you to do something about it today. Your mission statement ought to feel like a natural extension of who you are. Ask yourself the following questions.

1. *What do I want to be remembered for? What's my destiny? (Management guru Peter Drucker says that one of his formative experiences was when his religion teacher asked him and his teenage classmates these provocative questions.)*

2. What habits would I need to cultivate and what would I have to jettison from my present life to live out my true life purpose?

3. What are the most important personal accomplishments I can imagine in my life?

Once you've answered these questions, take an hour to write a page about your personal mission statement. Then, in fifteen minutes, synthesize that page into a paragraph. Once you've done that, choose three to five favorite words in the paragraph and create one sentence that summarizes your personal mission statement. Joie de Vivre used this process to develop our company's mission statement: creating opportunities to celebrate the joy of life.

You may be a little skeptical at this point. Don't be. You have years of conformist conditioning clouding your brain. Reigniting your rebel spirit won't happen overnight, but here are some exercises that will help you reinforce your sense of rebellious enthusiasm in the workplace on a daily basis.

LEARNING FROM YOUR JOB HISTORY

Take out a sheet of paper and make a job history of every job you've ever had (including that four-day gig with McDonald's at the fry station). List the positives and negatives of each job. Compare them with your current job. Do you see any common themes?

	Positives	**Negatives**
Paperboy	Freedom—no boss	Hated the rainy days
	Good money	Hands got dirty with newsprint
	Enjoy riding bike	Had to get up very early
Waiter	Good service = Good tips	Don't like smiling all day
	Short hours	My feet were always hurting

(continues)

(continued)	**Positives**	**Negatives**
Insurance Sales	Enjoyed selling things	Didn't like wearing a tie
	Liked commissions	Office politics
	Freedom	Insurance isn't creative enough
Advertising Executive	Enjoyed creating stories	Being inside all day
	Liked selling to clients	Occasional crazy client
	Casual and fun office	Don't own the firm

Based upon this profile, I wouldn't be surprised if this person didn't own a small advertising agency soon. He prefers creativity, performance-based compensation, and the freedom to control his environment. What does your history tell you?

When I looked at my own job history, I found that the common positive themes revolved around freedom to be myself, the ability to measure myself against others, and the opportunity for public recognition (working as a raw land salesman in Silicon Valley, research director for a congressional campaign). Environments that wore me down required too much linear thinking or repetitive work, a formal hierarchical structure, or they were situations in which I didn't feel I could make a difference such as working at McDonald's, my college paper route, working as an intern on Capitol Hill.

THE FRUSTRATIONS TABLE: HOW TO BRING ABOUT PERSONAL CHANGE

Most of us—consciously or unconsciously—know what's messing with our peace of mind. Yet few of us take steps to change the situation as frustrations, fear, and fatigue set in. This exercise will help you break out of your malaise.

Every Wednesday, make a list of your five biggest work frustrations (ranking them from first to fifth). After you've done this for four weeks or so, start plotting them on a chart to determine the recurring themes. Rebels aren't complacent, so they're unlikely to allow a first-tier frustration to last more than a few consecutive weeks. Letting chronic frustrations continue is the most common way we dampen our enthusiasm. After a while, you feel so powerless that you accept what was once previously unacceptable. Charting these frustrations weekly will make you conscious of them, and maybe a little angry. That's fine. (Doing this made me realize that we needed to completely revamp our food and beverage department because it had been sitting at the top of the list for nearly two months.)

Here's a sample frustrations table:

	Week 1	Week 2	Week 3	Week 4	Week 5	Week 6
Sales Manager Attitude	1	3	4	2	1	fired
3-Months Cash Flow	2	2	2	1	3	3
Joe's Exit Interview	3					
Poor Advertising	4	5				
Staff Morale	5	1	3	3	4	4
Accounting Ineffective		4				
Working Too Many Hours			1			1
Investors Are Antsy				5	5	5
Sales Not Meeting Quota			5	4	2	2

Based upon this profile, it looks like it made sense to make a change in the sales manager position since improvements weren't occurring and it was affecting sales quotas. Solutions for cash flow and morale need to be given immediate priority, with deadlines for improvement in each. Finally, it appears that every three weeks this person burns himself out. Figure out a way to break that pattern—get a massage every other week, take one weekday off every three weeks. Do something—or this will become a destructive, long-term pattern.

You can't make your business feel young again until you've sipped from the fountain of youth yourself. William Blake said it best, "He whose face gives no light shall never become a star."

Now that we've reestablished your relationship with the rebel within, let's look at how you can use your unique talents and passions in a leadership capacity at work.

2. What It Takes to Be a Rebel

There is a vitality, a life force, an energy, a quickening that is translated through you into action. And, because there is only one of you in all time, this expression is unique. If you block it, it will never exist through any other medium, and be lost. The world will not have it. It is not your business to determine how good it is, nor how valuable, nor how it compares with other expressions. It is your business to keep it yours clearly and directly, to keep the channel open.

—Martha Graham

Why do business rebels flirt with danger? During the last week of 1998, two of the world's best-known business rebels—Virgin's Richard Branson and Oracle's Larry Ellison—attempted death-defying endeavors that landed them in the Pacific Ocean. Branson flew a hot-air balloon that didn't quite make it around the world and Ellison won an Australian yachting race that sank or crippled nearly half the boats and killed a number of sailors.

Joe Costello, the former president of Cadence Design Systems and CEO of think3, a 3-D computer software company, says learning hang-gliding taught him the value of focusing your attention on the open field ahead of you. He discovered most plane or hang-glider accidents occur because of "negative target fixation," the pilot's tendency to focus on not hitting a certain object. The way to not fall into this self-fulfilling prophecy is to focus on the open field of possibilities.

Today's new generation of leaders are not indiscriminate risk-takers, but they do love "pushing the envelope." One part courage and one part faith, business rebels live their lives with the clarity suggested by Martha Graham. The rebel stands apart from the crowd by being authentic and courageous, by channeling some higher talent that has been bestowed upon him or her.

In the new economy, there's no room for the middle manager of yesteryear whose prime skill was loyally conforming to the long-term objectives set by top management. That manager got chewed up and spit out in the nineties.

In my case, I found that I was more of a rebel artist than a businessman. Both art and business are forms of expression, but my company's growth has resulted from my recurring need to find a blank canvas on which to create. Hotels and other hospitality businesses just happen to be my media of choice—maybe because I'm a people-pleaser from way back. For me, the freedom to create and make people happy allows those creative juices to flow from my heart to my head. Maybe that's why I can't stand wearing a neck-restricting tie—it cuts off the flow.

How can you best express yourself in the business world? In the previous chapter, we learned that knowing yourself is the first step toward figuring out your calling. In this chapter, we'll explore the common talents of rebels along with their habits and some leadership exercises that will help you to find your unique path.

PUTTING YOUR WHOLE BODY INTO IT

One distinguishing characteristic of rebels is a penchant for living their cause with every cell in their body. Their approach tends to be holistic, incorporating all of their senses. When rebels are "tuned in," their external and internal antennae are buzzing, their body and mind aligned with their mission.

For this reason, the human body itself serves as a useful metaphor for the four primary traits of today's new business leaders—each represented by a different body part. These traits reinforce the courage and authenticity that set the business rebel apart from his or her colleagues. I've outlined each of the traits along with the Rebel Maladies, the symptoms of a positive trait taken to the extreme, and some home-grown remedies that can bring the body and rebel psyche back in balance.

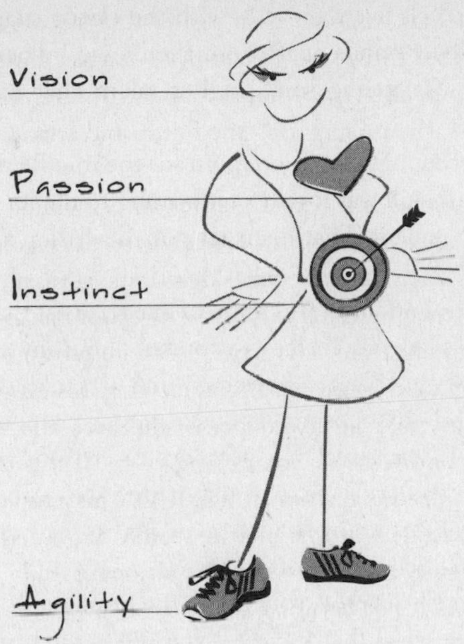

EYES REPRESENT VISION

This is the trait most associated with today's rebel entrepreneur. We live in a transformative time that rewards leaders who can imagine a personal computer in every home (unimaginable thirty years ago), a fax machine in every office (unimaginable fifteen years ago), or people shopping online (unimaginable five years ago).

Can you name the executives who ran America's great companies from World War II until the Reagan era? Probably not, since these were professional managers whose greatest strength was in planning and implementing relatively conventional business strategies. Today's era of business execs as pop icons began with Lee Iacocca at Chrysler, a rebel who earlier had helped create Ford's Mustang and re-create the convertible. Iacocca represented the new breed of business leaders who recognized that the power of their company brand was an extension of their reputation as a visionary leader.

The true rebel articulates a clear vision that people can rally around. The visionary rebel thrives on freedom, as it gives him a flexible mind, willing to entertain all sorts of notions and attitudes. This is an essential skill for someone who is imagining the future and articulating it on today's terms.

The visionary rebel is an experimenter and is willing to tolerate a certain amount of chaos. He must be willing to occasionally sound like a kook, for visions often can start out as delusions. Ultimately, the rebel's enthusiasm, persistence, and simple, precise direction make the dream tangible and give it momentum. His naïveté can be refreshing and inspiring. People are drawn to his presence and amazed by his clairvoyance.

Being visionary isn't all about personality. It's about connecting the rebel's creative mind with his compelling voice. If this leader can express an inspiring organizational vision, it will enable his people to move beyond their own preconceived limitations in search of something bigger than themselves. Imagine the Pied Piper. The visionary leader naturally finds a trail of believers in his or her wake.

REBEL MALADY

As with any of these talents, too much of one quality can be dangerous. Many start-ups fail under a founder who's constantly talking about vision but doesn't have a plan for execution. If you're a 10 on the 1-to-10 visionary scale, hire a chief financial officer or operating officer to keep you sober and to be on the lookout for icebergs on the horizon. While Bill Gates is a very practical visionary, he has recently accepted the fact that his sidekick Steve Ballmer, now the CEO of Microsoft, may be the better executor of the company's long-term vision. Jack Kenny, who has thirty years of hospitality experience, is Joie de Vivre's president because he can take my messy, overarching vision and root it in an organizational reality.

Entrepreneur Bill Gross discovered after he started Knowledge Adventure, the third-largest publisher of children's software, that he was better at starting companies than running them. "I love the invention part, but I wasn't paying attention to the details of making a profit," he says. Like many visionaries, Bill had the attention span of a gnat. Fortunately, his brother Larry has complementary skills and took control of the day-to-day operation as president and helped the company grow.

This gave Bill the space to create a business that accentuated his visionary talents. Idealab! was launched in 1996, backed by an impressive collection of investors dedicated to being an incubator for start-up Internet companies. This successful model has helped launch eToys, City-Search, and GoTo.com. The key to Bill's success has been to position himself as the visionary who surrounds himself with able practitioners.

There's another caution for the visionary leader. You fall in love with the limelight, and your vulnerability to grandiosity means you are propelled by a need to expand your organization rather than develop it. Dr. Michael Maccoby, a scholar of management, says that we live in an era that rewards productive narcissists as leaders: those who display a creative vision, a willingness to break the rules, and an ability to persuade people to follow them. Unfortunately, an out-of-balance narcissist becomes enamored with his image, which leads to a hypersensitivity to criticism, a lack of empathy, and an unwillingness to share the stage (in fact, Dr. Maccoby warns that the narcissist's faults become more pronounced as he becomes more successful). Such a leader is willing to take unreasonable risks because he or she becomes immune to traditional rules. Think Bill Clinton.

How do you create balance for the visionary leader in love with his image so that he doesn't have to take the Lewinsky tumble? Engage in a little psychoanalysis with him. Make sure he understands that his greatest qualities may not be those that are even seen by the public. For example, my colleague and muse Rob Delamater told me that I am most effective as Joie de Vivre's leader when I'm exhibiting "purposeful humility." Being more self-reflective (internal) helps balance the self-image (external) and can be antidoted by a healthy sense of humor and irony. Remind this visionary that the true sign of a sustainable company is when you create practical visionaries throughout the organization.

HEART REPRESENTS PASSION

While vision gives a rebel company direction, passion is the fuel that keeps it going. Like the heart, this passion pumps the rebel's energy to all corners of their organization. As companies have become less hierarchical and decision-making has become more democratic, this quality—passion—is all the more important, as it helps every employee think like an entrepreneur.

Unlike visionary leaders who can arouse cultlike followings, passionate leaders create loyalty to an organization more than to an individual. This is especially valuable at a time when employees tend to identify more with their work than they do with their company. A passionate leader is able to create "sticky people," employees who don't bolt for the revolving door. Consequently, turnover in a well-run, passionate rebel company is far lower than the industry standard.

Passionate leaders are great team-builders. They've mastered the left-brain/right-brain tango. They use both their analytical skills and their salesmanship to create a wonderful work climate. Along with their big heart, they may also have big ears, all the better to listen with. Passionate companies are the ones that are always described as having "a family environment." The passionate rebel is often Mommy and Daddy all rolled up into one.

REBEL MALADY

Fortune magazine recently published a story called "CEOs in Denial," detailing the fine line between optimism and denial. Two of the CEOs they profiled are classic entrepreneurs who built substantial companies through their passionate cheerleading of their cultures—Paul Fireman of Reebok and Jerry Sanders of Advanced Micro Devices. In both cases, their optimism and salesmanship brought employees, customers, and investors in the door, but their companies consistently overpromised and underdelivered.

Another related malady is the leader who is so passionate about what he believes that it leads to temperamental outbursts. I've seen small companies that both love and fear their leader. The staff may excuse the leader, saying, "He's just so passionate about what he believes. You have to accept his occasional outbursts when things don't go his way." After a while, the staff wises up, giving in to their own collective heartburn and leaving the would-be rebel in his own overcooked stew.

The mantra for an overly passionate rebel is "grace under pressure." If the rebel doesn't have the emotional stability for this, he needs to surround himself with trusted managers who can moderate his personality and feel safe delivering the boss bad news. Intel's Andy Grove suggests three steps for the CEO in denial: "Listen to people on the periphery. Let go of your ego. Undertake a task of justifying your case to the most challenging audience you can gather."

HOW TO MAKE SURE YOU'RE NOT A JERK

Many of the qualities of the rebel demand a certain amount of flamboyance, egocentricity, and thick skin. Consequently, some rebels can be great business successes, but lousy specimens of the human race.

The rebels who make a difference in the long run are those with *integrity.* Related to the words "integrate" and "entire," "integrity" means "the quality of being complete or undivided." As Tom Petzinger, Jr., writes in *The New Pioneers,* it's about knowing the effects of your actions on a wider circle and caring about those effects. Of course, this is even more important in our shrinking world and more integrated economy.

How do you know if you have integrity and how do you teach it? It's simple. Unfortunately, many of us think of integrity on a grand scale, as if you have only a few opportunities during the year to exhibit it—for example, when the supermarket clerk inadvertently overpays you in change. Instead, as my friend and entrepreneur Will Rosenzweig suggests, integrity can be demonstrated many times daily. It's all about knowing what to do, saying you're going to do it, and then doing it. Integrity is exhibited when appointments are kept, products are delivered on time, when feedback is given directly and respectfully. Sometimes too much vision and passion can get in the way.

The next time you're wondering about someone's integrity, ask yourself, "Do they exhibit good habits? Do they walk their talk? Do they deliver the goods?"

GUT REPRESENTS INSTINCTS

Trust your gut. Follow your instincts. Tap into your intuition. You've heard these clichés since childhood. But rebels do have an uncanny sixth sense that guides their decisions and an ability to concentrate on some innate talent. Strong instincts help cultivate that aptitude in themselves and others.

Just like vision and passion, instinct is a prized quality today. Who has time to commission a year-long study before entering a new market? How do you create a smart company so that common sense filters down throughout the whole organization? Leaders with great instincts can spend a half-day at a business, relatively blind to the industry, and ferret out the key challenges and opportunities that the CEO faces.

Steve Jobs proved this when he came in to mastermind the turnaround of Apple. Like a surgeon with a knife, he knew exactly where the business needed to be pruned, yet he also knew which divisions warranted life support. His ability to focus on just what needed attention—amid ambiguity, chaos, and finger-pointing—is one of the reasons he is so successful.

Rebels have a remarkable skill for elevating talent and brilliance. While vision points the rebel in the right direction and passion keeps the company moving, instinct helps the rebel chart a path without full information, sometimes when faced with enormous obstacles. Some people call it merchant sense, others call it tenacity. I just know it's not something they teach you in business school.

At twenty-three, I became a project manager midway through a large, ill-fated real estate renovation project. In over my head, a green M.B.A. graduate, I looked at the world with an exceptionally analytical mind. One day as I was trying to make one of three hundred snap decisions that were being "fire-hosed" at me, an old foreman on the job took me aside. Sal told me, "Son, the only way you're going to figure it out is by attending the school of hard knocks. Put your calculator away and start listening to your gut. You'll make a couple dozen bad decisions today, but your gut will learn quicker than your mind." It was great advice, for within a few months I'd built an instinctive confidence (wisdom) that was more typical of someone ten years my senior.

REBEL MALADY

What do you say about someone who has too much guts? They're crazy. They're careless and reckless. They don't plan sufficiently. They don't believe anyone but themselves. They're uncompromising. They don't share or effectively communicate their decision-making process. They're ruthless. They're selfish. They're not patient. They're a royal pain in the butt. Talk to any company with a rebel leader who's heavily reliant on his instincts and you'll hear some of these sentiments.

Bob Moog found that his strong instincts meant that he was a control freak at University Games. As with many entrepreneurs, he ruled by the axiom "If you want to get it done right, do it yourself." This worked when the company was small, but when they began introducing dozens of new games each quarter, he had to develop a system that helped build instinct into his people. Bob was able to mentor them by analyzing his own decision-making process and creating thirty questions that the product managers had to ask themselves before they launched a new game (for example, "Will the color on the cover of the box look okay under shrink wrap?"). This way his people could get inside his head—or more appropriately, his guts—to understand how he approached the creation and launch of a new game.

Instincts are hard to teach. It's one thing to instruct, it's another to coach. Coaching or mentoring requires a significant time commitment that many rebel leaders just aren't willing to make. Additionally, instinctual managers aren't always the best planners, so a new training program may never hatch beyond the initial idea.

If you want to build instinct in your organization, you have to create a vehicle for indoctrinating your people. Jack Welch has done this with General Electric's Crotonville leadership school, where his business strategies are taught to up-and-coming GE managers. Jack is the mascot for this training, but not the trainer (although he does teach many classes annually). Unfortunately, most smaller companies rely on the pronouncements of their instinct-based leader without the learning infrastructure to carry through their strategy.

FEET REPRESENT AGILITY

Agility is more necessary today than ever because of the pace of change in the digital age. Rebels have a bias toward immediate action and results. Fast and flexible, they tend to be opportunity-driven, while traditional managers are resource-driven (most managers work with the resources they're given, while rebels seek out opportunities beyond what they've been given).

The rebel combines the speed and dexterity of a gazelle with the determination of a stubborn water buffalo. Rebels must be dreamers, but they need their feet planted firmly on the ground. Undaunted by failure, rebels are great improvisers. They're the option quarterback, the auctioneer, the leader who can smell the finish line even before they've plotted a plan for getting there. As a result, they're great multitaskers and know how to prioritize.

Bill Gates has proven this at Microsoft, especially when he did an about-face on their Internet strategy in 1997. He was able to marshal tremendous resources and build a new strategy on the fly after previously neglecting the revolutionary relevance of the Internet. Charles Schwab did the same when he realized his discount brokerage company was vulnerable to the growing prospects of online trading.

Agility provides balance, the foundation for everything the rebel intends to accomplish. Without her feet, the rebel's other three qualities won't take her to the finish line. Henry David Thoreau said, "If you have built castles in the air, your work need not be lost; that is where they should be. Now put the foundations under them." The footwork is what assures that the foundations are in place.

REBEL MALADY

If you've ever worked in a company that's a little too agile, you know what the place feels like. Being light on your feet may be great for a ballerina, but it can wreak havoc with a business if the company's strategy is constantly changing.

"Fight or flight" is a primal instinct but also one that can plague an organization when it refuses to firmly plant its feet on the ground. A rebel leader or company that is too agile will be constantly distracted, in search of safer havens that are illusory. Rebel leaders who have a balanced talent of agility recognize that a rudder is a powerful tool that requires a certain amount of consistent stewardship or you're left with a seasick crew.

J. Peterman Company became one of the hot catalog companies in the 1990s but by 1998, the company slid into bankruptcy even though it had been even more popularized on *Seinfeld.* Like many fast-growing companies, J. Peterman lost its focus as it grew. The initial catalog, which included only seven precious and authentic items, became voluminous, trying to cover too many bases. Retail stores lacked the mystique and mystery that surrounded the J. Peterman brand. The company never championed any one retail concept or product long enough to make it a cash cow.

Consequently, this light-on-its-feet company produced a heavy thud when cash-flow troubles shut it down.

Sometimes it isn't just the amplified agility that creates a cultural dis-ease in a rebel company. Some start-ups that go the initial-public-offering (IPO) route end up with the idealism drained from the company since it's now forced to focus 100 percent on quarterly earnings. The focus used to be on creating great products, but now it's all about producing revenues as quickly as possible. The net result is burnout, cynicism, and products with short shelf lives.

Few people—rebels or not—possess all four qualities in full measure. Great eyes (vision) but awkward feet (agility) will lead to embarrassing organizational moments. A big heart (passion) but a confused gut (instinct) means a lovable but indecisive leader. A rebel out of alignment can create dis-ease not only in the rebel's body but also throughout the organization.

Just like any athlete, the rebel may favor certain body parts. But she can also develop her abilities, and when she combines all four aptitudes in a choreographed manner, the result is pure poetry.

★ ★ ★

BUSINESS REBEL HALL OF FAME PROFILE

Steve Jobs (Founder of Apple Computer and CEO of Pixar Animation Studios)

Steve is a classic rebel, as his innovations have transformed his industry. From being the cocreator of the first personal computer to insisting that the first Macintosh models include a user-friendly graphical interface with a mouse, Jobs has been the visionary pioneer who has brought computing to the masses.

When former Apple CEO John Sculley had Steve Jobs ousted in a bitter power struggle years ago, he remarked that he wanted to make Apple "more pragmatic and less religious." Well, nearly a decade later, with Sculley and two other ineffectual CEOs long gone, it is clear that Apple's renaissance has much to do with the enthusiastic halo around Steve Jobs's head. What's remarkable is how fast he was able to turn Apple around after the company lost $1 billion on annual revenues of $7 billion in 1996–97. Within a couple of years, Apple had nearly quadrupled its consumer market share and, by mid-2000, Apple's stock price was seven times the price at its nadir, shortly after Steve took over in 1997. And, Steve was able to accomplish this as the interim CEO while being compensated like a true rebel: $1-per-year salary with no stock options.

His bias toward action—cutting the clone business and the Newton project while reinvesting in the successful new iMac line—was crucial. Apple's "Think Different" ad campaign (a promotional plan that had "rebel" written all over it) helped to shore up confidence among its user base and built a bridge to many new customers who were impressed with the iMac's beauty and utility.

Finally, this charismatic visionary knows how to rally his troops as a band of renegades. He flew a skull-and-crossbones pirate flag over Apple's headquarters when they were first developing the Mac. Jobs told the *San Francisco Examiner* "The world's a little bit better place because Apple's in it. That's why I'm here. Someone has to make good computers. If Apple doesn't do it, I'm afraid nobody else will."

Your leadership style will follow your most natural talents and aptitudes. But there's one last note of caution for budding leaders: *Your words and actions magnify in direct proportion to your increased authority.* As you become a more successful leader, you become a role model to that many more people. Examine your behaviors, because just about everything your employees observe about you may seem larger than life and more important than you intended.

THE THIRTY-TWO TRAITS OF SUCCESSFUL REBELS: HOW TO IDENTIFY YOUR UNIQUE IMPRINT

I've found that it's easiest to determine your leadership style by referring to people you admire. A few years ago, I became a huge fan of the wonderfully wacky Herb Kelleher of Southwest Airlines. I read everything I could about him. At our 1997 annual management retreat, our top thirty-five managers discussed the book *Nuts,* which chronicles how Southwest grew their business while sustaining a remarkable corporate culture.

After studying Herb and his company, I was able to distill his management style down to four key talents. Since that time, I've tried to model myself after how I think Herb operates. It's almost like he's my guardian angel whispering in my ear. Similarly, Bill Gross found that one of his investors, Steven Spielberg, was his role model because of his creative ability to bring ideas to life.

Try the following exercise. Listed below are a collection of aptitudes that fall under the four categories of positive rebel traits. These thirty-two aptitudes define the way successful business is conducted in our new economy.

1. Choose four of the following aptitudes (you needn't select one from each category) that best represent your strengths.
2. Then think of a rebel role model from real life who best personifies this aptitude.
3. Next, think of a specific example of the way the role model outwardly expresses that aptitude and imagine the habits he uses in his everyday life to remain world-class in that talent.

When you're done, you'll have a list of your key aptitudes, a role model (or four different ones if you choose to have one role model per aptitude), and specific examples of how those role models use that talent. For example, Oprah Winfrey is a great storyteller who leverages diversity while Richard Branson is a cultural trend-spotter who charismatically creates buzz. Attaching personalities to the aptitudes may help you better understand the dynamics of those aptitudes.

VISION

☐ **Creativity and Innovation:** is an incubator and generator of new ideas

☐ **Cultural Trend-Spotter:** has the ability to use and synthesize ideas with one's own dream

☐ **A Sense of Mission Greater Than Oneself:** has a higher calling or destiny

☐ **Able to Aspire and Dream Globally:** even beyond rational expectations

- ☐ **Charismatic Buzz Creation:** has an ability to engage "influencers"
- ☐ **Persuasive Articulation of a Concept:** often visually, so people "get it"
- ☐ **Self-Confidence That Makes a "Presence":** you want to be in the person's company
- ☐ **Clairvoyance:** has a knack at seeing opportunities before they're evident

PASSION

- ☐ **Cohesive and Compassionate Team-Builder:** knows how to bring people together with a shared vision
- ☐ **Great Storyteller:** her life is an open book and a model
- ☐ **High Integrity and Trustworthiness:** he walks his talk, lives up to his commitments, and is a role model for the company's values
- ☐ **Emotionally Self-Aware and Empathetic:** shows his sensitive side, often with a splendid sense of humor; can step inside the shoes of customers and employees
- ☐ **Leveraging Diversity:** has the ability to understand and motivate wildly different people
- ☐ **Great Communicator and Listener:** knows how to leverage power and mobilize public sentiment through her candid personality
- ☐ **Infectious Optimism and Enthusiasm:** encourages the belief that anything is possible
- ☐ **The Contented One:** it's clear he loves what he does

INSTINCT

- ☐ **Willingness to Be Contrarian:** fights for what he believes in; popularity is no object
- ☐ **Grace Under Pressure:** makes sound and courageous decisions even amid crises and without complete information
- ☐ **Lifelong Learner and Teacher:** on a constant, steady path of self-improvement
- ☐ **Trusts Intuition:** great ability to read people and concepts quickly
- ☐ **Mr. Fix-It:** able to hold herself and others accountable for clearly articulated goals
- ☐ **One World-Class Idiosyncratic Skill:** something that is innate or comes naturally; demonstrates personal mastery

- ☐ **The Dealmaker:** has the ability to see the "true value" in things because of his merchant sense, and give people what they want
- ☐ **Battle-Hardened Veteran:** knows how to "work" the game and has impenetrably thick skin

AGILITY

- ☐ **Open Twenty-four Hours:** intense and tireless, nonstop resilience and persistence; physical vitality and stamina
- ☐ **Makes Things a Reality:** creates systems that allow a vision to flourish; spectacular execution
- ☐ **Spectacular Improvisation Skills:** has the ability to embrace change; adaptive, opportunistic, and flexible; a tolerance for ambiguity
- ☐ **Ability to Prioritize:** knows how to put first things first
- ☐ **The "Option" Quarterback:** is adroit and agile, the leader who moves the ball
- ☐ **A Resourceful Networker:** knows who to call upon for specialized assistance
- ☐ **Multitasker:** has the sense of balance to juggle chain saws; does not get distracted easily
- ☐ **Competitive Drive for Achievement:** has a tenacious focus on the finish line and a raw and powerful determination to achieve

FORM GOOD HABITS AND BECOME THEIR SLAVE

Keep my words positive:
Words become my behaviors.
Keep my behaviors positive:
Behaviors become my habits.
Keep my habits positive:
Habits become my values.
Keep my values positive:
Values become my destiny.
—Mahatma Gandhi

Your talents won't go very far if they're not habitually backed up day-to-day. While a discussion of habits may seem a little traditional, even rebels need a foundation of behaviors that reinforce their effectiveness. For example, Richard Branson has a habit of calling fifty customers a month each time Virgin Atlantic starts a new air route. His purpose is to stay close to the customer and to understand the challenges his staff is facing.

If you create effective habits that amplify your aptitudes, rest assured that you'll be a successful leader. In the chaotic world we live in, sometimes the only thing you *can* control are your habits.

Of course, your habits will be different than mine. Habits are most effective when they're specific and measurable. If your goal is to get healthy, you can't just say that your habit will be to exercise regularly. There's too much wiggle room in that. Instead, you might define your habits as doing three cardiovascular and two strength-building workouts weekly, eating no more than 2,000 calories per day. The key is to commit to some challenging but achievable changes that are driven by solid habits.

As of this moment, some of my current leadership habits include:

Catch someone doing something right: Write two complimentary notes per week to staff. Give positive reinforcement in real time.

Admit my mistakes: If people suspect I'm covering up my own errors, they'll hide their mistakes too. Talk about what I've learned from my mistakes when I'm giving constructive feedback to someone else.

Give gifts to the world: Give at least one gift a day to the people around me: a smile, a heartfelt compliment, a piece of gum, a nice note, a small book. The best gift I can give is my attention—tell the bellman he's got the most reassuring smile or tell my sales manager that I truly learned something from her today at the sales meeting.

At Joie de Vivre, we applied this personal approach at a corporate level by arranging a list of Management Habits to help reinforce leadership behavior. The list for hotel general managers was different than the list for the top accounting executives, of course, but the principles were the same. It's almost like going to etiquette school. We've found this to be especially helpful with our younger managers, as it provides a helpful form of group mentoring.

How can you create a habits list for your company? First, create a forum for your managers to discuss what key habits spell success in their particular area. We jump-started this process at one of our retreats by giving each functional group a list of forty positive habits (like "practice direct and respectful communication, being honest and humane at the same time"). We asked these groups to review the list, add their own proven habits, and come back to the whole group with a list of the ten that would most positively influence their position.

Of course, this caused some serious arm-wrestling in each of these groups, but the net result was a collection of consensus habits. Once these habits were presented to the whole group, we asked each manager to develop their own personalized list of ten essential habits over the next two weeks. Then each manager unveiled their list to their supervisor to assure that they had a parallel sense of priorities.

For example, our VP of sales expects our sales managers to spend 50 percent of their time finding new prospects. Ideally, half of their habits should reinforce this behavior. This process can be revealing and can precipitate conflict, but it also addresses these issues before the manager gets too far off course and fails. Most important, when you have a key subordinate with disappointing performance, you can refer back to the habits to see if (1) the priorities are right, and (2) the person is performing the habits on a regular basis.

Habits are the building blocks that define behavior—both for you and for your organization. And behavior changes reality. Habits . . . behavior . . . reality . . . It's remarkable how we neglect the impact of creating good habits.

HOW TO USE YOUR PAST TO GUIDE YOUR FUTURE

DON'T REPEAT THE PAST

Make a list of five to ten things that have been done to you in your professional life that deeply bothered you. Then make a list of five to ten things that have been done to you that you've loved. Take a look at the two lists. How can you create good habits to assure that you're able to emulate the positive acts and not repeat the negative?

YOUR DEFINING MOMENT

Reviewing your whole life, what one leadership accomplishment most jumps out at you as a reflection of your greatest talents? (This is a great interview question.) How were each of the four aptitudes you identified earlier in this chapter engaged in this accomplishment? Are you taking full advantage of these talents today?

LIFE AS A SOUNDBITE

Imagine that a reporter for the local paper joins you in the elevator for a sixty-second ride. She asks you, "You've been a successful business rebel—what's the key to your success?" What would you say? Would you focus on your role models? Your greatest aptitudes? An example of a success? Your key habits? An underlying philosophy or set of values? What is your distinct and unique approach to leadership? Remember, you have to be succinct: you only have one minute.

Ultimately, the business rebel has a remarkable knack for engaging her own talent and others', often in unconventional ways. Observers call this magic, but it's really just a matter of knowing one's self and fighting for what one believes in.

I hope you're feeling a few years younger now that you are two-thirds of the way through this section. So far, we've reestablished a connection to your childhood passion and identified your most important leadership qualities. In the next and final chapter we'll learn how inspired leaders like you can use their values to reach out to colleagues and employees and make rebels of them all.

3. What Do You Stand For?

I believe the real difference between success and failure in a corporation can very often be traced to the question of how well the organization brings out the great energies and talents of its people. What does it do to help those people find common cause with each other?

—Thomas Watson, former IBM chief executive officer

Perhaps the greatest gift Ma and Pa Conley passed on to me was a sense of values. The same could be said for the best rebel leaders. Employees long to be inspired and led. We all want to be connected to something larger than ourselves. In our transient, modern lives, the company has replaced the neighborhood (and often religion and family) as our primary community. Yet most business leaders don't realize they occupy a bully pulpit from which they reach more people than most preachers. Rebel companies are increasingly recognizing that the values they hold dear affect their ability to attract great employees and new customers.

I've found that my primary role as the rebel leader is to engage my staff so that they see not only the bottom line but also some greater purpose. Some companies create a simple motto that captures this. For example, Amazon's is "Work Hard, Have Fun, and Make History." Who wouldn't want to make a little history?

But historically companies have asked us to check our beliefs at the door. This created business leaders who were the ultimate "suits": efficient and productive, yet flavorless and banal. Business rebels, on the other hand, wear their values on their sleeves, whether they're Ben & Jerry, Ross Perot, or Ted Turner, and they attract troops who enthusiastically join the company as much for the values as for the company's product or service. In fact, many rebel businesses, like The Body Shop or Tom's of Maine, are more defined by their values than they are by their products or services.

James Collins and Jerry Porras studied diverse American corporations for their book *Built to Last: Successful Habits of Visionary Companies.* Finding an unmistakable positive correlation between the articulation of core values and sustainable profitability in companies like Hewlett-Packard, 3M, and Disney, they concluded, "It is better to understand who you are than where you're going in today's unpredictable world—for where you are going will almost certainly change . . . The crucial variable is not the content of a company's ideology, but how deeply it believes and expresses it in all that it does."

The Republic of Tea and Winetasting.com founder Will Rosenzweig calls this "brandthropology," or how the culture of an organization can build sustainable, high-performance results and relationships. It's about how a culture sees itself. Companies that don't know who they *are* beyond what they *do* suffer from an identity crisis. They're forced to operate the business using management by control as opposed to management through shared values.

Consultant David Sibbet told me the story of how Hewlett-Packard Labs was able to deepen its employees' commitment just by changing one word in its statement of values. In preparation for their "Celebration of Creativity," Manager of Worldwide Personnel Barbara Waugh engaged HP Lab's people in a conversation about what it meant for them to be the best industrial lab *in* the world. One engineer responded that what would truly motivate her was to be the best *for* the world. Just a one-word change, but this new statement packed quite a punch.

Soon another engineer had developed a graphic for the idea: a famous photo of the two founders gazing into the garage where HP was hatched, with the image of a beautiful blue planet earth, taken from the Apollo spacecraft, superimposed inside the garage. The picture symbolized HP's commitment to the world. It spread instantly throughout HP's worldwide organization, with more than 50,000 copies of the poster purchased. This image fit David Packard's original statement that "the Hewlett-Packard

Hewlett-Packard Company

HP for the World

company should be managed first and foremost to make a commitment to society . . . and to improve the welfare of humanity."

Values work like a common language to align a company's leadership and rank and file. Values can be interpersonal or ideological, social or political. They give meaning to our lives and the priorities we choose. As we discovered in the prior two chapters, the first step toward establishing values is personal. You can't ask, "What does your company stand for?" without first checking your own "conviction oven."

YOUR CONVICTION OVEN

I will not attempt to define the perfect personal value system. There isn't one. But inside each of us dwells a set of convictions that makes us passionate. These can be political, like animal rights, or interpersonal, like working in an environment that emphasizes diversity, or philosophical, like working in a strict meritocracy. The true rebel integrates her convictions into her career. Her life's work becomes her way of making the world a better place.

What do *you* believe in? Write a list of ideas, causes, or beliefs about which you feel passionate. Try to be as specific as possible—for example, "giving back to the community" is too vague. Just to get you started, think of controversial politicians, athletes, celebrities, or others who seem to represent something. Do you agree or disagree with them? What gets your pulse pounding when you read the newspaper? Which human qualities do you deeply admire?

Now create two columns: one labeled "Not at Work" and one labeled "At Work." Look at each of the values you've listed and indicate how—if at all—you *act* it out in each environment. Here is a widely varied example.

	Not at Work	**At Work**
• **Providing Urban Youth Opportunities**	Tutor at the YMCA youth program	Try to get the company to sponsor a kid at camp for the summer
• **Team-Oriented or Tribal Environment**	Play basketball with my team every week	Become team leader in the quality-control efforts
• **Animal Rights**	Vegetarian; lead fur protests	———
• **Strong Christian Values**	Lead church school every Sunday; try to live the proper values	Feel persecuted at work because of my beliefs; people make Christian jokes
• **Supporting Breast Cancer Causes**	———	———
• **Supporting the Arts**	Give $100 to the local theater company	———

Not surprisingly, most people find that they have many more examples in the "Not at Work" column than in the "At Work" column. This can be discouraging when you consider that more than half your waking hours may be devoted to work that's nowhere near your conviction oven. Or you may realize that your values are actually devalued at work. If that's the case, it's either time to find a new job or become a more vocal advocate for your cause.

INTEGRATING YOUR VALUES INTO THE WORKPLACE

At our annual management retreat, the highest recognition a manager can receive is the Living the Vision award, which is given to one manager each year who successfully integrates the company's values into their day-to-day business practices. This was my ideal when I started my company—to marry my personal purpose to my actual work. Not that it's easy—it's a perpetual challenge to run a highly competitive organization that allows for an authentic expression of individual values. Yet there's no reason you can't create your own Living the Vision award in your company.

Let's take an in-depth look at whether *your* values live in your workplace. Below, you will see a list of values that an individual or company can pursue or emulate. Find in the list ten of your most highly prized values; then identify and rank the ten top values found in your current workplace.

PICK TEN VALUES

1. Creativity and Innovation
2. Precisely Organized and Well Structured
3. Making and Keeping Commitments
4. Libertarianism: Free Markets and Free Minds
5. Building Win-Win Relationships
6. Connecting with the Earth
7. Helping Those Who Are Less Fortunate
8. Exhibiting Personal Integrity
9. Direct and Respectful Communications
10. Having Balance in Life
11. Building a Positive Reputation in the Community
12. Integrating Spiritual Principles into the Workplace
13. Loyalty and Trust with the Employees
14. Maximum Profits for Our Investors
15. Respecting Lines of Authority
16. Helping People Who Are Physically Ill
17. Meritocracy—Letting Bright, Ambitious People Rise to the Top
18. High Quality
19. The Importance of Art and Culture
20. Reliability and Predictability

21. Being an Advocate for the Customer
22. Being Likable and Well Regarded
23. Building a Safe and Nonconfrontational World
24. Opportunistic—a "Go for It" Attitude
25. Being Different Than the Rest
26. Feeling Proud About the Product or Service
27. A Collegial and Team-Building Environment
28. Giving Recognition Where It's Due
29. Supporting the Underdog
30. The Importance of Friends and Affiliation
31. Bottom-Line, Results-Driven
32. Golden Rule: Do unto Others as You Would Have Them Do unto You
33. Informal Relationships Without Rules
34. Consistency in Everything We Do
35. Individual Freedom and Independence
36. Compensation Enough for People to Provide for Their Families
37. Having Fun and Enjoying Life to the Fullest
38. Tolerance of Different Viewpoints
39. Patriotism and Altruism—Respecting Traditions
40. Fairness and Justice

How many of your top-ten values are mirrored by your company? Hopefully, if you're the rebel leader of your company, you see a strong alignment. If you're part of a larger organization, this exercise may be your wake-up call to realize that your advancement and happiness are at risk unless you leave the firm or change its culture.

HOW TO CREATE A VALUES INVENTORY FOR YOUR COMPANY

Let's take this investigation one step further. This "Values Inventory" will force you and your rebel cohorts to look at whether your walk matches your talk. Give this list of questions to key leaders in your company and have them jot down responses. Then spend an afternoon as a group, reviewing your responses and adapting your corporate behavior to make sure it's aligned with your values. (These are also excellent questions to ask a potential employer during a job interview.)

- What kind of people seem to succeed at your company?
- What particular aspects of their behavior are celebrated?
- Plato said that a society cultivates whatever is honored there. What annual awards are given within the company?
- What specific systems are in place to assure that the staff learns the basic principles of the company's ideology? What symbols do you use in the workplace to remind people of the company's values?
- When was the last time an employee pointed out a company practice that was not in concert with its core values? What was the follow-up?
- What are the listening posts you use that help you tap into whether the core values are being lived day-to-day?
- What makes your employees and stakeholders most proud of your company?
- If you surveyed your employees and your customers, what would the two groups cite as the most important value of your company?
- When was the last time your company received some credit in the community for doing something that was a reflection of your values?

Quite often, the merging of cultures can be corrosive. Richard Barrett, in *Liberating the Corporate Soul,* remarks that "due diligence" in a merger or acquisition rarely considers the cultural and values issues. When laid-back Celestial Seasonings was purchased by Kraft in 1984, the larger company imposed a hierarchy full of rigidity. In came the reserved parking spaces and mandatory drug testing, out went the family spirit. The end result was an expensive divorce.

★ ★ ★

BUSINESS REBEL HALL OF FAME PROFILE

Anita Roddick (Founder and Chairman of The Body Shop)

"Business people have got to be the instigators of change. They have the money and the power to make a difference. A company that makes a profit from society has a responsibility to return something to that society." Few business rebels have aligned their personal philosophy and their career in such a parallel fashion.

Anita started her first Body Shop at thirty-three, coinciding with the time that her husband began to fulfill his dream of riding on horseback from Buenos Aires to New York City—a journey that would take two years (and you thought she was the only rebel in the family!). From the very start, she had a knack for publicity. Anita's initial storefront was located near a funeral parlor whose proprietor objected to her name, The Body Shop. She took the story to a local newspaper in Brighton, England, which created some opening buzz for the store.

Anita's approach to running her business was revolutionary: avoiding traditional distribution channels, spending as little as possible on advertising, making sure the labels described ingredients rather than hyperbolic claims. She developed a loyal clientele that appreciated the education she gave them as well as her commitment to ethical business practices, including using products that were not tested on animals.

As she began franchising this concept, she also built a rabid following of unique entrepreneurs, 90 percent of whom were women without any previous business training. These franchisees became her "foot soldiers" and helped create the nurturing corporate culture that is associated with The Body Shop. Anita says, "The trouble with marketing is that consumers are hyped out. The din of advertising and promotion has become so loud, they are becoming cynical about the whole process. What we have tried to do is establish credibility by educating our customers . . . It humanizes the company, and makes customers feel they are buying from people they know and trust." This values-centered approach has helped make The Body Shop the largest and best-known skin and hair products retailer in the world.

CREATING YOUR COMPANY'S CORE VALUES

Once you've completed the earlier steps of this chapter, crafting a set of company core values shouldn't be difficult. The key is to make it a collaborative effort. The rebel leader can impose his or her values on the rest of the group, but of course the core values will become more deeply rooted if they grow from the rest of the company.

Lisa Thomas, cofounder and CEO of Clif Bar (the third-largest company in the energy-bar submarket), says that when you start a company many of the values are implied because you often choose employees who are similar to yourself. But as you grow, and the founding team is more disconnected from the new employees, your implied values must become explicit. Lisa says, "You can't assume your new employees are going to be as passionate and believing in the mission as your original team."

Clif Bar spread its values in two ways. Each of the executive team members was asked to take one of the seven company values and find a way to teach it throughout the organization, either in classes or with parties or philanthropic pursuits. Additionally, Lisa began using their cool company newsletter as a vehicle to explain Clif Bar's roots and folklore. This resulted in new employees gaining a better understanding of the company's values very quickly in their tenure.

You might want to create a Culture Club, drawing from diverse segments from your company. This task force should be vested with the responsibility of articulating the core values and developing, in concert with the HR department, activities that support the corporate culture and make the values tangible.

Here are some questions you can ask this Culture Club as it's developing your set of core values:

- What would we like this company to look like in twenty years?
- What would it feel like to the employees?
- What would it have achieved?

Joie de Vivre went through this process by offering a three-month class called "Creating Our Core Values" for any employee to attend. The goals were to develop a core ideology statement that would be presented at the annual retreat, to find corporate bad habits, and to consider new programs that would better align our corporate practices and values. Five essential values, which would never be compromised for financial gain or short-term expediency, resulted.

1. Pioneering hospitality innovation by promoting creativity and entrepreneurship
2. Honesty, integrity, and ethics in all aspects of business
3. A celebratory workplace built on teamwork that honors each person's individuality
4. A commitment to product and service that exceeds customer expectations
5. A connection and responsibility to community service

Every new employee receives this list at orientation, and these values are a critical component of our manager-evaluation system.

IDENTIFYING MISALIGNMENTS IN YOUR COMPANY

It's one thing to come up with values. It's quite another to identify the company's misalignments with the values and to find solutions for breaking the bad habits. The three-month class we convened also came up with a list of Joie de Vivre's good habits and bad habits, which at the time included:

GOOD HABITS

- We provide good value.
- We allow for autonomy.

- We promote a great family feeling and give back to the community.
- We have a spectacular niche focus in marketing.
- Our staff has an exceptional can-do attitude.
- We genuinely care about our employees and listen well.
- We promote a fun work climate.
- We maintain integrity in everything the company does.

BAD HABITS

- We have a bootstrap mentality.
- We don't do good follow-through because of a lack of operating systems.
- Our growth lacks prioritization.
- Bad planning leads to reactive thinking.
- We can't say no to new projects even if they don't fit our strategy.
- We don't fire well or enough.
- Ill-defined expectations lead to unclear accountability between managers and staff.
- Passion and creativity tend to overrule discipline and focus.

The group, which represented all parts of the organization, identified specific misalignments that were frequently cited by line-level employees. These included a lack of management resources in the food and beverage department, inconsistent timing of performance reviews, and a lack of follow-through from our training program Joie de Vivre University to the individual properties. We took these misalignments and placed them on a vertical axis. The bad habits went on a horizontal axis, creating a grid.

As we placed check marks under each bad habit that seemed to generate a particular misalignment, the grid helped us understand the cause-and-effect relationships. For example, our inconsistent timing on performance reviews was a source of frustration for many employees who felt that they weren't getting consistent feedback from their manager. While most managers wanted to give timely reviews, we had never developed operational systems that required a manager to turn in their employee reviews to headquarters so no one in the corporate office knew whether reviews were occurring, and the company's big-hearted reputation meant that some employees who would likely be terminated in an-

	Bootstrap	No Systems	Bad Priorities	Bad Planning	Can't Say No	Don't Fire	Unclear Accounting	Poor Communication	No Discipline or Focus
Lack of Resources in F/B	X	X	X	X	X			X	
Inconsistent Timing of Reviews		X				X	X		
Lack of JdV University Follow-through		X		X				X	X

other company were allowed to stay in their job too long, thus reducing the standards for everyone else.

While this three-month endeavor initially focused on articulating our core values, it had the equally valuable effect of showing how our corporate bad habits affected our individual and company performance. This in turn produced a list of key management behaviors (which we discussed in the habits section of the previous chapter), which we now use as a training tool and dedicated action plan to eradicate those bad habits.

CORE VALUES CREATE COMPANY VALUE

The *Cone/Roper Cause-Related Marketing Trends Report* shows that more than 80 percent of consumers polled would switch brands to align themselves with a good cause, assuming no difference in price or quality. This represents nearly a 15 percent increase since 1993. The Walker Research Foundation found that 50 percent of American consumers were willing to pay a premium for products whose companies were viewed as socially responsible. In another unrelated poll, a full 50 percent of graduating M.B.A. students said they would take a cut in salary to work for a socially responsible company.

Cause-related marketing has become an accepted and rewarded strategy for forging a connection between companies and consumers. In a crowded marketplace with product parity like never before, consumers are actually seeking companies that they can relate to or that share their values.

At Joie de Vivre, we've discovered that our values pack a powerful marketing punch. In early 1999, we were awarded the annual Humanitarian Action award for being the most socially responsible hospitality company in America (beating the runner-up Ramada at the industry's prestigious UCLA Hotel Conference). Here are three ways in which you can leverage your company's commitment to values into a reputation-enhancing marketing strategy:

1. Organize an event that highlights both your cause and your product in an unusual, media-savvy manner. By the time our first hotel, The Phoenix, was five years old, it needed another publicity shot in the arm. We'd been quite involved with a neighborhood afterschool program and other youth programs, so I devised a fund-raiser, the Celebrity Pool Toss, that helped raise money for the kids while letting the attendees act like kids. Fifteen high-bidders won the opportunity to toss fifteen local celebrities (like Robin Williams) into the pool. We scored national publicity for the kids' programs and our hotel, and this Fun-Raiser raises more than $250,000 annually for such worthy programs.

2. Ask yourself, "Which constituency is most impressed by our company's commitment to this cause?" Are they a potential customer? If so, figure out a subtle way for that constituency to learn that you're supporting the cause. When we launched The Hotel Rex, guests had the opportunity to donate $5 per night of their stay to one of thirteen different local arts organizations who were struggling because of cutbacks by the National Endowment for the Arts. This philanthropic PR helped reinforce the Rex's position as San Francisco's "arts & literary" hotel and built a following among the local arts community, all while giving money and a high profile to arts organizations.

3. Invite leaders of your favorite cause to spread the word in your company and industry. Most recently, we invited the leaders from Huckleberry Youth Programs, the original runaway shelter in the country, to a corporate breakfast with CEOs from two dozen local hospitality companies. This breakfast highlighted their "Dinner at Huckleberry's" program, in which companies can donate $1,500 to pay for a month's worth of dinners for runaway teens at the shelter. With their strong presentation and my gentle persuasion, we were able to pay for a year of dinners just with this breakfast fund-raiser alone. While this event received no outside publicity, the influential attendees certainly spread the word about Joie de Vivre's commitment to the community and the plight of runaways, because I received a half-dozen calls from other industry leaders shortly afterward asking why they hadn't been invited.

FINDING MEANING IN WHAT YOU DO

Rebel companies inspire their employees through embracing shared values. Employees in these companies are proud and enthused to contribute to an organization with such integrity. The more an employee feels that she has influence over the company's values, the bigger commitment she'll make to the company. The natural result is a strong team spirit that translates into positive PR and good works in the community. Yet the more values-oriented the company, the more risk when the actual practices deviate from those values. A sacred trust can be broken if your employees or the community feel manipulated by the proverbial "wolf in sheep's clothing" that portrays itself as value-conscious but acts in a misaligned fashion.

III. CREATING A REBEL REVOLUTION: THE FOUR TRAITS OF GROUNDBREAKING LEADERS AND COMPANIES

4. Birthing a Rebel Company

Great spirits have always encountered violent opposition from mediocre minds.

—Albert Einstein

Starting a company begins with a crescendo of emotion and instinct, and from that comes the "conception" of an idea. With the creation of that fragile embryo begins a gestation period. Depending upon your situation, this could last from two to twenty months. (In my case, it lasted about nine months.)

Pregnant with joy and pain, your body and mind start acting strangely. Your dreams are rich. Your heart is full. You're blissful in your imagination of what can be, but you lose track of those around you, focusing instead on that lovely, kicking beast inside. When your "labor" begins, you hold onto anyone who will give you their arm or ear. Violent and peaceful, you try to find a rhythm that synchronizes with this flow of life. Finally, with every last ounce of energy, you deliver a messy bundle of love from deep within you. You are a parent. You are an entrepreneur.

Just like children and mothers, no two businesses or entrepreneurs are alike. All new companies follow a unique arc and experience a different outcome. And rarely does a rebel's venture begin with a rational decision. Engineer Pierre Omidyar founded the Internet auction company eBay after creating a successful Web site for his girlfriend to trade Pez dispensers.

CHIP'S STORY

At the age of twenty-five, I began building a business plan for what would become my hotel company. There was nothing rational about it. I had never worked in a hotel. My entrepreneurial experience was limited to selling calf-nursing bottles full of booze at Stanford football games. I had no money.

Even before I knew what I was going to do, I decided to call my company Joie de Vivre ("joy of life" in French), because that's what I was seeking. Only two years out of business school, I wanted to tear off my tie and do something I really enjoyed. I wrote a screenplay that gathered dust, and trained to be a massage therapist, but how was I going to pay the bills?

I did have certain basic skills. I'd worked as a commercial real estate salesperson in Silicon Valley during college, so I understood how to buy property. I'd received my M.B.A. from Stanford at age twenty-three and worked for Morgan Stanley in New York during the summer, so I knew how to wear (and be) a suit. And I'd worked for two and a half years for a maverick San Francisco real estate development company as a project manager, so I understood building renovations and the peculiarities of the San Francisco real estate market. But by conventional standards I was not prepared to start a hotel chain.

My initial business plan boldly projected I'd have ten hotels by Joie de Vivre's tenth anniversary. I guessed wrong. We had thirteen.

Hotels seemed a natural direction for me because hospitality is truly a people business, and success can come from creatively packaging products. My real estate experience wouldn't hurt and tourism was San Francisco's number-one industry. Frankly, I was tired of having visiting friends lament about the lack of fun hotels in town. My goal was to create a company with hip hotel concepts that appealed to a younger customer base—people like me. And I was going to do this without a necktie strangling me.

Everyone thought I was crazy.

Appropriately enough, my first hotel's core market consisted of real rebels. The Phoenix, once the notorious Caravan Lodge, San Francisco's pay-by-the-hour "no-tell motel," stood at the gateway to the Tenderloin, one of San Francisco's seediest districts. Even so, I fell in love with this ugly duckling, insisting it was one of the few places in San Francisco where you could throw a poolside party. Synchronized swimmers, a band playing surf music, beautiful people grooving nearly naked by the pool while MTV filmed the whole thing . . . I was choreographing the party to beat all parties in my mind.

I got so excited about a grand opening party that my skeptical M.B.A. brain had literally shut down. For my first project, I was buying a foreclosed and broken-down motor lodge on a relatively short land lease in a rough part of town. With no hotel experience, I was ready to devote the next three years to helping the soon-to-be-Phoenix rise from its ashes and become a lodging landmark. One friend said I had chutzpah—most said I'd lost my mind.

I remember my first day: January 1, 1987. With the debris of New Year's Eve still cluttering the pool area and garden courtyard, I sat down with the ragtag staff and boldly articulated my vision of resurrecting this motel. I was just hitting my stride when the beanstalk-thin night desk clerk, Gordon Anderson, stopped me. Gordon, twice my twenty-six-year-old age, smoked like a chimney, probably had never earned more than $8 per hour in his life, and was ready to deliver my first piece of bad news.

"Your idea for turning this *motel* into a cool and hip *hotel* is all well and good," Gordon said, "but how are you going to get rid of the hookers?"

Just as Gordon posed that question, a 6'4" drag queen who would have put Dolly Parton to shame stumbled across the courtyard screaming at the top of her lungs as a spindly young marine ran after her in his underwear.

Gordon and I locked eyes. He smiled. I sighed.

The truth was that the former owner had dramatically increased occupancy rates in the months leading up to the sale by renting rooms to neighborhood "street merchants." The private courtyard off the street made for a wonderful illegal marketplace. In my naïveté, I had thought I was buying a property with financial momentum; the revenue had been growing steadily. Needless to say, as soon as I cleared the property of its hookers, pimps, and drug-dealers, our occupancy fell well below break-even. And unfortunately, I hadn't capitalized my venture with nearly enough money to handle such a downturn.

Over the next couple of months, I had a series of painting parties with friends who came over to swim, paint a bit, drink a few beers, and tell me how crazy I was. Just call me Tom Sawyer, Jr. There were entire weeks during this renovation when I felt like such a deluded fool. The committee in my head treated me mercilessly: "Who do you think you are starting a hotel in your mid-twenties with no experience?" I was no longer imagining the MTV shoot by the pool.

Given my frantic state of mind, I even resorted to visiting a psychic. The psychic informed me that the mythical phoenix bird was the guardian animal of my astrological sign (Scorpio). She reminded me what I already knew—the phoenix rises from its own ashes fierce and strong. She suggested patience. A couple of weeks later, with spring arriving, The Phoenix Hotel opened just as we were running out of cash. Patience wasn't going to make the payroll.

At about that time, I realized that there existed a market niche of San Francisco visitors who would appreciate the retro-hip look of a fifties-style motor lodge like The Phoenix and wouldn't mind the edgy location. You see, some months before, while trying to negotiate a real estate development deal with legendary concert promoter Bill Graham, I learned that musicians, comedians, filmmakers, dance and theater companies, and visual artists and their oddball entourages represented a large untapped market that had a hard time finding non-cookie-cutter hotels that they could afford.

So, as I was smiling at our Grand Opening Party, my trampoline mind was jumping ahead to determine just how we could capture the arts-and-entertainment market—and fast. A couple of days later, like a vehicular angel from heaven, a sixty-foot pink tour bus pulled into the motel parking lot. And who popped-out? A pint-sized pop legend with a foot-high pink beehive—Brenda Lee. Her group was driving through San Francisco and hadn't booked a hotel. Fate had somehow steered them to our lobby. Brenda and her entourage stayed a couple of days—long enough for her to run into another aging rock icon, Arlo Guthrie, who booked a few rooms at the last minute while he played a gig a couple of blocks away. I sat down with both of these road warriors, told them my story, and asked them what they looked for in a hotel. Sometimes naïveté pays off. They welcomed my questions and started teaching me how to become the world's greatest rock-and-roll hotelier, or at least a guy who could make his payroll.

The Phoenix not only rose from its ashes; it soon rose from its cash-flow woes by creating services and amenities that addressed this market's needs better than any other hotel in town. For example, when then-unheralded Sinead O'Connor stayed a few months later (she had her first American press conference in our tiny hotel suite-cum-conference room), she was losing her voice. We knew right then it was essential to have an ear, nose, and throat doctor on call for our performer-guests. The dancers who stayed with us appreciated our massage staff. The visual artists enjoyed the fact that each of our guest rooms featured the work of an emerging local artist. Band members watched our "band-on-the-road" video collection of the world's greatest music-oriented feature films. And everyone's bus drivers loved our roomy, free parking. The complete package, including many other unique services such as free passes to underground clubs and staff-written guides to their favorite hot spots, wasn't suited to your average traveler, but it fit the needs of this market to a tee.

The Phoenix is a case study in niche marketing, one of the methods by which an aspiring business rebel can compete with the big guys. Niche marketing works well when you have a limited budget, when you want fast word-of-mouth (members of a subculture talk among themselves), when you seek targeted media, and, most important, when your product has flaws for the general marketplace (an inner-city motel is probably flawed for the general public).

In our case, we found it easy to tap into the channels of distribution because there were three primary decision-makers that determined where a band or theater company might stay: (1) an entertainment-oriented travel agent, of which there were only twenty or so in existence, mostly in Los Angeles and New York; (2) the venue where they would be playing, many of which lay within ten blocks of The Phoenix; and (3) the management company or agent that supervised the act. We made direct sales to these three groups simply and inexpensively. We began by asking them what they looked for in a rock-and-roll hotel. Ultimately, the answer could be summed-up in one word: respect. Most hotels look disdainfully (or fearfully) upon bands and entertainment groups because of their reputation for wild living. So we recruited and trained a staff not from the traditional hotel schools or training programs but from recording studios and concert venues.

I knew The Phoenix had become the lodging landmark I dreamed it could be when that paragon of mainstream respectability, *People* magazine, ran a three-page feature during our third year of operation. More important to my investors, the hotel has consistently enjoyed an occupancy rate far above the citywide average ever since.

What have I learned from the experience of creating the world's most

★ ★ ★

BUSINESS REBEL HALL OF FAME PROFILE

Nick Graham (Founder and Chairman of Joe Boxer)

In 1985, when he was twenty-seven and had less than $1,000 of start-up capital, Nick started a small business making men's novelty ties. Possessing a highly developed sense of humor and a penchant for the irreverent, he soon moved to men's underwear. Since then, Joe Boxer has become a leader in fashion, producing more than a thousand eye-catching designs annually.

What sets Nick Graham apart as a rebel is the way he has revolutionized the way the fashion industry promotes itself. Using irreverent, over-the-top promotions, Nick departed from the traditional in-bred, stilted approach most fashion retailers use to define their brand (think runway models). For example, in a joint campaign with General Mills, free boxers were offered on the back of Frosted Cheerios boxes to entice eaters to have "Breakfast in Your Boxers." In concert with buddy Richard Branson and Virgin Atlantic Airways, Nick staged the first-ever in-flight underwear fashion show.

Joie de Vivre partnered with him to create a "Joe Boxer Pajama Party" at The Phoenix, where we staged monthly poolside parties in which all the guests come out to play in their underwear (and receive a fresh pair at turndown service instead of a chocolate on the pillow). Leveraging his company's hip name and reputation, Nick says, "The brand is the amusement park . . . the product is the souvenir."

celebrated rock-and-roll motel? A rebel business leader needs to be a visionary, able to imagine what doesn't exist today. I dreamed about the great parties I could throw and the sense of community celebration we could create around the pool, paying no attention initially to the potential hotel market. I ran no focus groups or feasibility studies. I simply knew I was creating a niche product that my competitors would never imagine copying.

HOW TO WRITE A FOOLPROOF BUSINESS PLAN

Guy Kawasaki, formerly chief evangelist at Apple Computer and the founder of Garage.com, says the perfect business plan can be summarized in a thirty-second "elevator pitch," something short enough for an eight-floor ride with a venture capitalist (e.g., We want to create "The Gap" of hotels: a mid-priced product that offers style to the mainstream). Yahoo!'s landmark business plan was only twenty pages long.

Investors are looking for the following key elements in a business plan, in order of importance:

1. Management Team: *A brain trust that includes a passionate visionary, a "get-your-hands-dirty" operator, and a responsible finance-minded executive.*

2. Concept and Market: *Focus is on the potential size of the market and how you create barriers to entry. If you're starting an Internet business, investors will look at three key factors in your business model: its ability to get big quickly, its potential for building customer loyalty fast, and flexibility. The ultimate question is, Do your customers really care about what makes your product or service so different?*

3. Financial Projections: *If you get the first two elements right, the numbers ought to look good, but don't make the classic mistake of proclaiming that you're going to capture X percent of the market. Instead, focus on the average price per sale and the cost to acquire customers. Additionally, investors want to understand the "exit plan," how they're going to cash out, whether it's a sale, refinancing, or an IPO. The short-term projections are as important as the long-term since they'll show your "burn rate" (how much working capital is spent to get you to the point you show a positive cash flow).*

4. The Risks: *The best business plans tackle the most challenging obstacles head-on and describe how the new company will overcome them. This tests the practicality and thoroughness of your brain trust, and, it satisfies your investors that you've planned for the downside too.*

Writing a business plan serves dual purposes: it raises you the necessary capital and it forces you to have some discipline in your planning. I prefer seeing a one-page executive summary at the start that encapsulates the whole thing (this is the last part of the business plan that you'll write).

HOW TO CREATE YOUR OWN BUSINESS MODEL

It's hard to imagine any rules in today's entrepreneurial economy, but the fact is that successful new businesses, whether they're within the context of a big company or are a start-up, tend to follow these Birthing Tips (just remember to breathe!):

CHOOSE YOUR MATE WISELY

One of the typical mistakes novice entrepreneurs make is creating a company with friends. It sounds like a good time. You know you can trust them. You have a similar vision. Why not? Yet, how many successful businesses can you point to that have the same three to five partner-friends three years after the business was launched? Unfortunately, usually the friendships and the business end. Instead, focus on economy. Avoid redundancies. Make sure each operating partner is an expert in a different segment of the business. If you're a creative marketing guru and you want just one partner, look for someone who's an operations or finance specialist. Define the distinct roles for the key players from the start. You'll avoid misunderstandings later.

SOMETIMES BABIES NEED INCUBATORS

Business incubators are a strategy for accelerating the start-up and growth of new companies. They provide cheap office space, shared support staff and office equipment, and hands-on business management skills. In 1980 there were just twelve business incubators in North America; now there are more than six hundred. These baby business owners report that it is really the informal networking, collegial learning environment, and opportunities to do business together that make the incubator effective.

Claudia Viek, president of the Renaissance Entrepreneurship Center, a

San Francisco incubator targeted to women and minority business owners, cites that 85 percent of their incubator graduates either are still in business after five years (or their businesses were sold for a profit). This statistic is typical for most business incubators and essentially inverts the common mortality rate of 50 to 80 percent failure for small businesses within five years.

Claudia says, "One of the greatest benefits our people get is a sense of confidence and empowerment. The incubator tenants bounce ideas off one another and often wonderful synergies develop. When you create a sense of community, people want to give back." Sal Chavez, the co-founder of Bidcom, an Internet database software that streamlines construction management is one of Claudia's star incubator graduates. Sal got his break when a Renaissance board member introduced him to the president of a large local construction firm, which tested the software and ultimately led to $13 million in venture financing. Claudia says, "At the same time, Sal was helping Derrick, another incubator tenant, set up his customer database for Apex Driving School. Where else can you get this kind of expertise and inspiration? An incubator is a great tool for building an entrepreneurial culture in diverse communities."

Sounds a little like a Lamaze class, doesn't it?

To obtain a list of incubators, send a self-addressed, stamped envelope to the National Business Incubation Association (NBIA) at 20 East Circle Drive, Suite 190, Athens, Ohio 45701. Or visit their Web site at www.nbia.org.

IGNORE THE CONVENTIONAL WISDOM AND BEWARE OF PLACING LIMITS ON YOURSELF

Wal-Mart's founder Sam Walton says, "Swim upstream. Go the other way. If everybody else is doing it one way, there's a good chance you can find your niche by going in exactly the opposite direction. But be prepared for a lot of folks to wave you down and tell you you're headed the wrong way." Sam grew Wal-Mart into the biggest retailer in the world based upon a rebel premise that most experts said was absolutely wrong: creating a big-box discount store in small-town America.

Sam also recounts in his book *Made in America* the 1960 article written about him called "Success Story of the Year." It described how Sam had built an empire of nine variety stores (now they're up to 3,000 stores) and quoted him as saying that Wal-Mart probably wouldn't grow much more because he believed in personally supervising the stores. At that time, he thought any more stores would be "unwieldy" to manage.

This reminds me of the Zig Ziglar story about the fisherman who throws back all the big fish and keeps the small. When a curious observer asks the fisherman why he's throwing away the fish best suited for a feast, the fisherman points to his tiny frying pan and shrugs his shoulders. Don't shortchange yourself! Go get a bigger frying pan if you need it.

I completely understand Sam's perspective. When I had three hotels, it was unfathomable for me to imagine having six. But, now with twenty-five businesses, I have potential capital partners approaching me asking, "Why aren't you twice your size?" Jay B. Hunt, a valuable member of Joie de Vivre's Board of Advisors, is constantly asking me for a strategic plan that details the quantification of our next five years (how many hotels, how much capital required, etc.). I'm always stumped by this, as I remember Sam's strategy: "We're going to take it as it comes." While forecasting future growth is an important business practice (and certainly on the minds of your investors), don't let this ruin the magic of your vision. Do the right things on a daily basis and your business will grow to a size you'd never imagined.

MAKE YOURSELF AVAILABLE TO FATE

University Games founder and CEO Bob Moog has learned that when you're trying to sell a customer, you're really just trying to solve problems for him. The more problems you solve, the stronger relationship you'll build. Each time he'd venture from California back to the New Jersey headquarters of Toys "R" Us (his company's largest purchaser of games), he made a point of trying to further the relationship, not just close another sale.

On his December 1998 trip back east, Bob decided he'd focus this trip on giving Toys "R" Us some suggestions about how they could jump-start their Internet presence. His suggestions fell upon deaf ears—no one was interested. In April 1999, he was back there again. Once again, he wanted to act as a valuable resource to Toys "R" Us, so he targeted a fellow Stanford M.B.A. who worked there to discuss his online vision for the company. By this time, Toys "R" Us stock was being heavily penalized for the company's lack of Internet strategy and eToys had issued its successful

IPO and now had a market capitalization that was beginning to rival Toys "R" Us. This time, Bob was treated as the messiah.

Within a week of his April trip, the chairman and president had flown to University Games's small Bay Area headquarters to meet with Bob and some Silicon Valley venture capitalists. Within another week, Bob was offered, and accepted, the position of CEO in a start-up, Toysrus.com, even though he truly wasn't looking to leave his own company. Opportunities can often come knocking in a faster and more furious fashion when you are open to what fate may offer you.

This story has another interesting wrinkle. Two months after Bob took on the job, he resigned as it was becoming clear that he didn't fit the Toys "R" Us culture. He also wasn't sure if the company was truly committed to this online venture. Just a few weeks after Bob resigned and the venture capitalist for Toysrus.com pulled out, President Robert Nakasone was ousted as the company's market share experienced a precipitous free fall because of their blown Internet strategy. We live in an era of toppling icons. Those who aren't paranoid about new competition like eToys may find themselves playing with toys in the backyard quite soon.

THE TEN QUESTIONS ANY ENTREPRENEUR SHOULD ASK HIMSELF BEFORE GETTING INTO A NEW BUSINESS

Once you've birthed your first business, you can use your learning to help master the next pregnancies. To do this, I've created a filter for how I look at new opportunities. Based upon my business birthing, I've developed the following ten questions as my guiding principles for starting any new business. If at least half my answers suggest that this deal shouldn't be done, I don't pursue the new business.

1. If I pass up this opportunity, will I see a similar deal (or this one) later?
2. What's the opportunity cost of this deal? In other words, does this deal impinge upon some precious resources (my time, money, the company infrastructure, other opportunities)?

3. Is this the kind of project that has me smiling in the shower, or the kind that will keep me up late at night?
4. Are these the kind of partners I'd choose to do business with, or is it just a marriage of convenience?
5. How bad is the downside scenario? What impact would it have on the rest of the company?
6. How competition-proof is the business plan? How do we create barriers to entry?
7. Who's going to run the business day-to-day? If they're unsuccessful, then who's going to run the business?
8. Are there synergies or economies of scale with our existing businesses?
9. Does the business build a bridge to new opportunities we wouldn't see if we didn't do the project? What are we going to learn?
10. Can we double our money in two or three years?

Remember, each new baby has its own personality. My children challenge me: the overachieving hotel, the developmentally disabled restaurant, the precocious spa—and, of course, I love each one for its individuality.

5. Communicating Your Vision

Obstacles are those frightful things you see when you take your eyes off the goal.

—Henry Ford

The rebel's job is to make the complex simple. Tolstoy suggested that everything in the world should be expressed in such a way that an intelligent seven-year-old can understand it.

This is especially true when it comes to your vision. A verbose vision statement will have your employees reaching for the remote control. If you think they'll "stay tuned" if you just create great sound bites, you'll also be disappointed. Sound bites are like popcorn. They seem filling, but an hour later you're hungry again.

The visionary who isn't able to effectively communicate his vision will be awfully lonely. Your co-workers are more likely to embrace your vision if it

- Energizes and inspires people to greatness
- Belongs to everyone and can be succinctly described among the workforce
- Is clear to each person what their specific part is in it
- Gives people an idea of the future payoff for all
- Is tangible and lived out by key role models

There are three primary methods of assuring that your vision resonates with your people: visual, verbal, and aspirational.

THE VISUAL VISION

With the advent of television and computers, young people have grown up in a more visual culture. The truth is, we're all distracted. Attention deficit disorder is a sign of the times. The key skill for working in the twenty-first century will not be a longer attention span but rather the ability to multitask—to do many things at once, well.

Your rank and file may be younger and quite possibly bilingual. They need a message that's universal and memorable. You need to make it visual.

We found out the hard way. We launched our mission statement, "creating opportunities to celebrate the joy of life," with our employees a few years ago, and along with it we circulated a lofty, nine-sentence vision statement. It went right over the heads of our back-of-the-house staff, 80% of whom speak English as a second language. I knew we had to communicate this important message in a different fashion.

Over the next few days, I started sketching visual depictions of how Joie de Vivre runs its business. At our new employee orientations, we talked about being an employee-driven company, but what did that really mean? We asked our staff to lead with their hearts, but did they truly understand this, let alone remember it?

Finally, I had a visual brainstorm. We'd said for some time, "Service is the heart of Joie de Vivre," so I drew a simple heart with four arrows going in a clockwise direction. At the base of the heart, I wrote, "Creating a Unique Corporate Culture," because my highest priority is to preserve our fun-loving, family culture. Following at the left side of the heart was "Building an Enthusiastic Staff," the natural result of our attention to culture. At the top of the heart, I put, "Developing Strong Customer Loyalty," because our staff, not our stylish architecture or pretty brochures, brings return guests to our properties. Finally, at the right side of the heart, "Maintaining a Profitable and Sustainable Business" showed the end result of developing a fiercely loyal customer base. The final arrow goes from the dollar signs back to the culture as our profitable business reinvests in company culture to keep the blood circulating in this cycle.

Thus was christened the Joie de Vivre Heart, a pivotal component of how our employees come to understand what our company is all about. I knew we were onto something when, during a job interview with a potential candidate from one of our biggest competitors, the future employee pulled out of his pocket our Heart and said, "I want to work for you . . . the blood in the company I work for now flows in the opposite direction."

Poor financial performance is almost always a lagging indicator, a function of dissatisfied customers who may have been turned off by disgruntled employees. And low employee morale can almost always be corrected by improving the work climate and company culture. Invest in climate and culture and you'll see improvement in the bottom line—sometimes within a quarter, probably within one year.

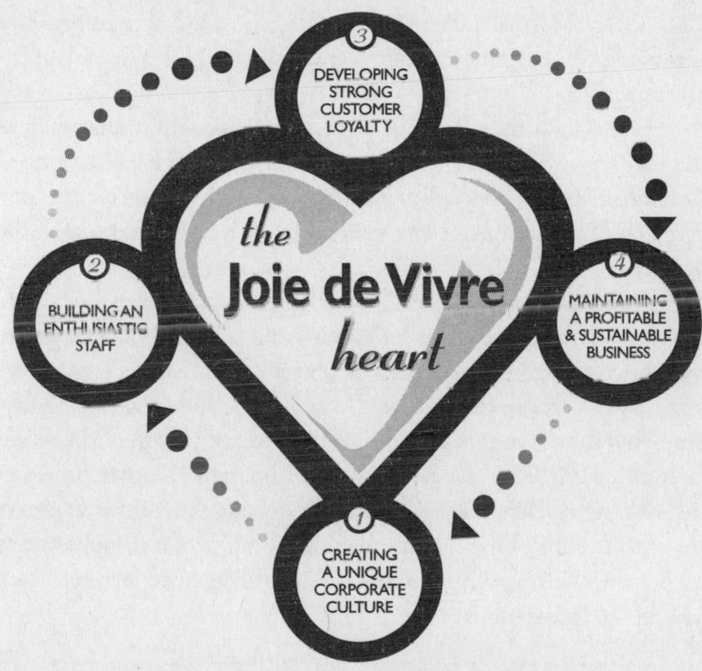

HOW TO CREATE YOUR OWN VISUAL ICON

The Joie de Vivre Heart communicates what the company is all about. This simple image tells you more about our company than any of our individual products ever will. How can you create a visual icon that becomes the rallying point for your company? There are three different questions you can ask to determine what the icon will look like:

1. *People have a deep desire to be connected to something from the past, so is there anything from your founders' or company's past that can help define the company's future?* For example, Hewlett-Packard achieved this connection of past to future with their image of the founders gazing at the futuristic world in their garage. When new CEO Carly Fiorina took over in 1999, she used this image in a worldwide advertising campaign to reintroduce H-P's history of innovation.

2. Some industries have an underlying philosophy that defines success. *Is there an object or shape that best defines your preferred method of operation?* In the hospitality industry, service from the heart is one of the chief aspirations of any general manager, thus it became the focus of our icon.

3. *Does your company already "own" a recognizable icon that can be used to make your point?* Former Coca-Cola CEO Robert Goizueta used this approach by asking his employees to visualize a large sixty-four-ounce Coke bottle. He would then tell them that this bottle represents the amount of liquid that the average person of the world consumes a day. Then he asked them to imagine the two ounces at the bottom, which is Coca-Cola's market share of worldwide beverage consumption. That visual image helped Goizueta emphasize to his behemoth company that there was still a huge market share available to be captured.

THE VERBAL VISION

Some of today's best rebel business leaders are great storytellers. The best means of getting your vision across is to communicate on a one-on-one basis or in small groups with your employees. In a small company, this may be an option, but many rebel companies have outgrown this approach, and sometimes, they find their visionary's words twisted.

★ ★ ★

BUSINESS REBEL HALL OF FAME PROFILE

Howard Schultz (Chairman of Starbucks)

Ten years ago, who could have imagined that coffee could become so sexy? While coffee was always a delicacy in Europe, Americans' idea of good coffee was still dictated by Maxwell House. Visionary Howard Schultz dusted off this old commodity and invested in dramatically improving the coffee-drinking experience. He aspired to "take something old and tired and common—coffee—and weave a sense of romance and community around it." What's revolutionary is that Howard was able to demonstrate that if you upscaled the coffee experience, not only could you increase the price, but you could also broaden the market.

Howard joined the company at twenty-seven and engineered a buy out to become chairman at age thirty-one, when Starbucks had fewer than 100 employees. Since then, the company has grown to billions in sales with more than 25,000 employees worldwide. In order to control the quality of Starbucks's product, Howard insisted that the company control the process from start to finish—from the selection and procurement of the beans to their roasting and blending to their ultimate consumption. This "out-of-the-box" approach was met with skepticism by industry observers at first, but it's part of the reason Starbucks has the most loyal customer base of any American food and beverage retailer.

When he rejoined the company in 1987 to take over operations, Howard needed to reconnect with employees who were skeptical about his plans. It was a pivotal moment in the company's history, requiring a well-crafted message to build team momentum. Howard used three simple rules to get his point across. These will be valuable to any rebel with a vision. First, speak from your heart. Second, put yourself in your employees' shoes. And, finally, share the big dream with them.

My advice? Develop a vocabulary that becomes the mantra for your rebel organization. Language guides culture. At Disney, it's guests, not customers. At the Republic of Tea, customers are called citizens. At Joie de Vivre, we call the service staff "hosts," because that implies that they are ambassadors to the hotel and the city.

We often use words with each other and wonder why our cohorts don't get what we're talking about, so use key words carefully. In my own case, I found three words consistently popping into my Joie de Vivre discussions. I also realized that these words—better than any others—described my vision for the company. I spent thirty minutes at our 1998 midyear management retreat talking about what each word means to me.

When it comes to how we treat our people, I want us to create an *inspiring* environment. To be inspired is to feel connected "in spirit," and that feeling is more powerful than anything else we can create. An inspired employee is worth a pot of gold.

I want products and promotions to be *compelling*. Marketing is meant to be a call to action. Anything compelling is hard to resist.

When it comes to how our leaders manage, I expect them to be *effective*. Peter Drucker's landmark book, *The Effective Executive,* explains that effective executives focus on results, not on work. Periodically, managers should ask, "What can I contribute that will significantly affect the performance and the results of the institution I serve?" The emphasis on contribution puts the executive's unique gifts first, in contrast to "What work should I do?" which puts the work first.

Those three words—*inspiring, compelling,* and *effective*—trip out of my mouth more often than I'd like to admit. But now my associates know that the words define benchmarks used throughout the organization to determine whether our practices are aligned with our vision.

Once you've got the language down, it's time to do your Oprah impersonation. One of the best methods of spreading your vision is in Town Hall meetings. Wal-Mart popularized this idea with their Saturday morning meetings at the headquarters in Arkansas that is transmitted by satellite to their stores around the world. Sam Walton used these meetings to share information, build teamwork, and celebrate the successes.

While Wal-Mart's weekly format is purposely unpredictable to keep peoples' attention, there are a few basics that you'll see at these now-famous meetings. They'll study one particular store in detail to highlight some positive lessons to be learned throughout their stores (the store manager may be flown into Bentonville, Arkansas, from anywhere on the planet to take a bow at the meeting). This is the place where the Wal-Mart leaders may declare an audacious goal that seems unattainable and then ask the team how they can make it work. This is also the place where they talk about strategies for attacking their competitors with the follow-up occurring at the store level as soon as the simulcasted meeting is complete.

Sam Walton said, "The Saturday morning meeting is where we discuss and debate much of our philosophy and our management strategy: it is the focal point of all our communication efforts." This is an amazing evolution from the typical discussion at the water cooler to this tool that spreads the vision for the world's largest retailer.

THE ASPIRATIONAL VISION

Another method for spreading the word is to choose an ambitious award or goal that gets people's attention. Doing this can help build *clarity* about the vision and *solidarity* among the team members.

At our 1998 annual management retreat, I described a letter I'd received from an up-and-coming young manager who'd just flown our coop to join a much bigger national company. Eric Sinoway said that he enjoyed his time with Joie de Vivre and believed that we ought to apply for the *Fortune* magazine annual "100 Best Companies to Work For." I asked our management team what they thought. Not surprisingly, they were eager to go for it, as it suited perfectly our Joie de Vivre Heart and philosophy of business.

During the course of the next few months, we received informative measuring tools from the Great Places to Work Institute and Hewitt Associates, the companies that determine *Fortune*'s top 100. This helped our employee development department learn quickly which practices, beyond what we already offered, were necessary to make the final list. What we found was that the "100 Best" companies invest more money, effort, and time in their people by offering broader and more meaningful benefits programs, a share in the company's success, and a commitment to personal growth. Striving for the award made tangible our message that being one of the best places to work in America remains a pivotal part of Joie de Vivre's vision.

Finally, when Jack Welch took over as leader of General Electric in 1981, he knew his role was to make the complex simple. This was not an easy task, as this diversified company was in products from electric turbines to television networks, with more than half GE's $27 billion in revenue coming from slow-growth businesses. Welch created a concrete, to-the-point aspiration for the company: We're either number 1 or number 2 in every business that GE is in, or we fix it, close it, or sell it. Over two decades, GE has divested itself of nearly $20 billion worth of businesses, but has spent more than $50 billion in acquisitions that better fit its goal of being a leader in each field it's competing in.

What audacious award or goal can you shoot for? I promise you it will get your people's attention.

6. Creating a Passionate Culture

How I thought it worked was that if you were great, like Martin Luther King, you had a dream. Since I wasn't great, I figured I had no dream and the best I could do was go listen to those who did. But what I now believe is this: It's having the dream that makes you great. It's the dream that produces the greatness. It's the passion we have for what we want that draws others around us and attracts the resources it takes to accomplish the dreams.

—Barbara Waugh,
manager of worldwide personnel,
Hewlett-Packard Labs

Rebel companies produce dreamers. And those dreamers create an organization that may fly in the face of conventional wisdom. A quarter of a century ago, that meant Southwest Airlines doing everything it could to be outrageous: painting its planes funny colors, predating Ally McBeal with professional miniskirts on their flight attendants, and promoting a culture based upon fun and frivolity in an industry traditionally obsessed with its enormous hard-asset investment. A decade ago, that meant Starbucks offering full-time and part-time employees health insurance benefits and stock options when this was unheard of in the convenience retail business, which had historically treated its workers as a highly replaceable asset.

Rebel companies translate the founder's vision into the people's passion. You can feel the vibe when you walk in the door. I'm sure you remember the first day at one of your past jobs. By the end of that first day, both the subtle and obvious attitudes and actions of your coworkers told you whether this was a "whistle while you work" workplace. Your coworkers carry around a report card pasted on their forehead about what they think of their workplace.

Justice Telecom, the fastest-growing American company in 1998 (based upon *Inc.* magazine's annual list) has created a counterculture culture with free dog care, subsidized commuting bicycles or skateboards, and a companywide lunch the day before each payday. This cutting-edge telecommunications company has become the nirvana for many Southern California Generation Xers who could barely imagine that they'd be able to work in such a lifestyle-oriented environment. It may help that founder David Glickman was just thirty-three years old when his company was featured in *Inc.*

The culture at rebel companies can best be described as "work hard, play hard." Rebel companies dare to be different and their cultures show it. Since "thinking outside the box" has become nearly an "inside the box" convention in most companies, we are seeing more experimentation than ever in the creation of employee motivating tools. But it is essential that a company's culture be a natural extension of who the company is. Rapid change requires that companies have a stable center. The company culture is the nucleus of that ricocheting, amplified playing field we call the workplace.

John Mackey, CEO of Whole Foods Markets, believes that if you get the company's purpose and values right, a vibrant corporate culture will naturally follow. It doesn't have to have the dot-com, youth-focused flavor that we see emblazoned on popular business magazine covers. You don't have to allow dogs at work or skateboarding lunch breaks. Your company's culture should be as distinct as you are. The key question to ask yourself is, "Does your company's culture support your company's values and allow sustained profitability?"

The most culture-focused companies almost *treat their work climate as a brand* because it reinforces their image in the marketplace. Hewlett-Packard is known for the high level of respect it pays its people, and this carries over to the customer. Nordstrom and Ritz-Carlton built corporate cultures based upon empowerment, giving their service staff extraordinary flexibility in solving customer problems. Southwest and Disney are all about creating an enthusiastic environment to work in, and their customers are the beneficiaries.

Successful companies may have a cultural leader (quite often the founder or president), but the responsibility of sustaining the culture is the domain of the HR professionals. Why is it then that the average company's human resources department is so totally disengaged from this process of creating culture? Most companies focus on the science rather than the art of managing people, and their HR staff might as well be located in the insurance department because it's all about risk aversion. Consequently, companies bleed good people. In a knowledge economy, when you're bleeding good people, you're bleeding value.

Barbara Waugh believes that most companies experience a huge lost opportunity when they assign HR to paper-pushing and the policy police. The company hierarchy only thinks of HR as a transaction processing department (payroll, benefits, recruiting, evaluations). Most HR folks go into the field because they are "people people." If charged with challenging the status quo, they can identify and feed the rebels, the risk-takers who are going to lead the innovation in your organization. HR accomplishes this by standing up for the rebels. Barb calls this "amplifying the positive deviants" and believes it's a key responsibility of HR departments. Instead of trying to make the misfits *fit in* by rounding their jagged edges, Barbara focuses on creating a culture that prizes its misfits.

Usually, the HR department wants the employees to conform. They don't foment revolution. Rarely is the HR director seen as a "friend of the people," and consequently the department spends most of its time with crisis management, whether it's wrongful terminations or sexual harassment claims.

It becomes a self-fulfilling prophecy. If your HR staff spends all their time creating rules to deal with potential negative employee situations, that's the world they'll play in, and, that's how your employees will use the department. Take this approach and your company culture will be stunted. To unleash your people's passion, you first have to build their trust. But you have to start by building the trust of your HR professionals.

HOW TO FIGURE OUT YOUR EMPLOYEES' PRIORITIES

Before you rush out in search of that dot-com feeling for your company, consider what's unique about your people. You can make your business feel young again if you ask "What motivates our people?" You might be surprised what you learn if you ask them. You might also find that you don't have to start all over again building a new corporate culture—you may just need to get in touch with what made your company great in the first place.

Over the course of two years, while teaching a class to our employees called "Creating Your Own Personal Mission Statement," I asked employees to rank motivational tools from 1 to 14 based upon their priorities. Here are the composite results from our anonymous survey of nearly one hundred employees:

1. *Recognition for My Achievement*
2. *Company and Personal Sense of Mission*
3. *Freedom and Creativity*
4. *Ethical Harmony*
5. *Sense of Teamwork*
6. *Intellectual Stimulation and Learning*
7. *Opportunity for Career Growth*
8. *Variety in What I Do*
9. *Compensation*
10. *Flexible Work Schedule*
11. *Power and Decision-Making Authority*
12. *Work Environment Aesthetics*
13. *Job Security*
14. *Status and Prestige*

Do these rankings surprise you? Historically, most managers have assumed that compensation, power, security, and status were the top motivational tools. Yet these ranked in the bottom six. Only when companies fail to address the first eight issues do their people revert to those traditional motivators—the higher salary, the better title, the gold watch at retirement. In Frederick Herzberg's classic 1968 article, "How Do You Motivate Employees?" he found that the motivating influences in a job were intrinsic to the job: achievement, recognition for achievement, the work itself, responsibility, and growth or advancement. Job dissatisfaction tended to come from factors he called hygienic, those that were outside the employee's specific job responsibilities: company policy, relationship with supervisor, salary, status, and security. This landmark article suggests that job enrichment (now often called "empowerment") is the key to success in building high employee morale.

If your HR department can tap into your employees' highest needs and their unspoken desires, you will find ferocious passion erupting from deep within your company.

CREATING A KING OR QUEEN OF CORPORATE CULTURE

Southwest Airlines chairman Herb Kelleher once said something that ought to be tattooed on every HR director's door: "The tragedy of our time is that we've got it backwards. We've learned to love techniques and use people." Some HR personnel become jaded after a while because they feel underutilized. Like lawyers and police officers, they develop a healthy suspicion of human nature because of the sticky personnel situations that they're constantly asked to resolve.

First determine whether your HR leaders are open to a shift in perspective. Spend a few hours brainstorming with them about the impact HR could have if it were broadened beyond matters of administration. Is your HR team enthused by this prospect? You may be surprised by the unspoken dreams these people have for their work, but you need to convince them that you're talking about long-term changes in the department (and appropriate staffing to accomplish the mission), not just band-aids. To send the message of change, consider renaming the department Employee Development or the People Department (as Southwest Airlines' calls it).

Once you've enlisted this department in the cause of developing the corporate culture, it is essential that you define what will make them successful. Beyond changing the title of the department and determining the receptivity for change by the department head, you need to make sure that all *other* department heads see the importance of Employee Development. Many see it as a passive department that responds to problems rather than a proactive department that cultivates the culture and builds employee passion for the company.

In the end, it's a matter of deciding what gets attention in this department. There will always be administrative distractions that will take time away from truly developing employees. Invest in buffers that allow the science of HR to be accomplished efficiently while the art of HR is allowed to flourish. Provide this department the time and space to create outrageous employee events, innovative training programs that engage your people in the enterprise, and remarkable incentives that assure that everyone has a stake in your company's success. Gauge HR's quantitative success not just on their ability to reduce employee turnover or limit wrongful termination claims, but also judge the department by how they raise employee morale in your employee satisfaction surveys.

Your other department heads need to understand the positive results they'll experience once Employee Development gets humming. Operations will likely see less staff turnover and more motivated employees. Accounting will see lower labor costs. Sales and marketing will find that advertising can be decreased because customer satisfaction has sparked a remarkable word-of-mouth campaign (training and advertising costs tend to be inversely proportional in many companies, especially in the service industry).

DEVELOPING YOUR OWN CULTURAL PROGRAM

Creating a unique corporate culture is at the foundation of our company's success, yet few companies invest in culture as if it's a pivotal part of their strategic plan.

Jane Howard, our vice president of employee development, is our queen of corporate culture and Samantha Bryer is our princess. Jane and Saman-

BUSINESS REBEL HALL OF FAME PROFILE

Herb Kelleher (Cofounder and Chairman of Southwest Airlines)

One of the foundations of Southwest's financial success is the fact that they keep their airplanes in the air approximately 30 percent more hours than their competition thanks to the simplicity of their strategy of short-haul flights with one primary type of aircraft, the Boeing 737. Herb's profitable business model is now being emulated by other airlines around the world.

But Herb's gift as a rebel is due to his mouth being full of his heart. Herb was one of the first American CEOs who started talking about a relationship-driven, rather than a performance-driven, organization. "The customer always comes second . . . our employees are first." "The heart of the service journey is spiritual rather than mechanical." It's no wonder the company's New York Stock Exchange symbol is LUV, as this rebel company is one of America's models for the twenty-first century.

Southwest has created a celebratory culture that has, amazingly, become more solid as the company has grown. They're the most profitable airline, with the highest customer satisfaction scores in the business, and the most rabidly passionate employees in the industry. It's not surprising Southwest was named the #1 Company to Work for in America by *Fortune* magazine.

tha are responsible for creating a cohesive and consistent culture amid the chaos that reigns in this rebel company. We look to them as the experts on what fits and what doesn't fit our culture, as well as how we motivate and tailor-make perks to the changing desires of our employee base.

Jane uses many benchmarks to determine how we're doing versus model companies, including *Fortune*'s annual review of the 100 Best Companies to Work For, which comes out at the start of each year. It lists all kinds of unique perks, and since Joie de Vivre competes for this award, we're able to compare our scores with the best companies.

Additionally, the employee development department forecasts the results of our annual work climate surveys for each of our businesses before the data are tallied. This tells them whether they're close to the heartbeat of our employees. There are other opportunities for this department to "hear" from employees, including quarterly open forums with Jane and me and nine employee retreats per year.

Jane also analyzes Joie de Vivre University participation (there will be more on this in the next chapter) since her department created and manages this ambitious program. A final benchmark Jane uses is the twice-annual composite review her department receives from the general managers of each of our properties to determine whether her department has been responsive to their needs.

Jane's department supervises Employee Recognition Week, creating and running more than a half-dozen fun, major events during this celebration as well as other wacky activities throughout the year. The HR department's influence on a company's culture doesn't have to be limited to planning the holiday party.

This may sound like a lot to expect from your HR department. They can't do it alone. Whether you have a Culture Club or, as Ben & Jerry's calls it, a Joy Gang (complete with a Grand Poobah), your company can rely upon other passionate employees to organize fun activities for the whole gang. This is all part of creating a corporate culture.

I'm a big believer in fun, especially when it's connected with recognition. Wells Fargo Bank created a "You're Good Company" coupon that allowed employees to award each other with a $35 bonus for great performance. The employees who received the most coupons qualified to win outrageous awards at a dinner hosted by the bank's top executives. These awards included a day supervising and training the company president in *their* job, a balloon bouquet delivered to their office every month of the year, and a menu item named in their honor in the Wells Fargo cafeteria.

The employee who receives the award or attention certainly gets a positive sense of recognition, but this carries over to other employees too. When it's done right, a sense of pride builds in the organization and leads to improved customer service and a more profitable business. It's simple. Consider lending a bouquet of flowers—keep it on your desk for a half-hour and then present it as a gift to another employee and ask them to do the same. Or rename your conference rooms after the nicknames of your most gregarious employees. Or give your employees a surprise day off or an afternoon shopping spree (but ask them to go in pairs to celebrate together). We announced a free day off for all employees at our annual holiday party, based upon their contribution to our strong financial year. We also offer a "Joy Pass" for a free afternoon off once a quarter for our home office staff. This paid dividends in increased employee loyalty.

Here's another tip for your king or queen of culture: don't forget the family! Much has been written recently about how many employees have substituted the workplace for home as the primary locus of their sense of family. It's no wonder when you find increasingly more personal concierges, luxurious gyms, and gourmet cafeterias at corporate headquarters. But the more you make work feel like home, the more you risk alienating the family.

Xerox created a LifeCycle Assistance Program that funds employee work-family benefits in the areas of child care, mortgage assistance, personal emergencies, and extended household health care (each of which were very topical problems for their employees). Each employee is given a "virtual" $10,000, which they may draw upon anytime during their employment in $2,000 annual increments. It's almost as if Xerox acts like a parent to the employees, always available to fund some of those rainy day situations that naturally arise.

What else can your HR department do to foster passion in your people? Create teamwork by amplifying the significance of groups and celebrating small wins. These small wins build confidence, which leads to more small wins. Before you know it, you've developed a passionate, winning spirit that becomes a legacy for your organization.

The power of a highly focused team cannot be overestimated. In the high-tech arena, most of the engineering breakthroughs have come from small teams. Unix was developed by two people. Sun Microsystem's Java was created by a team of less than five, and Netscape's Mosaic was started by only four people.

Eric Schmidt, CEO of Novell, who helped develop Java while chief technology officer at Sun, believes that teams are more effective when they're small and that maturing companies have to guard against the natural growth in the size of teams. The smaller the team, the more the sense of ownership of its members and the less likelihood for bureaucracy. His simple rule for keeping techie teams small: don't allow the team to be any larger than the ability of the company's largest conference room to accommodate them.

Over the years, our employee development department has used many team-building games to facilitate collaboration. The following three are my favorites, although they are truly rebel exercises since most companies wouldn't pursue them because they can be emotionally challenging and make your people feel vulnerable (but that's part of the reason these exercises can be so effective—the barriers come crashing down). In order for these to work, the participants must feel an inherent trust in the people leading the exercise. You can develop that trust by letting the group create the ground rules (confidentiality, respect, communication, etc.) and by making sure the leaders of the exercise take the lead in exposing their feelings and beliefs.

THE EMPATHY EXERCISE

This exercise is particularly helpful when you have two groups that are feuding within the organization. Split up into two groups: group A and group B. For example, half from the corporate headquarters and half from the satellite offices. Each person spends time individually writing answers to these questions about his current job:

1. What are your greatest professional challenges and fears?
2. In what areas at work do you need more support or more tools?
3. At what task or activity do you spend the most amount of time on an average day?
4. What most frustrates you about dealing with the people from the other group?

Then each person from group A draws a name of someone from group B (headquarters folks draw satellite managers' names and vice versa). Now you're faced with the challenge of trying to answer these same questions from their perspective. Once you try to get inside of the mind of the person whose name you've drawn, they then read what they wrote about themselves at the start of the exercise. This is an effective bridge-building tool for groups that need to understand and respect each other more.

THE THING I LIKE ABOUT . . .

This exercise focuses on what's going right in the organization when you need to build morale. Each person takes a piece of paper and anonymously writes down the name of another person in the group along with a professional characteristic she admires about that person. All the pieces go in a hat and are chosen randomly by the participants. When you choose a sheet, you go stand in front of the person who's receiving the accolade and talk to them as if you were the one who wrote the positive comments.

HE SAID, SHE SAID

Conflict occurs in even the best of companies. Sometimes the best solution is for all participants to admit their faults freely so that no one seems righteous. This exercise forces each participant to look at their own part in the mess that may have been created. Sometimes conflict can develop during this exercise. That's fine as long as all parties are respectful. There's a myth that Employee Development is all about warm feelings and talking nice. Not necessarily. The facilitator's role is to provide a safe forum for openness, vulnerability, and conflict resolution.

Draw a four-box grid and list a situation in each box when:

Box 1—You did something wrong and your coworker did something wrong in return.

Box 2—You did something wrong, but your coworker did nothing wrong in return.

Box 3—Your coworker did something wrong, but you did nothing wrong in return.

Box 4—You and your coworker did nothing wrong and worked well together.

While it may be challenging for a person in conflict to come up with a situation for every box (especially Box 2, in which you are at fault but your coworker isn't), the process of thinking this way opens each person up to the possibility that they aren't always in the right.

. . .

Finally, while creating fun, celebrating families, and fostering teamwork are essential responsibilities of the HR department, the almighty buck still hasn't lost its impact in producing employee passion. The rebel company recognizes that in just the past decade the number of employers offering incentive compensation grew from 50 percent to 75 percent.

An entrepreneurial culture can be sustained even in a multibillion-dollar company like Microsoft. When you realize that the 16,000 Seattle-area employees of Microsoft earn an average of $250,000 annually (including stock options and benefits), you can understand that compensation is a critical ingredient in creating passion.

Or consider this. In 1974, 200,000 workers owned equity in their company. By 1999, this number had grown to 10 million.

Yet many companies don't have the luxury of offering skyrocketing stock options to their employees. What's an HR director to do if she's on a tight budget? Go buy Bob Nelson's book, *1001 Ways to Reward Employees.* He's got a great list of zany rewards that can help spread positive word-of-mouth throughout your company, like writing five Post-it notes thanking someone for a job well done and hiding them among the employee's papers, or hiring a catering service to bring lunch to a special employee for a week. He also recommends renting a sports car for a week for your star employee, but ARCNet, a telecommunications company took this one step further.

ARCNet leased BMWs, with fully paid insurance, for all of their workers who had been on the job for at least a year (more than half of their fifty-seven employees). The company chose this unusual perk because it was less expensive than new rounds of recruiting and training. E-Trade gave this idea a rebel spin at a performance-celebrating party by handing the keys of thirty Harley-Davidson motorcycles to employees who met aggressive goals.

Jeff Bezos, Steve Jobs, Martha Stewart—these rebels are passionate about what they do. The trick is to assure that their people feel that passion and carry it into the workplace with them daily. While the bells and whistles of employee perks will always get your employees' attention, it's the culture that is enduring. If you think of your work climate or culture as its own brand, you'll be far along in unleashing the "tiger in your tank" that spells success for your rebel company.

7. Building Corporate Instinct

In the society of organizations, it is safe to assume that anyone with any knowledge will have to acquire new knowledge every four or five years or become obsolete.

—Peter Drucker

Gut instinct. For me, there's some weird connection between my solar plexus and my brain. When my gut is right, I have peace of mind. When it's off, I suffer unceasing doubt and my mind chatter keeps me up at night. For the gardener, gut instinct is knowing when to pull the carrots. For the chef, it's knowing when the cake is baked just right. For the rebel, it means knowing just how to defy conventional wisdom in a way that will work.

Why did Fox founder Rupert Murdoch believe he could create another American television network? In 1985, the three established networks were in the early stages of what would become a long decline. The infrastructure costs to create a network were staggering. Yet, Murdoch hired another instinct-based rebel, Barry Diller, who masterminded Fox's successful plan.

The rebel can't do it all on his own. And simply hiring a rebel CEO isn't enough either. Each company has a collection of time-tested rules of thumb that can't be found in any employee manual. For example, Cisco Systems CEO John Chambers knows that any new corporate acquisition should be valued at about $2 million per engineer for the acquired company. Rebel companies create mini-CEOs throughout the company by teaching a business point of view to their people so that these valuable rules of thumb become common knowledge.

Your most valuable assets probably don't appear on your balance sheet. Two of the rebel's three key intangible assets—reputation and relationships—are addressed in other chapters. Those two pivotal assets determine how a company is perceived and how it connects with the world. The third, indigenous intelligence, provides a company with more than just knowledgeable people. It establishes a framework for creating corporate instinct and causes that knowledge to proliferate throughout the organization.

You can instantly tell the difference between a company that's learning twenty-four hours a day and one that's half-asleep. Employees in a learning company are always asking questions, questioning assumptions, and reveling in their chance to grow. You might see an inherent contrariness in the people, but it's balanced by a childlike innocence about what could and should be.

There's an inherent assumption within the rebel organization that building corporate instinct is a good long-term goal for the company. Management needn't fear that it will train employees only to watch them leave to join the competition. No, the rebel leader doesn't fear "brain drain." As long as the inquisitive culture thrives, its legacy of learning allows a powerful corporate gut instinct to grow.

Most companies are full of what Professor Haim Mendelson calls "islands of knowledge," small receptacles of key information that aren't available to everyone else. For example, the purchasing department may know that a particular supplier produces a poor product and they always miss their delivery date. Unfortunately, a line manager may not know that information until after they've gotten burned by the supplier. The key is to turn these islands into concentric circles where information is shared, whether it be between departments or individuals.

In a rebel company, the *desire to know more* is more important than *what* you know. So, how do you teach instinct? Aren't some people just born with a people or merchant sense? Concepts discussed in this chapter will come more easily for certain employees. But instinct always begins with knowledge, making your first step a concerted effort to build the company brain trust. And there is no better way to teach your people business sense than by using open-book management.

OPEN-BOOK MANAGEMENT

Rebel companies are incubators for entrepreneurs. The ideal company engages all its people to think like owners. At Joie de Vivre, we strive to improve the business literacy of everyone involved in our enterprise, from managers to maids and bartenders to bellmen. At our 1999 management retreat, each of the managers of our twenty-five businesses (as well as all department heads in the home office) was responsible for presenting his plan for incorporating open-book management into their operations.

("Open-book management" was popularized by Jack Stack in his book *The Great Game of Business* in 1992, in which he told the story of how he turned a nearly bankrupt company, Springfield ReManufacturing Corporation, into a profitable model for employee empowerment. Management chose to "open the books," to share all of the financial information of the business in a fun, educational format that helped to engage the employees in the process of turning around the company. Author John Case has written a couple of excellent follow-up books, *Open-Book Management* and *The Open-Book Experience*.)

In-room Service Manager Ana Maria Sanchez at The Maxwell Hotel provided much inspiration for the growth of open-book management in our company. For months, Ana Maria had been frustrated by her housekeeping and maintenance staff arriving late for work. While her initial reaction was to threaten the employees with being fired, she knew that this would be difficult given the union rules. She tried lecturing the group and writing individual written warnings, but her employees did not seem to understand why this was important to her. So Ana Maria calculated the financial impact of her employee's tardiness on the hotel's net income.

At a meeting with her thirty-five employees, she presented her findings and led a group discussion on the subject. Her employees' interest was stimulated. But only when she introduced a new game did she have them in the palm of her hand. Ana Maria announced that for the next month, a tally board showing on-time attendance would be installed next to the time clock. Previously, only 80 percent of the employees on any given day were arriving on time for their shift. She set a goal of 94 percent (in later months, when this caught on, she encouraged her staff to set the monthly goals) and told them that she would list those employees on a daily basis who were not on time. She announced a prize of a lunch for the whole group if they made their goal for the month.

Not only did they make their goal that month (scoring almost 100 percent), but they beat their new goal the next month, which won them the right to be served dinner by the CEO (me), the general manager, and a few other corporate hotshots who weren't used to wearing an apron. The photos from this celebratory dinner still grace the walls of their break room a year after the event. Ana Maria says the most interesting result was that staff members began holding each other accountable in a direct yet respectful manner. The us-versus-them (management and labor) atmosphere began to dissipate at this unionized property, where the average staffer had worked for nearly twenty years.

There's another story about The Maxwell Hotel that shows the power of open-book management. Before we took over this hotel, the operation had never aggressively pushed their room rates during the busier time of the year. Lee Rolfe, the reservations manager, had been with the hotel for seventeen years before we began operating the property. No one had ever explained what impact he alone could have on the value of the hotel.

In one of our early training sessions, we asked Lee and his colleagues to play a game. Let's say that Lee booked fifty room nights per day as a reservationist. Based upon his improved perception of the hotel as well as some training in "upselling" (persuading potential guests to upgrade from standard to deluxe accommodations, thus increasing their average room rate), we'll say that Lee was able to increase the average rate for his hotel reservations from $122 to $130, or $8. Doing this for one year, how much does Lee's work increase the value of the hotel? (You can try noodling this one yourself, although there are some industry standard value calculations you may not know.)

After a couple minutes of calculating, Lee and the others raised their hands and said that Lee could have nearly a $100,000 impact on the hotel's value. (This was based upon 50 room nights multiplied by 5 workdays per week multiplied by 50 workweeks per year multiplied by $8 per room night. This equals $100,000, and since there are virtually no direct costs associated with the higher rate aside from slightly higher credit card fees, the increase in net income is virtually equal to the increase in revenue.) A buzz began in the room. This was a large number, but they didn't know the half of it.

I told the employees that real estate investors begin with the net income of a property—and "capitalize" it—to determine the property's value. The "cap rate" for a San Francisco Union Square hotel might be 10 percent, which means that the investor would take the total annual net income for the property, which might be $2,000,000, and divide it by 10 percent (.10), which would calculate to a value of $20,000,000. Using this formula, Lee's upselling skills, which generated $100,000 in increased net income, could justify a $1,000,000 jump in the *value* of The Maxwell Hotel. Jaws dropped. The reality set in. One person can have an enormous impact on a business's value. In the year following that meeting, the average rate of Lee's reservations actually grew by more than $12 instead of $8!

One hotel, two examples of how open-book management can teach employees to make a significant difference. It proves the great rebel maxim: *If you want to improve something, start measuring it.* And, if you want to sustain it, make sure your employees are well rewarded for their performance. Here's a simple sequence of steps that can make such a program work:

1. Identify the critical numbers that your staff can impact and the status of your current numbers.
2. Post the critical numbers regularly on a scoreboard (preferably in a fun, visual format).
3. Conduct basic financial training and develop strategies for making an impact.
4. Review the success of those strategies and identify "best practices."
5. Play a game with a critical number (when possible, let them create the goals).
6. Set up a reward bonus system (make sure your employees thoroughly understand it) and give recognition as often as possible.
7. Communicate the results throughout the organization.

Two final notes of caution on open-book management. First, beware of sharing proprietary numbers or trade secrets with employees who don't understand the strategic necessity for discretion.

Second, be careful substituting open-book management incentive compensation for competitively driven base pay. In doing a market wage survey at one of our hotels, we found that the hotel was paying 10 to 20 percent below the average market wage for employees. But we also knew that this hotel was going to pay sizable year-end bonuses to staff (based upon the hotel's strong profitability) in a couple of months equal to nearly 15 percent of each employee's total annual pay. Rather than decisively upgrading base pay immediately, we sheepishly chose to wait to do this until after the sizable year-end bonuses were paid.

Unfortunately, due to year-end accounting delays, these bonuses weren't paid until the end of February, by which time a handful of great employees had already been poached by other hungry employers. Ironically, this hotel (which paid the company's highest per employee bonuses of the year) ended up experiencing the highest turnover of any of our businesses during that quarter. The moral of the story: don't starve your people while distracting them with a big carrot.

THE "HUNCH KNACK" WINS THE GAME

Building corporate instinct is all about improving your staff's ability to imagine the future. It's a game called hunch, in which your employees learn to forecast future performance based upon their intuition about current trends. We've learned that rebel companies build this instinct at all levels of the organization by sharing the numbers. (Whole Foods Markets shares such detailed financial and performance information that the Securities and Exchange Commission (SEC) has designated all 6,500 employees "insiders" for stock-trading purposes. That's a "transparent company.") Before your people can improve their hunch knack, however, they need to know the benchmarks. That's where you come in.

It is essential that every person in your organization have an agreed-upon measurement of what's expected of him—*and* a method for measuring how he's doing relative to the benchmark. But the benchmark needn't necessarily be driven by the bottom line. It could be linked to customer service or safety or employee satisfaction. It's always helpful to teach your staff what benchmarks are used at your competitors. This provides a reality check, assuring your staff that you're not setting unreasonable goals. It also serves as a rallying cry for the team, which will typically want to beat its competitors' numbers.

Once the benchmarks are clear, it's time to start building your employees' hunch knack. When they are asked to forecast, three positive things happen. First, they take responsibility for understanding the numbers. Second, they learn how they can affect the numbers. Third, they build a sense of camaraderie as they strive to succeed.

And there's one additional benefit for you. By using this process, you quickly learn whether a manager or a division is "getting it." When one of your managers is constantly off on his forecasts, it tends to reveal bigger problems: he doesn't understand or care about the numbers, his staff is misaligned or unmotivated, or there are major market forces making predictability impossible.

Make a game out of it with a Hunch Knack Snack break. Have each of your employees guess what the monthly revenue (or anything else) will be and give a $100 bonus to the winner. Or design the forecasting competition between various divisions to build teamwork within each group. Either way, the net result is gaining your peoples' attention and focusing them on the same numbers that concern you.

USING DASHBOARDS TO SPREAD THE MESSAGE

The introduction of dashboards sprang from another Joie de Vivre dilemma. We have some seven hundred employees working throughout our various businesses in Northern California and approximately thirty employees in our "home office." We grew from four to twenty-five businesses in the course of about four years. For one eighteen-month stretch, we opened a new hotel or restaurant every ten weeks in San Francisco. For those in the franchise world, this may sound like no great achievement. In our "boutique" hospitality business, that's fast growth, since each of our businesses is handcrafted and follows no single business strategy or marketing plan.

During the course of this growth, we found that our old form of communication—talking to managers and expecting them to spread the news—began to break down. Our company newsletter, *Pillow Talk,* helped a little, but it didn't capture the specific strategy necessary for each individual business. We tried to hold our managers accountable, but they swore they were passing on such vital information to their staff as new hire orientations at the home office and monthly service and financial goals.

Our solution was to buy a bunch of bulletin boards (we call them dashboards), one for each location, and affix six category headlines with enough space under each to fit at least a letter-sized piece of paper. We produced six headlines that represented the key information we wanted our managers to communicate to their troops: (1) last month's financial performance, (2) financial goals for this month (along with any short-term incentive program), (3) last month's customer service scores, (4) home office communication (upcoming courses, job openings, newsletter), (5) property-specific communication (complimentary letters from guests, recent media about the property), and (6) a manager's monthly message, which highlighted current priorities and featured a specific employee's positive contribution.

We call this our dashboard because this instrument panel monitors the key success factors in navigating a business. Putting up these boards encourages our managers to walk their talk and allows our vice president of operations, Fred deStefano, to tour a property at will and see what's being communicated to the staff. Even though our home office department leaders can no longer attend every property staff meeting, this technique gives us a sense of what priorities are being presented to the employees. This is now a performance measure for managers. Outdated, bare, or boring dashboards get lower scores in their evaluations.

Visit any rebel company and take a look at what's posted on the walls in the employee common areas, especially in the kitchen or coffee area where people mingle. You're likely to see capitalist propaganda decorating the walls—performance data, cheerleading letters from the CEO, positive correspondence from customers. The purpose is to create dialogue amongst the employees about how we operate the business.

According to the Center for Workforce Development, up to 70 percent of what employees know about their jobs they learn informally from the people they work with (formal training accounts for the other 30 percent). Upgrading the business literacy of your workforce will pay dividends for years to come, as the newfound knowledge spreads to workers throughout the organization.

★ ★ ★

BUSINESS REBEL HALL OF FAME PROFILE

Michael Dell (Chairman and CEO of Dell Computer Corporation)

How could a twenty-year-old college student have the instinct to grow a company from a start-up in his dorm to a $20 billion worldwide enterprise? With wisdom well beyond his years, Michael masterminded Dell's growth with a simple unprecedented idea that has now become the norm: bypass the middleman in the personal computer industry and sell custom-built PCs directly to end-users. In fact, Michael was one of the first major computer retailers to emphasize online sales of their equipment. The company also was years ahead of its competition by creating a process to provide mass customization to their customers.

When Dell was added to the *Fortune* 500, Michael, at thirty-one, became the youngest CEO to join the list. The company's stock grew by about 30,000 percent during the 1990s. Michael is that rare founder who's made the transition from bootstrap entrepreneur to executive leader. His commitment to learning (not surprising, since he's about the age of many graduate students) and teaching is legendary. And Dell's approach to training is cutting-edge. Online training at the well-respected Dell University has grown from 25 percent of all education to 75 percent from 1996 to 1999. Michael calls this "stealth learning"—education that is so seamlessly incorporated into the company's work that employees don't even realize they're learning.

LEADERS ARE LEARNERS WHO TEACH

General Electric CEO Jack Welch runs a $100 billion company that is enormously admired for its market leadership in the fourteen different market segments in which it competes. Business leaders from around the world pay big bucks to hear Jack speak at conferences and symposiums. Yet he still has time to train new managers at his own company's management development institute. After each GE training session, Jack asks participants to send him a note explaining what they learned and which issues still seem unresolved. Jack reads each note and personally answers each participants' questions. Incidentally, GE spends nearly $1 billion annually on leadership programs for their staff.

Ingvar Kamprad, founder of IKEA—the European company that innovated the business of making and selling furniture—recognized the importance of building a learning culture. Knowing that he couldn't do it alone, Ingvar identified high-potential employees whom he designated "culture bearers." Through week-long training sessions that he personally led, he ensured that these key players internalized the company's values and operating systems. By the early 1990s, IKEA had assigned more than three hundred of these "ambassadors" to key positions worldwide, creating a dense personal network that could collect, interpret, and relay information without the distortion that formal systems often introduce.

HOW TO CREATE A SMART COMPANY

The terms "intellectual capital" and "learning organization" have become clichés in the business world, but companies that want to grow rapidly need people who can keep learning swiftly. Does your company encourage learning and build instinct quickly enough to keep up with the change around you? Take the following test, scoring 1 for "yes," 2 for "sort of/maybe," or 3 for "no."

1. Do you have an institutionalized program that asks managers to share "best practices" with each other on a regular basis? To answer this question, think about the following: How are your failures studied? Do you have a feedback loop that asks (a) what were our objectives, (b) what was our performance, and (c) how and why did we deviate from plan?

2. If we asked ten managers within your organization who your company's role model is (another company), would at least five of them mention the same company? Have you studied their best practices?

3. Do you have a corporate university that trains not just managers but people throughout the organization?

4. Do you ask your employees at least once per year what additional tools or training they need to do their job more effectively?

5. Are key decisions in your organization pushed down to the lowest level possible because these employees are likely to have the most information?

6. Are you testing the value of your training by measuring changes in the behavior of trainees? For example, do you ask this of subordinates within ninety days of the formal training of their manager?

7. Do you have a formal method of teaching what you've learned from your customers through surveys or meetings to employees to make them more market-responsive? (A 1988 study showed that more than 50 percent of product innovations come from customers or end-users. Your customer service department may be a great untapped source of valuable information.)

8. Can the people at the lowest levels of your organization recite your benchmarks and this year's strategic initiatives? (Not sure? Think about your receptionist, your janitorial or mailroom staff.)

9. Do you use technology as a prevalent tool in your training efforts?

10. Do you spend as much money on company training as you do on advertising your products or services?

If you scored 16 or above, you should reevaluate your company's commitment to learning because you're probably falling behind the competition. For a much more in-depth analysis of your company's "organizational IQ," pick up Haim Mendelson and Johannes Ziegler's book, *Survival of the Smartest,* which measures a company's ability to process information quickly and make effective decisions. High-IQ companies have external information awareness, ensure that decisions are made at the right level, disseminate knowledge quickly, keep a unified organizational focus, and operate in this same manner with key networked partners.

CREATING YOUR OWN CORPORATE UNIVERSITY

A few years ago, it was becoming apparent that our traditional method of training and mentoring was becoming outdated. For years, my partner, Larry Broughton, and I would spend enough time at each of our properties that our employees learned our mission and priorities from observing our actions firsthand. However, when we grew to more than a half-dozen businesses, osmosis no longer worked. New employees were becoming further and further removed from our historical culture. We even started losing some of our young stars, who had no fast track for learning beyond the school of hard knocks.

Many options were available. Contracting with outside training companies would assure that we covered our bases, but it was expensive and would almost surely miss the unique corporate culture of Joie de Vivre. Hiring a full-time employee to run the university sounded good until we realized we couldn't afford it. Allowing the managers at the individual properties to oversee their own training kept costs down, but it didn't ensure consistency or an immersion in the overall company culture.

So we created a "virtual university."

Our employee development department develops a quarterly catalog with approximately twenty-five classes. Eighty percent of these classes are taught by managers and employees within the company. The focus is on skill-building classes, and on lifestyle enhancement courses, such as yoga, boxing, holiday card-making, team-building through group sculpture, and creating your own personal mission statement. Our average employees don't make a fortune, so anything we can do in the university to enhance their life is a good thing. The most popular class is English as a second language, which helps our back-of-the-house staff communicate better with our customers. Best of all, our university's approach aligns perfectly with our company mission of creating "joy of life." Some of our employees take as many as five to ten classes per quarter.

Whenever there's an important issue that needs to be addressed in the organization, we create a class around it. When Chief Operating Officer (now President) Jack Kenny arrived, he found that many of our junior managers needed time-management training, so that became a class the following quarter. All it takes to create your own university is a group of employees who want to learn and another who want to teach.

For more information on launching and enhancing a corporate university, check with Corporate University Xchange, Inc. (CUX)—which includes one of the only consortiums of Chief Learning Officers Worldwide. The organization's Chief Learning Officer Xchange is a member-driven research and benchmarking forum for deans of corporate universities. Check them out at www.corpu.com.

THE IMPORTANCE OF SHARING KNOWLEDGE

Today your workers are probably as interested in your learning environment as they are in the company's traditional benefits package. Portable skills are prized in this "free agent" economy, where employees do well to learn as much as they can as quickly as possible, improving their own marketability. Here are a few ways, some inexpensive and some expensive, you can create a dynamic learning culture.

TAP INTO YOUR "FRESH EYES"

Most companies waste an enormously valuable resource—new employees. During their first few weeks, new employees have "fresh eyes." They can observe business practices that don't make sense yet remain embedded in the culture. Your new employees look at your business in much the same way as your customers. But typically during an employee's first few months, communication is a one-way process. You already conduct a review of the employee's performance after ninety days. Why not do a thirty-day review, in which the new employee can ask questions or provide comments about things that don't seem to be working? We've tried this and found it works extremely well as long as the employee feels safe with respect to the person with whom they're communicating.

CREATE A "GONG SHOW"

Michael Eisner has used this approach to foster new ideas at ABC, Paramount, and Disney. Once a week, a cross-section of the brain trust is invited to an unruly brainstorming meeting. People come prepared for fun. Each person is responsible for throwing out a new idea for a show and the rest of the group gives them the thumbs-up or the gong. Ideally, each person leverages some of the best ideas that have been mentioned prior to their turn. This approach helped Disney create *The Little Mermaid* and *Pocahontas.*

SWAP KNOWLEDGE

Smart companies create programs to swap knowledge. Wal-Mart calls it their seven-day learning cycle. Their key sales managers spend each week flying around to their stores and visiting competitors. The sales managers regroup each Friday night at corporate headquarters to compare notes. This helps to set the agenda at their weekly Saturday morning powwow, where they might unveil a new competitive counterattack that was cooked-up on Friday night. Wal-Mart does this every week. At Charles Schwab's headquarters, a tradition started with key technical employees doing a fifteen-minute team meeting every morning to talk about what they learned the prior day.

WRING THE SPONGE

When you create a new business, your frontline employees need to be a sponge of learning, responsive to what's working and what's not for your customers. This is especially true when you open a new business and elicit feedback from your customers. Information overload became a problem for our hosts at the front desk of one of our new hotels because we didn't have regularly scheduled meetings in the first few weeks for them to "wring out" all the information they'd learned. The result was a remarkable staff that felt like a wet sponge. After we started instituting regular download meetings with the front desk staff, their stress levels dropped and they were able to start "sponging up" new information from our guests.

GIVE YOUR MANAGERS A MAGAZINE

Sound simple? It is, and it's cheap! We did this at a retreat. We asked each of our forty managers to select one of eight diverse business or lodging-industry magazines. We bought them a subscription for the year, which cost $25 on average. The whole effort cost $1,000, but it sent the message that we want our managers to intensify their intelligence-gathering.

STUDY A ROLE MODEL OR A COMPETITOR FROM TOP TO BOTTOM

As I've mentioned elsewhere in the book, we spent one three-day retreat just studying Southwest Airlines' business practices. We bought each of our managers a copy of the book *Nuts!* so that they could learn how this unique company actually strengthened its culture during rapid growth. That was our core issue for that particular year. While this was a lavish use of our company leaders' time, it didn't actually cost much, and it helped frame our goals for the year. (You're welcome to use our company as a role model and buy carton loads of this book!)

WRITE A BOOK

No, not like this one. We learned this lesson from the Pointe Hilton on South Mountain in Phoenix, and we have created our own version as part of a Joie de Vivre University class on extraordinary service. Our home office created a template on disk in the form of a book with seven chapters. Each chapter portrayed a fictional guest in the hotel and showed how the guest experienced hospitality, using dialogue to reveal how the little things we do makes a guest's stay that much more enjoyable. For example, there's a chapter about a married couple whose marriage is on the rocks and they come to the hotel for a second honeymoon. Small, thoughtful details—like a carafe of bubble bath in their room or the way the bellman addresses them warmly—makes their experience so memorable that it helps save the marriage. Each story focuses on a different part of the hotel and, consequently, the actions of a different set of employees. Since we have such diverse properties, we made the template flexible enough so that each hotel could tailor-make the stories around their superior service offerings. Ultimately, the staff of some of the hotels helped write their own unique book and each employee received a copy of the book. New employees are issued a copy of their hotel's book. From their first day, they understand how their work can have a profound impact on our guests—whether their job is tending the garden or taking reservations.

. . .

How a company spreads knowledge is one of the defining differences between twentieth- and twenty-first century companies. Business rebels recognize that instinct-based companies breathe different air than their competitors. An atmosphere of learning and fresh inspiration permeates every nook and cranny of the organization. The rebel company creates rising stars who've tapped into a rich vein of worldly wisdom.

8. Promoting Fast Footwork: The Agile Company

It's not the big companies that eat the small; it's the fast that eat the slow.

—Wall Street Journal

In the past, war in the marketplace was fought in the equivalent of tanks, lumbering juggernauts with thick skins. Today companies wage war in jet fighters, reacting with lightning quickness to changes on the competitive landscape. Even big companies like Microsoft are agile. They *adopt and adapt.* They may not be the initial inventors of a product, but they adopt the best attributes of that product and get it to market as quickly as possible. Then they adapt over time based upon the reaction of their customers. This is called "churning" and it's a way to build momentum like a locomotive.

Vision sets the direction, passion fuels the enterprise, and instinct enables each employee to think on his or her feet. But today's unpredictable competitive landscape demands fancy footwork, or what author Louis Patler calls "acrobatic leadership systems." Of all four aptitudes, agility seems the most relevant, so much so that when the world's second-biggest computer-maker, Hewlett-Packard, split off its measurement company in 1999, it chose the name Agilent Technologies. Bill Hahn, Agilent's vice president of strategic programs, says the name is meant to connote a sense of being "nimble and well coordinated," as well as being "mentally quick and resourceful." He says, "We believe if we act in an Agilent manner, great things will happen."

While "agilent" isn't likely to become a household word overnight, there's no doubt that speed and intelligence define today's rebel companies. Andy Grove, who helped steer Intel to greatness, says in his book *Only the Paranoid Survive*, "Ultimately, speed is the only weapon we have."

In the Internet generation—when the incremental cost of distributing one more electronic page of information is virtually zero—size no longer matters. In fact, traditional notions of economies of scale are a thing of the past for many new companies. The Internet economy is forcing every company to take a step back and reevaluate how they do business.

Think about catalog shopping. In the past, a retailer would spend years developing a hit list of prime customers, months creating a seasonal catalog, weeks sending the catalogs out in the mail, and then hope that the phone would start ringing. Now, you have companies like RedEnvelope.com, one of the largest online gift companies, that can hyperaccelerate the whole process of starting this type of business (the company was founded in less than sixty days in 1999). Moreover, RedEnvelope and its competitors can track what's selling on an hourly basis and then reformulate the online catalog mix of featured merchandise at will. The Sears Catalog must be spinning in its retail grave!

The rhythm of change itself has changed. J. Neil Weintraut, general partner with 21st Century Internet Venture Partners, says a would-be Internet entrepreneur only has four months to transform an idea into an actual product that's available on the Web. So we're searching for helpful partners as if it were the last dance at the high school prom. Take the popular PalmPilot. Originated by a tiny software company, Palm Computing, it was designed by what was then the Palo Alto Design Group. Its parts were manufactured in Taiwan, and Flextronics, a Singapore subcontractor, assembled the parts. Yet this brilliant new management tool appeared on the market less than a year after its conception.

INSPIRING INNOVATION IN YOUR PEOPLE

Rebels know how vital it is to get a product to market quickly. When a rebel's instinct tells them there's a market, they start a "conversation" with their customers by introducing their product and adapting it rapidly, based upon consumer reaction. If this is done right, it can even build customer loyalty, for the customers feel they've helped develop the product. It also forces the competition to adapt the rebel's strategies.

Instinct married with agility creates an expert surfer. A neophyte surfer watches the wave as it approaches the shore but fails to see what's behind the wave—the swells, the set. The rebel surfer has developed expert eyesight to look beyond the surface to see what's next. This surfer ensures the wave he's riding has sustainability to it, a long-term trend rather than a short-term fad; the novice rides wave after wave going nowhere. The best surfers rely on their dexterity and sense of balance—a propensity for improvisation—to ride the wave all the way to shore.

This surfing model accurately describes the innovative process in rebel companies. But innovation doesn't just happen in the high-tech arena. Joie de Vivre was able to "hang ten" by creating innovations that inspired change in the hospitality industry.

CREATING A NEW CONCEPT BASED UPON CULTURAL TRENDS

Contemporary television commercials are a window into the hearts and minds of America. In the early nineties, car ads were about soccer moms and minivans. That changed in the last half of the decade as automobile advertisements focused on escape and soft adventure. Sport utility vehicles became more popular than minivans because SUVs represented freedom at a time when we were feeling progressively more overworked. At the same time, outdoor gear, such as North Face daypacks, Patagonia all-weather jackets, and Trek mountain bikes became commonplace on urban and suburban streets. Adventure travel companies like Backroads and Abercrombie & Kent carted more stressed-out urbanites to exotic, luxurious destinations in the wilds around the world than ever before. Put simply, people were looking for an opportunity to get away from it all, back to nature, but without getting their hands dirty.

In 1999, we introduced the country's first luxury campground, Costanoa, one hour south of San Francisco on panoramic Highway 1. We created a "natural playground," where a two-income couple could introduce their kids to camping while using their outdoor "toys" (in fact, one of the things we learned was that one of parents' rites of passage is taking their kids camping, but this generation was feeling stymied by doing it the old-fashioned way).

As Nike did for running shoes and Starbucks for coffee, we reinvented a staple: camping. We found that camping is one of the few products or services in which upscaling the product actually broadens the market—what economists call "positive elasticity."

Clearly, price has not kept Yuppie families from camping. Staying overnight at a typical state or federal park campground site costs less than taking the family to a Sunday matinee. No, they're camping less than their parents' generation did because (a) it's time-consuming and expensive to buy the gear; (b) our lives are more oriented around comfort, causing traditional camping to lose appeal relative to other forms of recreation; and (c) most camping facilities are stuck in the 1970s with no style and limited services. Additionally, most public campgrounds are overrun with crowds because of a lack of government investment in new facilities. Bottom line: demand exceeds supply.

We saw an opportunity to create a new product: the kind of place you might find in Costa Rica, India, or South Africa, but situated in the United States. Costanoa offers a 40-room lodge, 12 cabins, and more than 125 furnished tent bungalows reminiscent of the safari scenes in *Out of Africa.* There's no need to buy or bring gear. These stylish tents have it all (including room service). It's sort of like *Outside* magazine meets *Metropolitan Home.*

The family can have an afternoon of biking, hiking, horseback riding, windsurfing, berry-picking, and tidepooling and return to Costanoa for the farm-animal petting zoo, to be pampered in the spa, or to prepare a gourmet barbecue with the help of our upscale market and deli. The communal bathrooms have radiant heat floors, enormous stone fireplaces, saunas, and indoor-outdoor showers. This is not your parents' campground. It's Gen X's answer to the golf resort, an escape without the formality of rules.

CREATING A NEW CONCEPT BASED UPON DEMOGRAPHIC TRENDS

It's remarkable how most product development teams focus on past demographics. This is inherently dangerous in a world that is changing so fast.

Joie de Vivre has recently opened three stylish hotels in Silicon Valley (Hotel Avante, the Wild Palms, and La Plaza), which previously didn't have anything but bland and predictable business hotels. When we first started creating cool, sophisticated boutique hotels in the Valley, everyone told us we were crazy since these high-tech companies were so engineering-driven that their visitors were likely to be nerdy techies who couldn't tell the difference between a Four Seasons and a Holiday Inn.

But if you watched television over the 1999 Christmas season, you knew the times were changing as nearly 50 percent of all advertising in some metropolitan markets was by dot-com companies. Virtually overnight, high-tech had gone from being engineering-driven to consumer marketing–driven. In fact, the *Economist* magazine reports that the rule of thumb in many new Internet companies is that 70 percent of the operating budget goes to marketing. So now the visitors to Yahoo!, eBay, and other Silicon Valley firms are advertising execs and media consultants from New York and L.A. These people hated the existing collection of generic Silicon Valley hotels. In 1999, we heard a chorus of discontent from travel agents who begged Joie de Vivre to open some boutique hotels similar to what we'd created in San Francisco.

With some foresight and against the conventional wisdom of hotel industry execs, Joie de Vivre was able to become the favorite hotel alternative for this huge new collection of Silicon Valley visitors. Our surfer eyes saw the next wave of visitors coming to town. Joie de Vivre owes inspiration to Steve Jobs, who proclaimed that the people deserved stylish choices for the computer box on their desk (or, for that matter, their choice in hotels). Techie no longer has to be tacky.

CREATING A FAST AND FLEXIBLE COMPANY

One of my favorite business rebel friends, Seth Godin, who sold his company Yoyodyne to Yahoo! (did they have the same naming consultant?) notes that one cool thing about the Internet is that from day one, the entrepreneurs have beaten the old guys. Yahoo! and AOL are the winners, leaving CompuServe and Prodigy behind. Small companies can't typically compete for access to capital or sheer clout, so the rebel creates a field on which speed and flexibility count. In no time, the large opponent's size becomes a point of vulnerability. Big companies don't usually have fast reflexes, unless they're smart enough to keep their department or unit sizes streamlined enough to be nimble.

Of course, this is especially apparent in the high-tech field. Innovation has led to shorter product life cycles, which means that the first company to reach the market garners the bulk of market share while the remainder are left to compete on price (with the exception of Microsoft, which has done a remarkable imitation of 1980s Japanese companies by taking other companies' inventions, making small but meaningful innovations quickly, and blanketing the market).

Microsoft proved their agility in the Internet arena when, in late 1995, Bill Gates finally declared they were going to become "hard core about the Internet." Before then, Microsoft had been distracted with trying to get their Windows 95 out to market and was assuming that their inferior product, Microsoft Network, would be able to compete with all the Internet start-ups. Then, Bill Gates proved he could turn a multibillion-dollar company on a dime. Microsoft adjusted its development cycle to Internet time, launched a collection of state-of-the-art Internet software, and revamped Microsoft Network so that it was now based entirely on the Web.

Big companies *can* move quickly if decision-making power is concentrated and based more on instinct than on market research that can take months to accumulate. Virgin Atlantic Airways was airborne just five months after Richard Branson first discussed the idea. And Virgin Trading, the consumer goods company, was created just days before Virgin Cola was launched. In each case, Virgin partnered with an existing expert in the field and performed virtually no marketing focus groups, relying instead on Richard Branson and his brain trust's gut and ability to create a business plan quickly.

Back in 1994, Southwest Airlines was suddenly frozen out of two major airline reservations systems. This required Southwest's brain trust to act quickly since their customers now found it more difficult to book their tickets. Almost overnight, Southwest introduced ticketless service, which has now become the norm for many shuttle airlines. Soon after launching ticketless travel, Southwest's passenger volume increased 15 percent as customers took to this new easy-to-use system. Once again, if you create a rebel company with strong instincts, your "agility ability" will be a natural by-product.

GETTING PEOPLE TO EMBRACE CHANGE

Authors Joseph and Jimmie Boyett suggest in *The Guru Guide* that 50 percent to 70 percent of all corporate change initiatives launched in the 1980s and 1990s failed to achieve their objectives. In 1993, the Wyatt Company asked the CEOs of 531 U.S. companies that had recently undergone major restructuring to name one thing they would change about their effort. Overwhelmingly, the CEOs said they would alter the way they communicated with their employees about the change.

Clearly, it is a waste of time attempting to implement change initiatives without considering the employees' temperament for change. It's the rebel leader's duty to convince his people that change is inevitable.

IBM tried to solve this fear of change by creating a handbook called "Changing the World," filled with tips from employees about how people can break through their mental barriers. Six thousand of these handbooks were distributed to IBM's labs and offices around the world with ideas like "Brainstorm with someone ten years older and someone ten years younger" and "For a day, switch places with your boss."

Below is a list of *warning signs* that the business rebel should recognize as an indication that their organization is losing its receptivity to change:

- Everyone is good at identifying problems but less proficient at or interested in coming up with solutions;
- People are always reminiscing about what it was like in the past;
- Managers are more focused on the number of people reporting to them than the results of their people's hard work;
- Computer models and financial projections typically dominate 50 percent of the discussion during strategic meetings;
- Customers are seen as a necessary evil, or there's a "we're better than them" attitude, and staffers are forgetting that customers' tastes change over time;
- Key mascots (the role models for other managers) within the company either leave or make sure they don't put in as many hours as they used to;
- Employee participation at the annual holiday party is in steady decline; and
- Excuses become a way of life throughout the company ("too bad about the economy . . .").

Don't be surprised if resistance to change isn't made blatantly obvious by your people. Few of us want to admit we're afraid of the future's uncertainty. You'll find it comes in negative statements like, "Management is expecting more than the customers"; "We don't have time for this b.s.!"; or, "This might make sense for other divisions, but not ours."

Resistance to change is all about fear: people legitimately fear that they'll lose their job, be humiliated because they can't adjust, or have to work harder. Unfortunately, the one question that is rarely heard when a company embarks upon rapid change is, "What happens if we *don't* change?" This question and its answers should serve as a healthy reminder to your employees that the rest of the world is not static.

In a rebel company, believe it or not, the word "change" is seldom spoken. Change is simply expected by people seeking constant improvement. In fact, when employees are surveyed, they make it clear that they want to be a vehicle for positive change. These surveys also suggest that people are eager to accelerate their personal rate of change and learning. So the essential task in creating an agile organization is to address employees' fear of losing control.

HOW REBEL COMPANIES MAKE WHOOPEE

The information economy demands a quick response time. This often means that a company's competitive response is to partner with someone

HOW TO CREATE CHANGE

Get rid of fear or at least refocus it. That's what Andy Grove did at Intel: he turned fear into paranoia into motivation to improve.

Fear works when outside forces demand immediate action. You can create a sense of urgency by focusing on a competitor's savvy moves or an example of a recently failed project within your organization, or by bringing up a horror story from a customer. Dissect the problem and quantify the risk of not fixing it. Will the ultimate result be the failure of the business? How soon? That ought to provide a wake-up call. Develop the action steps to get it fixed—that will assure that no one will be paralyzed by their fear. Most important, identify what sacrifices or steps key management is taking to facilitate the change, whether it's with their own salary cut or rolling up their sleeves and getting more operational. This will help everyone understand that the change initiative is not just falling on the shoulders of the employees. Don't forget to define and emphasize the positive pay-off if the change succeeds, because fear can only motivate for so long.

Barbara Waugh says, "You don't manage change. You help to create the conditions for it. Your people need to learn that the process of change is not bad, any more than the product of change is good. Your employees need to be reminded of past changes that helped them and the company."

Don't get discouraged if you don't see change overnight. Barbara told me about a special bamboo that grows in northern China. The farmer plants it and, for the first four years, nothing happens. The fifth year, the bamboo shoots up eighty feet. Sometimes change requires roots to form before you see progress.

else in their network. Most companies now define their core competency and outsource everything else. Sometimes these strategic alliances are purely "hit-and-run" quickies designed to create instant gratification: a leg up in a new industry, an ability to share a new technology, a short-term boost to the stock price. Other times, these partnerships are the start of an exclusive long-term affair.

One of the consequences of this frenetic focus on innovation is a need for a more networked organization. Strategic relationships tend to fall into one of five categories:

1. *Sharing Resources or Information:* Like Sun Microsystems, which exchanges new technology with key developers so that the alliance members can ensure that their technological road maps are parallel
2. *Sharing Brand Identity:* Like Virgin, which was approached by a soft drink company with a new cola formula that wanted to leverage Virgin's independent-spirited image—thus creating Virgin Cola

★ ★ ★

BUSINESS REBEL HALL OF FAME PROFILE

Dee Hock (Founder of Visa International and the Chaordic Alliance)

More than twenty-five years ago, Dee Hock oversaw the creation of a business, Visa International, that has become the model for the future company—agile, responsive, diverse, and ingenious. One of Dee's favorite tricks is to ask an audience, "How many of you recognize this?" as he holds up his Visa card. Of course, everyone's hand is in the air. Then, he asks, "How many of you can tell me who owns this company, where it's headquartered, how it's governed, and how I can buy shares?" Everyone is bewildered, and Dee is satisfied. That's how an organization ought to be—the less obvious it is, the better.

Dee became Visa's CEO in 1970 with the intent of creating a highly decentralized and collaborative organization. He and Visa succeeded beyond his wildest dreams, as sales volume now exceeds $1 trillion annually and continues to expand at an annual growth rate of nearly 20 percent. A quarter-century before "networked organizations" had become the rage, Visa expanded around the globe using a blend of competition and cooperation to provide cohesion among their member institutions despite the challenges of different cultures, currencies, and customs. At the traditional height of his career (age fifty-five), this rebel resigned as Visa's CEO, "trading money for time, position for liberty, and ego for contentment."

Yet this avuncular gentleman is more of a radical than he'd like to admit. Nearly a decade after he left Visa, he founded the Chaordic Alliance (the mixture of "chaos" and "order") to help revolutionize the nature of organizations. Using Visa and the Internet as a model, Dee is showing organizations how a more organic system—one based upon self-organizing, rather than top-down hierarchy—can govern business better in our modern world.

With respect to change, Dee says, "We tend to fall in love with the things that we think are true. We treasure those truths. Gradually, they become old and shabby, and they lose their utility. But they are comfortable, and we can't bear to part with them. We clutter our mind with so much old stuff that there is no room for anything new. We can't discard mental 'stuff.' But we can create a mental attic and put a sign on the door that says, 'Things that are no longer so.' Until you understand your thinking about a certain thing, you'll never change. So question that habit of mind, and lug it to the attic if it's no longer useful. Don't try to get rid of it; just refuse to dwell within it any longer."

3. *Manufacturing Networks:* Like Dell, which maintains tight links with its suppliers, insisting that they warehouse most components within a fifteen-minute drive of a Dell factory
4. *Marketing Networks:* Like Yahoo!, which has become akin to a television network on the Web, collecting original content from independent sources
5. *Mergers and Acquisitions:* As we're seeing more and more in the Internet world, when it makes sense to take advantage of the long-term synergies of a relationship

How do you know when to partner? The benefit of outpacing your competition has to outweigh the pain and suffering of linking the two organizations. In Karen Southwick's book *Silicon Gold Rush,* venture capitalist Don Valentine points out that as Cisco Systems became the dominant computer networking company, its distribution channels became so powerful that "acquisition had an incredibly high revenue impact." The acquired company's products suddenly had the added value of Cisco's clout with customers. This acquisition model, which is found all over Silicon Valley, has led to many entrepreneurs creating new businesses (or, in some cases, just a network of free agents) with the sole purpose of being acquired within two years by one of the Silicon Valley big boys. Some of the biggest investors in high-tech companies aren't the venture capitalists but instead are the Intels and Microsofts of the world, who acquire the little guys because their technology is complementary. Additionally, it means the traditional research-and-development function that has historically represented up to 10 percent of some large high-tech firms' annual sales can be partially farmed out.

Are there any key rules to remember in this new mating ritual? The first and second rules come from Guy Kawasaki, CEO of Garage.com, which marries entrepreneurs and investors. He says, "You have to make sure that the middle and bottom of both organizations are motivated to make the alliance work. That is, it's not just something the airhead CEOs dreamed up while playing golf in Carmel. The second rule is that there has to be a balance of benefits. One-sided alliances never work."

The third rule is think like a pessimist (or a lawyer). Imagine the partnership not working. What does that look like? How do you disband this relationship if it's hurting your brand identity or if it's a clear money-loser?

Finally, accept that there may be a certain loss of autonomy when you create a relationship. My father used to tell me, "Marriage is a compromise." Are you the compromising type? For me, I revel in my space to be creative, and thus for years passed up numerous long-term partnering opportunities for fear that I might sacrifice freedom.

SEVEN TIPS FOR IMPROVING YOUR COMPANY'S AGILITY

Now that we've agreed that change is inevitable, let's look at some small ways you can promote flexibility in your organization.

CELEBRATE FAILURE

Gavin Newsom is a youthful member of San Francisco's Board of Supervisors and one of the rising political stars in California. He's also CEO of the PlumpJack companies, a well-respected Northern California brand with wineries, resorts, and restaurants. Gavin realized that most people fear making mistakes, and therefore don't try anything new. To encourage his employees to learn from their failures, he created the Magical Moments Failure Award. Each month, the award ($600 in PlumpJack merchandise) is given to the employee who came up with the most creative way of solving a challenge, even if it failed (as long as it was an attempt to add value to the guest experience). Recently, one of his employees at their PlumpJack Resort near Lake Tahoe won the award because he tried to eliminate the mosquito haven that popped up in the pond next to the restaurant. This enterprising employee put catfish in the pond to eat the mosquitoes. Great idea, but he forgot about the raccoons. The morning after adding the catfish, the maintenance staff found catfish parts strewn throughout the resort as the raccoons got themselves quite a meal. While this was a mess for the resort guests, it was a creative, if flawed, solution worthy of an award.

CREATE A TEMP AGENCY

Given the vibrant Northern California economy and Joie de Vivre's rapid growth, our general managers were having a difficult time filling shifts at our hotel front desks. Sometimes this meant that our managers were required to work the desk—not a bad idea occasionally, but too frequently it's a distraction from their primary responsibilities. So we created an in-house "temp agency" of supertrained desk hosts who can parachute into any of our hotels on a moment's notice to pick up shifts. Now our quality is improved and our managers' time is used more efficiently.

DESTROY YOUR ORGANIZATIONAL CHART

Convene a half-day meeting with a cross-section of employees in your company. Put your current organizational chart on the wall and start throwing darts. Ask them if your current structure does the following:

- Keep you close to the customer?
- Allow for constant, informal communication among key departments?
- Acknowledge the relationships that currently exist in practice, if not on the chart?
- Allow flexibility for project teams or outside consultants to play a part, as needed?
- Focus on innovation for survival over the course of the next five years?
- Give enough credit to the line-level employees who are the backbone of the company?

When you're done answering these questions, you may find that your old chart no longer serves a purpose and it's time to create a new organizational chart.

LISTEN TO OTHER VOICES

Sun Microsystems started a "Voice of the Supplier" program with their suppliers to improve their supply chain efficiency. Sun learned that many of their suppliers felt frozen out of the product development process and didn't understand Sun's approach to forecasting demand. With their suppliers' input, Sun adapted their processes, and this program became an ongoing rating process in which suppliers rate Sun as a customer.

APPLY THE PRINCIPLES OF ANOTHER INDUSTRY TO YOUR OWN

That's what Frederick Smith did when he started Federal Express. He used the central clearinghouse system that was used in the banking industry as well as the hub-and-spoke system used in the airlines to create the United States' first national overnight delivery company, an idea that seemed preposterous before FedEx launched the service.

DISPATCH TWO TEAMS

Michael Brown, CEO of Quantum Corporation, was faced with a dilemma in the 1990s: how could a big company with one primary technology focus acquire the agility of a start-up to maintain its competitive edge? Michael assembled two teams (of eight people each below the vice president level) to develop long-term strategy for the company. He assigned them full-time for six weeks and brought them from around the world to their Silicon Valley headquarters to tap into some of the Valley's best and brightest technology experts. Neither team was allowed to talk to each other because Michael wanted to see whether they would arrive at the same conclusions. In the end, both teams came up with comparable strategies that the company is now pursuing.

TALK TO YOUR DISSATISFIED CUSTOMERS

This sounds logical, yet many executives don't do it. Recently, I contacted a few corporate accounts that had stopped using some of our hotels to determine why we weren't seeing as much of their business. I got an earful from two of them. But rather than get defensive, I listened and ultimately set up a meeting in which they could explain their frustrations directly to the relevant hotel management team. Hearing an important customer complain is a bold way to convince your managers and employees that rapid change is needed.

IV. BECOMING A MAGNET FOR GOOD PEOPLE

9. Recruiting and Coaching Rebels

As a fast-growing company, we're looking for E-cubed: People who are entrepreneurial, enthusiastic, and energetic. We want people who have a point to prove and who are insatiably curious.

—John Kilcullen, chairman and CEO of IDG Books Worldwide

People. People who need people. No, I'm not going to break into a melancholy song, but here in the Bay Area recruiting is a melancholy subject. We've lost a handful of capable employees to the dot-commies. The competition for good people has never been more fierce.

There's nothing more important to a rebel company than recruiting and nurturing people, yet few companies recognize the relationship between recruitment and retention. How do rebels become recognized leaders in attracting and keeping talent? It starts with a little old-fashioned analysis. Expert recruiting can only take place after you know your company's needs. And once you've hired the proper team, you need tools to analyze their effectiveness on the job. Only then can you inspire heroic performance from your rebel recruits.

Most rebel companies are so busy growing that they fail to focus on these issues. Maury Hanigan, founder of Hanigan Consulting Group, says in *Fortune* magazine, "If a $2,000 desktop computer disappears from an employee's desk, I guarantee there'll be an investigation, a whole to-do. But if a $100,000 executive with all kinds of client relationships gets poached by a competitor, there is no investigation. No one is called on the carpet for it."

Two independent consulting companies—Hewitt Associates and the Saratoga Institute—have estimated that the cost of replacing a worker runs between 1 and 2.5 times the total annual salary of the open job. The more sophisticated or senior the job, the higher the cost. Do the math yourself. How many people does your company have to replace annually? What is the annual average salary for each of those jobs? Multiply the product of those two numbers by anything from 1 to 2.5, and you'll recognize the importance of this chapter.

Lenny Nash and Jonathon Barsky, who started Market Metrix (a company that creates customer and employee surveys), believe one of the first steps in analyzing your retention efforts is to survey your existing employees. Next time you survey your employees about their workplace satisfaction, ask the following question, "How long do you intend to stay with the company? (a) less than a year, (b) from one to three years, or (c) more than three years."

If you tabulate this question with the length of tenure of the employee, all of your employees will fall into one of five categories shown on the graph:

- Promising: employees who are relatively new to the company (answer *a* above), but intend to stay a long time (*c*)
- Loyal: employees who have longer-term tenure (*c*) and intend to stay (*c*)
- Mismatch: new employees who aren't likely to stay (*a* and *a*)
- Disenchanted: longer-term employees who are likely to leave in the next year (*c* and *a*)
- Uncommitted: employees who've been with the company for one to three years and plan to stay another one to three years (*b* and *b*)

Determining what percentage of your employees fit into each of these categories is an important step in analyzing the fragility of your workforce. We found that 68 percent of our employees fit into the first two categories and that only 1 percent were disenchanted. But, we also found that 22 percent of our employees were uncommitted, meaning there was some risk

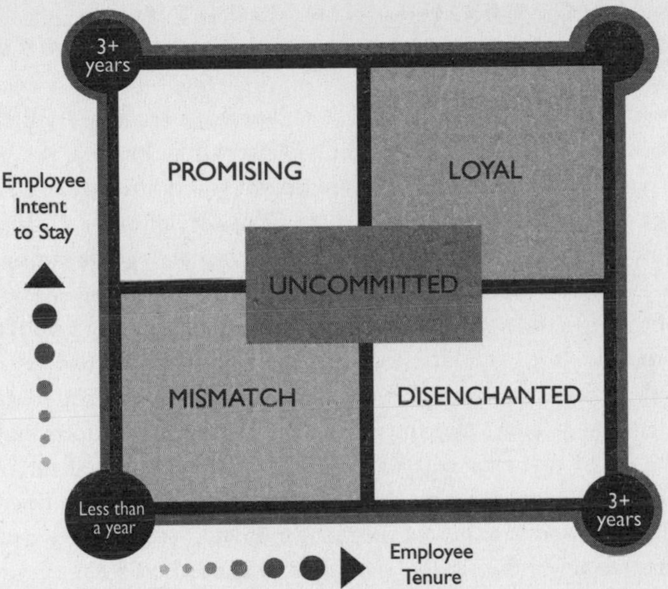

they would leave in the not too distant future if we didn't develop a more compelling career path or work environment.

The rebel company creates a work environment that is lifestyle-driven and combines both tangible and intangible attributes. Some of the tangible attributes you find in today's successful companies include (a) identifiable paths for job growth, (b) compensation linked to what you contribute, (c) job descriptions that focus on specific results rather than a collection of tasks, (d) freedom to move between projects to advance the learning project, and (e) programs that foster open communication and information-sharing.

Additionally, there are some common subtle, values-driven elements in today's most popular companies: (a) employee perks that meet the staffs' spoken and unspoken needs, (b) reduced status distinction between various levels of employment, (c) an appreciation for balancing work and personal life, (d) a sense of pride in the company, and (e) a sense of connection to a "tribe" and a sense of meaning in what the tribe does.

If you can create an environment that incorporates these issues, you'll have no problem attracting and retaining people.

CREATING THE RIGHT MIX: IDENTIFYING YOUR RECRUITMENT NEEDS

Recruitment of individuals is often considered in a vacuum—without any consideration for the team a person will play with. Imagine if a professional basketball team took this approach when it drafted college players. The team might need point guards, have plenty of power forwards, and be too slow throughout its roster to compete against younger teams in its division. The best NBA squad is not a sum of its individual talents but a result of the powerful chemistry that comes from just the right mix of talent.

When we hired our first vice president of sales, we had two hotel industry dynamos compete for the position—one with greater national experience and stature and the other with more local contacts and relationships. The first candidate was like a Mercedes—polished and professional—and the second was like a classic Mustang—fun and personal. Most firms would have picked the first candidate, yet we ended up choosing Peter Gamez, the second candidate, because he fit our culture and management team perfectly. While we did have national aspirations, our short-term goal was to build our regional presence, which Pete did.

How does this apply to your company? If you're in a youthful start-up, this is an especially important concept, as you may desperately need some maturity to balance out your team. At Yahoo!, Jerry Yang and David Filo brought on the more-experienced Tim Koogle as CEO, who had previously spent a decade with Motorola. The smaller the organization, the more important the mix, for there's no room for redundancy.

Before choosing an individual, you need a way of gauging what would add to your company's ideal mix. At Joie de Vivre, I use a Key Player Analysis to promote this chemistry. Here's how it works.

Make a list of every key professional in your division or company. (If your list exceeds thirty people, streamline it or break it into multiple lists to maintain focus.) Rate each person on a 1-to-10 basis (10 being extraordinary) on two scales—experience and growth potential or capacity. Once you've rated each employee, add the two ratings and identify each person as fitting into one of the following six categories:

- *Key Players:* Total score of 15 or higher, with capacity being at least as high as experience

- *Wise Ones:* Experience of at least 8; capacity of 6 or lower
- *Future Superstars:* Capacity of at least 8; total score lower than 15
- *Silent Majority:* Total score between 11 and 14
- *Underperformers:* Total score between 8 and 10
- *Weak Links:* Total score lower than 8

The more growth-oriented you are, the more you'll need to recruit Future Superstars. The more stable your business, the more important the Wise Ones and the Silent Majority.

Here's a quick rundown of the role each player should fill in your organization:

Key Players. Give them a primary voice in developing the company and plotting its future.

Wise Ones. Gain information from them and occasionally use them as role models or mentors. They are better suited for managing existing projects than conceiving new ones.

Future Superstars. Cultivate and mentor them with Key Players. Provide a growth-oriented path for them or they'll move on to new opportunities sooner than you expected.

Silent Majority. The backbone of the organization, they are easily forgotten. Let them act as the cultural team leaders with line staff. Develop a two-to-three-year plan for them so they don't atrophy.

Underperformers. Accountability, accountability, accountability . . . either their performance or attitude needs to improve within six to twelve months or they should leave the organization.

Weak Links. A chain is only as strong as its weakest links, so these managers need to be removed from the company as quickly and respectfully as possible, before they poison morale and motivation.

One note of caution: This information isn't meant to be shared widely within the organization. Keep it to yourself to guide your recruitment efforts.

HIRING TIPS FOR THE HARRIED REBEL

The number-one question I ask myself when I'm evaluating our existing staff or interviewing potential candidates is "*What if this person worked for our biggest competitor?*" This is a telling question because it addresses whatever you most cherish in your people—decisiveness, diplomacy, raw talent—and forces you to look at people in the all-important context of competitive positioning.

Dee Hock gives some of the best advice I've ever read on the subject of hiring: "Hire and promote first on the basis of integrity; second, motivation; third, capacity; fourth, understanding; fifth, knowledge; and last and least, experience. Without integrity, motivation is dangerous; without motivation, capacity is impotent; without capacity, understanding is limited; without understanding, knowledge is meaningless; without knowledge, experience is blind. Experience is easy to provide and quickly put to good use by people with all the other qualities."

There's an art to hiring. Most companies do it the old-fashioned way—they don't start looking for candidates until a position opens up; they place an ad in the local paper; they review résumés, placing the highest priority on education and comparable experience; they interview the best candidates; and they hurry to hire someone because the position had to be filled yesterday.

This sets off a chain reaction during the new hire's first days on the job. If they're replacing someone who gave two weeks' notice, they probably joined the firm after that person left, so they receive no transfer of knowledge. If they're filling a position that has been empty for a long period of time, their in-box is already full, and people are expecting immediate results. All this doesn't allow for much in the way of company orientation or training. It's no wonder that "buyer's remorse" kicks in within the first thirty days for many new employees.

Rebels renovate the hiring strategy by taking unconventional approaches to finding good people. Cisco Systems brings a group of employees to the annual Stanford-Berkeley football game, knowing that the stands are full of qualified potential employees. After each touchdown, the group waves placards that spell out WWW.CISCO.COM/JOBS. According to Cisco's director of corporate employment, the visits to the college recruiting section of their Web site always jumps 10 percent after the game.

Here are some rebellious rules for finding and evaluating candidates:

Look for people in unconventional places. Don't rely solely on the want ads in the local paper. The "loser" quotient is just too high. Where are the winners? How can you emulate Cisco's approach to getting your face in front of those strong candidates? Each year, I deliver thirty to forty speeches to groups that would logically include potential job applicants, such as hospitality schools, and groups that seem far afield, like the regional youth hostel conference where we found our VP of creative services, Rob Delamater. All I do is talk about our company's inspired vision, about the Joie de Vivre Heart of Service, and about all the fun we have along the way. No matter whom I'm talking to, I assume that they know someone else who's a perfect fit for Joie de Vivre. We estimate that more than a dozen of our top forty managers and department heads learned about the company at one of my speeches. If your CEO isn't a compelling speaker, put someone else on the circuit.

Don't stop looking. Rebel companies expect everyone in the firm to be part of the recruiting team. Make a list of your top five competitors and the key personnel at each competitive firm. Learn more about these people. Ask your suppliers, your customers, and employees at the other firms about them. Then, with your company brain trust, do a simple evaluation of your competitors' personnel. Imagine how each person might fit into your organization. This process will turn up a few potential candidates. Start cultivating those relationships. Keep them in the loop about your company by inviting them to open houses or by sending them company newsletters.

Audition first. I once hired a chief financial officer who stole my heart. I liked her job history (although she didn't have much accounting experience), and her Harvard M.B.A. She showed me a one-page letter that she'd submitted to her Harvard reunion book—I was impressed because her values matched mine, and she didn't mind looking like a lunatic in such a serious crowd. After a detailed set of interviews, I hired her, yet I realized after the first day that I'd made a mistake. While her values fit the company, her experience was purely corporate. Our seat-of-the-pants entrepreneurial operation was a bit of a shock to her. But most important, it became clear that we needed a CFO with a strong accounting background to help develop systems. Unfortunately, this CFO's experience was lacking in that area. If I'd brought her in for a day (or a week) of work *before* hiring her, she and I both would have spared ourselves the pain. Now, whenever we can, we try to hire someone as a contract employee or consultant for one to three months before hiring them full-time.

Don't neglect the candidate's greatest weakness. Have you ever tried comparing candidates by rating them on a set list of different talents? This otherwise useful approach can be dangerous when it fails to identify a candidate's most glaring weaknesses. One way to prevent this is to make a rule that any candidate who scores below a ___ (you pick the number) on any one area of talent is disqualified. While you intend to hire and coach someone to maximize their strengths, the fact remains that certain people aren't cut out for certain positions.

Take an unconventional approach to interviewing. Southwest Airlines asks people to tell a joke or draw on a paper bag to demonstrate their lightheartedness or creativity. Other companies present potential professionals with a real dilemma that the company faces and ask them to address it with a one-page memo and an oral presentation. Go to a baseball game or shopping with the candidate. Ask the candidate to lunch, but tell them to pick a place that best reflects their personality. We've asked potential managers to be interviewed by a group of potential subordinates to ensure the right chemistry. Ask tough questions like: "What was your greatest failure and what did you learn from it?" "If you were to fail in this job, what would be the warning signs that it was going to happen?" "What's your greatest professional fear?" "What would your current boss say about you on a bad day?" The point is to get underneath that neatly polished exterior to understand how they behave under pressure. Don't make it too uncomfortable or you'll lose the candidate. But don't be afraid to subject them to a free-form obstacle course. After all, that's probably an accurate metaphor for their job.

Consider the exit plan for your employees even before they've entered. This is particularly important when you're offering a low wage job in a tight employment market. A local Burger King in Grand Rapids, Michigan, teamed up with Cascade Engineering, a plastic parts manufacturer. Applicants who don't have the experience for the more skilled Cascade jobs are directed to interview with Burger King. And, successful Burger King employees who are looking for a raise and more responsibility are connected with the HR department of Cascade. Burger King is able to attract more entry-level workers because there's more upside career potential, while Cascade Engineering has a new recruitment vehicle. With whom can you team up in your community?

HOW TO BECOME THE BOSS YOU ALWAYS WISHED YOU'D HAD

The first half of the battle is recruiting great people. The second half is retaining them. As with recruitment, retaining employees begins with sound analysis—specifically, analyzing performance in a way that enables you to coach them to realize their potential. Leading your people to accomplish

HOW TO INTERVIEW YOUR POTENTIAL EMPLOYER

Rebels are not just interviewers. They can also be interviewees. Here are a few questions a job-seeking rebel would do well to ask when evaluating a potential employer:

1. *What is the most compelling and inspiring attribute of this company, and, what one word best describes its employees?*
2. *Will I have a mentor?*
3. *Can I interview anyone in the company, including the CEO, to learn more about the job?*
4. *What is the primary reason people leave the company? Can I talk to them?*
5. *Can I spend a day at the company just observing the work environment?*
6. *How is learning facilitated at this company?*
7. *Who are the heroes (don't assume it's the CEO—sometimes it's not so obvious) in this company, and why are they considered heroes?*
8. *How would this company deal with failure?*
9. *Is this company willing to have a contrarian, a risk-taker, an oddball in its midst?*
10. *What's the next logical career step if this relationship fails? (This question is better kept to yourself.)*

★ ★ ★

BUSINESS REBEL HALL OF FAME PROFILE

John (Jack) Welch, Jr.
(Chairman and CEO, General Electric)

You might ask, "How can the CEO of a $100 billion company make this list?" That's a good question, but if you look at the crucial combination of vision, passion, instinct, and agility that Jack brings to his job every day, you realize that there are few rebel executives in the world who are as gifted as he is (he became GE's CEO at age forty-five, almost two decades ago). In fact, Jack runs GE with the dexterity and drive of the leader of a little Internet start-up.

General Electric has long been known for attracting and developing some of the best leaders in business and for creating some of the most widely practiced business techniques (the results and relationships evaluation grid introduced later in this chapter has its roots with GE). General Electric is the most admired company in America (1999 *Fortune* magazine winner), and anybody who knows the company well knows that Jack is the force behind this success. He is considered a "man of his people," as he was one of the first CEOs to regularly teach in the classroom in GE's executive programs. He was also one of corporate America's first leaders to spread the wealth within his company. During the last half of the 1990s, GE's employees saw a capital gain in their options equal to twelve times their annual salary.

In short, Jack helped revolutionize the world of work—creating incentives throughout the organization and making it more informal and dynamic. He says, "I can remember twenty years ago in this company when you went to a meeting, the lights went down, you read a script, you gave your pitch, and you got the hell out of the room. That was the game. Today you're in there having an open dialogue with self-confident people, real exchanges about real things." Professor Noel Tichy, a longtime GE observer, says that along with Alfred Sloan of General Motors, Jack is one of the two greatest corporate leaders of this century: "And Welch would be the greater of the two because he set a new, contemporary paradigm for the corporation that is the model for the twenty-first century."

extraordinary things is the most certain way to ensure that they'll stay. No combination of employee perks, bonuses, incentives, or notes from the boss can match the deep satisfaction one has when one smells the freshness of his own talent. Great bosses are great evaluators and motivators of talent.

The ideal rebel company is full of balance: the balance between achieving (accomplishing results) and connecting (maintaining relationships), the balance between core values and financial performance, the balance between home and work. Yet the most tangible way that most companies evaluate a manager is based upon a monthly financial statement. Sure, once or twice a year there's a performance review that rates the manager on his or her ability to communicate or inspire the workers, but that amounts to a small score on a larger review.

At Joie de Vivre, we've developed an evaluation format that addresses this oversight that is common in most companies. Our ideal manager is equal parts results and relationships. Hopefully, the combination of the two is synergistic: rebel managers build strong values-based relationships, which inspire their employees, producing customer satisfaction and profitable financial performance. So we created a grid that juxtaposes results and relationships in a precise fashion for evaluating managers. We call it the Triple R grid: Rebels' Results and Relationships.

To begin with, we needed to decide on the measuring tools. On the results side, that was easy. These measurements include the P&L versus budget and prior year; the quality of the monthly P&L reviews the manager authors; customer service scores; spotter reports ("mystery shoppers"); status of capital improvements relative to budget; and competitive market analysis (are we picking up market share or not?).

On the relationships side, we determined that the following metrics helped determine managers' proficiency with people: work climate surveys (which will be discussed in greater detail in the diversity chapter); employee turnover statistics; employee exit interviews; a peer and industry review of their reputation; the quality of their dashboards; Joie de Vivre University staff participation; and examples of how managers incorporate the company's core values into their property. As you can imagine, it is harder to evaluate relationships and values, as some of the criteria tend to be subjective.

Ultimately, each manager is rated from 1 to 4 (1 being superior, 4 being poor) in the aggregate on both a results and a relationships basis. The sixteen possible results are shown in the diagram below. This exercise is not easy because everyone ends up in a box (and no one likes being in a box), and there is the risk of performing "fortune cookie management" by not deeply exploring why the manager is in that particular box. But this visual approach does allow you to have a shorthand approach for giving ongoing feedback to your managers.

To allow this manager review to be an open dialogue, ask your managers to review themselves and determine where they believe they belong on the grid before you sit down with them. (Unlike the Key Player Analysis that I discussed earlier in the chapter, this evaluation technique works best if shared with your employees.) One of the benefits you'll find from this evaluation technique is that it will allow for more specific feedback: just what most managers and employees are looking for from their boss.

Once the manager has been rated, there is a simple prescription (which shouldn't replace an in-depth discussion that is more specific to the manager) for each of the sixteen boxes that can help you coach the manager to greater success. I have included summary descriptions on pages 265 to 270, organized by quadrant.

To summarize, a manager in quadrant one is primed for career growth in the company. In fact, we will rarely promote a manager that isn't scoring in this quadrant. Quadrant two finds managers who may be good cheerleaders but need some additional "hard-skill" training. Quadrant three is more complex, as managers may be performing well on paper but their relationship skills or lack of attention to the company's core values could be cancerous. Finally, quadrant four requires immediate attention, for this manager is failing on both accounts—results and relationships. For more details, see pages 269 to 270.

INSPIRING HEROIC PERFORMANCE

Now that your people understand how their talents fit on the results and relationships grid, it's time to be specific about how to coach them to greatness. There's nothing worse than receiving an evaluation from your boss without any guidance or immediate follow-up on how you can improve.

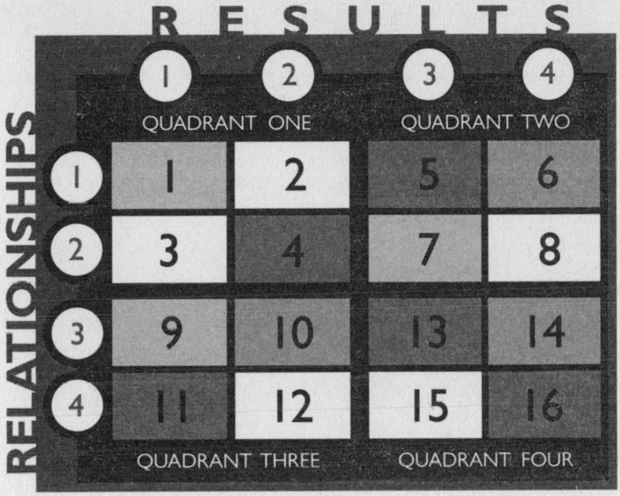

RESULTS

RELATIONSHIPS	1	2	3	4
	QUADRANT ONE		QUADRANT TWO	
1	1	2	5	6
2	3	4	7	8
3	9	10	13	14
4	11	12	15	16
	QUADRANT THREE		QUADRANT FOUR	

One of my first bosses said to me, "Don't believe the classic manager myth that incompetence begins just one level below where you are." That boss also taught me about maximizing people's strengths while minimizing their weaknesses. If you coach your people well, the result will be happier employees, less turnover, and a more profitable company. And, selfishly, it will make your life easier.

Here are some of my favorite coaching rules:

Make sure your people know the steps in your coaching style. For example, the classic coaching approach is to (a) explain the purpose of what you're trying to teach; (b) role-model it; (c) observe the person in practice, providing immediate and specific feedback; and (d) place special emphasis on what she is doing well (catch her doing something right) to build confidence, and focus conversations on these right actions so the person knows what constituted her heroic performance. Once people understand your process, let them hold you accountable if you're not coaching them correctly.

Be clear about how you want your people to communicate with you: meetings, voice mail, presentations, memos, etc. Every manager has a preference. If a specific employee doesn't know how to write a concise, one-page memo, teach him. Let him review some of your better memos. Never forget: you're a role model.

Encourage people to take responsibility. We live in a victimized society in which it sometimes seems the buck stops with no one. Help people regain their sense of authority (and make sure you give them a matching amount of responsibility) and their willingness to make mistakes. If an employee isn't taking the initiative, ask him, "What can I or the company do to help you be more effective?"

Bad news is good, surprises are bad. Make sure everyone understands that bad news needs to be revealed (in its entirety) as early as possible in order to learn and react. The earlier bad news is digested, the fewer surprises an organization experiences. Teach your people the gift of managing expectations.

Ask questions and don't give answers. JdV President Jack Kenny is great at this with our younger managers. Ask an equal amount of "why" and "how" questions. Don't always fill in the uncomfortable pauses in conversations. Let your people mull over a tough question. It's the only way they'll learn. Don't be afraid to ask them questions about what direction you should be taking with your job—they'll be flattered to be included in your strategy-making. Be willing to show some vulnerability. You really *don't* know it all.

Look for feedback. Remember in the film *Jerry Maguire* Tom Cruise's frantic explanation to Cuba Gooding, Jr., of his role as agent? "Help me help you!" Ask your people, "How can I contribute to making you more successful this year? Give me three specific actions I can take." Let your employees evaluate *you* on the results and relationships grid.

Be tangible. Make sure you share common expectations about what defines success and what are the measuring tools. This is obvious, but many managers aren't specific enough with their employees about the exact goals they're seeking. Always use a date or quantifiable reference point. For example, "As director of sales, you are responsible for attracting five new accounts each month who, in total, will represent at least 20 percent of our annual business this year."

Be sensitive. Sometimes a shoulder is all your staff needs: one to cry on in times of need and one to stand on to see a brighter future. Occasionally, a coach needs to provide "placebo management"—giving a person a shot of self-confidence by assuring him that he had an impact on a recent company success. Mark Twain wrote, "Keep away from people who try to belittle your ambitions. Small people always do that, but the really great make you feel that you, too, can somehow become great." Sometimes we just need someone to believe in us.

Know your employees' "breaking points." Consultant Maury Hanigan has identified certain junctures in employees' tenures at which they are at greatest risk of quitting. Those tend to be (a) a new-hire crisis: when the employee realizes the grass isn't always greener on the other side; (b) a promotion crisis: when the employee has been in the job approximately two years and hasn't earned the promotion she was looking for; and (c) a boredom crisis: an employee's attention wanders after four or five years. Addressing these breaking points proactively will improve employee retention.

Consider redesigning key jobs to reduce turnover. Certain key positions in your company may have revolving-door loyalty. Just when you have a treasured employee fully trained, he hits the road. If you see this pattern repeat itself, you may need to redesign the position. UPS found that when they redesigned their drivers' position so that it no longer included the thankless job of loading the trucks, they were able to dramatically increase the length of driver employment. UPS made a strategic decision. They determined that the drivers were the face of the company and that their customers didn't appreciate meeting a new driver every six months. Alternatively, the company figured that the loading jobs were lower-skilled and likely always to be high-turnover jobs. This didn't concern them, because the training period for the loading jobs was much shorter than for the driver jobs and the customer contact was minimal. Sometimes employee retention is just a matter of strategic thinking.

Coach values, not just performance. As we discussed, most employee reviews focus exclusively on short-term performance (financial statements), but this can be dangerous since it neglects employee attributes for organizational success, such as an ability to communicate and create a clear vision, skill at building morale and teamwork, integrity and reputation. This is especially important in the rebel company that's driven by its values.

Now that we've established the ground rules for recruiting, evaluating, and coaching rebels, how does this apply to younger employees? Are there different rules for Generation X employees than for baby boomers? Read on.

10. Collaborating with Young Talent

Work is not work. It's a hobby that you happen to get paid for.

—Richard Barton, thirty-one, head of Microsoft's Expedia

Imagine you're on the stage at Woodstock in 1969. As far as the eye can see, a seething mass of youthful and exuberant humanity, 500,000-strong, is doing its thing. Now fast forward thirty years. Once again, imagine standing on that stage and surveying the crowd. Today you see five times as many young, idealistic people at a different type of gathering. This crowd of more than 2.5 million represents the number of Gen Xers who started businesses in the United States last year. The workplace has replaced Woodstock. It's where decorum deviates, passion predominates, and rebellion resonates.

We're in the midst of the greatest generational shift of wealth and power that this country has ever seen. Remarkably, people between the ages of twenty-one and thirty-five are one of the driving forces behind the nation's flourishing economy. In fact, more than 50 percent of all businesses being created today are started by people thirty-five or younger. And more than 75 percent of America's fastest-growing companies (*Inc.* 500) have CEOs forty or younger.

This rebellious, performance-driven generation has tossed out the typical business rules of the past: the hierarchical organizational chart, thick employee manuals, and five-year strategic plans. In place of the old rules has risen a new business model, one that merges the Woodstock generation with the Internet generation. Free minds and free markets is the rallying cry. People want to make a difference in the world at the same time they're making money.

It's remarkable that this "wired and desired" generation was widely derided as "slackers" just a half a decade ago. And then came along the dominant technology of our generation, the Internet, and almost overnight, the Gen Xers had a huge leg up in the digital derby (in the Internet's early days, it seemed like a private club for Xers). While your head may be spinning from the technological changes of the nineties, just imagine how Internet innovation will be leveraged in the next decade. Until just recently, most of the changes in high tech came from baby boomers who were introduced to computers in their teens. Now we have a generation that learned about computers at the same time they were potty-trained.

Demographics are also on Gen X's side as boomers near retirement age. The number of American workers aged thirty-five to forty-four—typically the group that is tapped to replace departing leaders—will decline 5 percent between 2001 and 2005, according to Census Bureau data. Therefore, Generation X will take an even larger role in defining the business world. Unlike many boomers, who couldn't imagine studying business in college, these young entrepreneurs have come to realize that business is the most powerful and, potentially, the most progressive social force in the world.

Boomers can't afford to misunderstand Gen Xers, because they represent such a tsunami of talent. So let's identify some ways that boomers and Xers can collaborate effectively.

★ ★ ★

BUSINESS REBEL HALL OF FAME PROFILE

Master P (Percy Miller) (Founder of No Limit Records)

Freestyle, internally motivated, impatient, and self-confident, Gen Xers have a number of newly minted rebel multimillionaires who could have been profiled here. But, since rap music is the true dividing line between boomers and Xers, I chose New Orleans-based Master P as the Gen X rebel poster child. In 1998, he was on *Forbes*'s list of the highest-paid entertainers—there was only one musical group or individual who made more money that year ($56 million) than Master P—the Rolling Stones. But, Master P is more than an entertainer—he's a conglomerate who breaks the rules.

It all started when, growing up with his grandmother in the San Francisco area projects, he inherited $10,000. Percy Miller used this money to open an independent record store (No Limit Records) in the East Bay, and while selling records, he built his company. With his label headquartered far from the hip-hop meccas of New York and Los Angeles, Master P refused to take the path of the other hip-hop elite—like Sean "Puff Daddy" Combs—who linked up with major record companies even though it diminished their upside and freedom.

P built a following with no major distributor and a stable of unknown artists. He trailblazed the record industry by going directly to the consumer, with street merchants handing out his new music directly to the people. His company has followed in the footsteps of Richard Branson, David Geffen, and Chris Blackwell, becoming America's most successful independent label. In the process, *Fortune* magazine estimates his net worth has grown beyond $350 million.

Master P is a cross-promotional genius, as No Limit was one of the first media companies in which the video films promoted upcoming record releases. P's currently building the largest recording facility in the country. He produces, writes, and stars in his own movies. He has created a No Limit clothing line, a controversial sports agency, and a real estate business. He's played professional basketball in the CBA. This is a true Renaissance Rebel!

In a recent interview with MTV News, he expressed the values of his generation: "I'm not going to limit myself. That's what No Limit is all about. Whatever you feel you can do, you got to believe in yourself, and plus you got to prepare yourself and you got to make it happen . . . Some people only think or dream about what they can do. I'm going right there and taking the step. It's easy to put something on paper and never make the step . . . Master P and No Limit is living the American Dream, and whatever I feel I could do, I'm gonna do it."

BOOMERS VERSUS XERS

What happened? How did these slackers become moguls overnight? There are two explanations: (1) the slackers weren't really slackers after all but were perceived as such in the early nineties due to the anemic economy, and (2) our whole society is experiencing "icon-toppling" like never before—shifts in the balance of power facilitated by new technology that allows anyone to access information that previously only the elites controlled.

Does Abbie Hoffman's admonition that you can't trust anyone older than thirty apply to these youthful business rebels? No, what predominates in the young, rebel companies is a meritocracy. Put up or shut up. No generation corners the market on wisdom—age is irrelevant. In fact, baby boomers and Gen Xers share a common rebel spirit: the questioning of authority, the reverence of individuality, the desire to create a legacy.

Remarkably, the Woodstock celebration and the Internet generation share virtually the same birthday. That legendary concert in the fields of upstate New York lasted the weekend of August 15–17, 1969, and the Internet was birthed just two weeks later, when on September 2 the first two computers were connected to form ARPANET, the network that grew into the Internet.

Can boomers and Xers make beautiful music together? Consider this family story. Blue Mountain Arts is a greeting card publisher founded in 1971 by self-described flower children Stephen Schutz and Susan Polis Schutz. These arts-minded hippies (take a look at their Web site at www.bluemountain.com and you'll see photos of them on their way to Woodstock with their car named Freedom) created silk-screened posters of inspirational poetry and sold them out of their car as they trekked across America. Over time, their business grew as Susan's poetry and Stephen's mystical artwork won a loyal following.

While this counterculture company prospered, even becoming a small but formidable competitor to Hallmark, it took the World Wide Web for it to skyrocket to fame and fortune. In 1994, the Schutzes' son Jared came home from Princeton and taught his eleven-year-old brother about Web pages. Jared's father, Stephen, an MIT graduate with a Ph.D. in physics from Princeton then learned how to construct Web pages from his eleven-year-old. The next step was obvious. To stay in touch with Jared on the East Coast, Stephen, living in Colorado, created an online greeting card.

A year later, the family decided to host a free greeting card service, an Internet business Jared founded during college. The idea was such a hit that the family went on to launch bluemountain.com—their intent to create the Web's first center for sending poetry and communicating emotions.

To call bluemountain.com a success is an understatement. Twelve million people visit their site per month, and at one time it was ahead of even Amazon and eBay. Tapping his parents' artistic talents, the Net-savvy Jared has been the family's guiding entrepreneurial force, combining the three killer C's of the Internet world: content, commerce, and community. In the process, Jared helped win bluemountain.com a whopping 65 percent market share in the Internet greeting card market. In 1999, Excite@Home bought bluemountain.com for $780 million.

Given the growth of the Internet, the press is having a field day trying to establish a competition between boomers and Xers. The truth is that they have more in common than you might think. As J. Walker Smith and Ann Clurman write in the book *Rocking the Ages*, "The diversity of Xers is nothing but the 'individuality' of boomers carried to the extreme."

Boomers have to admit that Xers exhibit some of the most admired traits in today's workplace: flexibility; a hunger for learning; innovation; an appetite for change; the ability to solve problems independently; a strong multitasking orientation; a preference for diversity; and a genuine passion for making a difference. And Xers have to realize that boomers possess the wisdom and instinct that come from experience, while also sharing many of the same values. Both boomers and Xers support the idea of corporate meritocracy, banishing nepotism and old-boy cronyism. With that comes a shared belief in personal responsibility. Both groups want to be held accountable and be rewarded for their area of responsibility. Additionally, both boomers and Xers are comfortable with the idea of short-term, project-oriented teams.

LEARNING TO XERCISE

Are there any secrets to working effectively with Generation X employees or employers? No. There are just some basic rules of thumb. Incorporate these philosophies into your leadership and you'll find yourself at the helm of a lean, mean, and committed team of fiercely loyal talent.

MANAGING VERSUS LEADING

Traditional structure and rules are stifling. No one wants to be micromanaged. As one Xer says, "Tell me what to do, give me the resources, and then let me create." In other words, don't waste my time with lots of meetings and rules. Yet underlying this independence is a desire for learning. Many sociologists believe these young people are thirsting for heroes and role models. They want someone to lead by example, someone they can emulate. You might call them Generation Why? They have lots of questions, and they're looking for a mentor who can give them answers. Not the kind of answers that come from a rule book, but the wise words from someone who's been around the block a couple of times. Young people are looking for a leader who makes his or her expectations clear. They don't mind well thought out processes that effectively run the company. What they won't accept is linear reasoning based on the tired "that's how we've always done it" premise.

VALUES-BASED LEADERSHIP

Because many young people find their sense of community and home in the workplace, a powerful bond develops. Encourage this by making the company something you can both be proud of. Joie de Vivre has done this by setting up a quarterly philanthropic project that our employees create and implement, whether it's a beach cleanup with sixty employees or the seven staff members who were given an extra week of paid vacation to participate in the annual AIDS ride fund-raiser from San Francisco to Los Angeles.

THE NEW EMPLOYMENT CONTRACT IS BASED UPON LEARNING

The old, implicit employment contract between labor and management was based upon job security. In our hypertransient modern lives, security is an illusion. Young people believe their ultimate security comes from building a collection of portable skills that makes them superemployable. The new contract goes something like this: We will make you a prized free agent by offering you good compensation, a challenging project, and a chance to learn some valuable skills while you're with us. The more entrepreneurial the learning, the better.

QUALITY OF LIFE IS MORE IMPORTANT THAN STANDARD OF LIVING

Is this new generation "nouveau riche?" No, you might as well call them "nouveau unleashed" because what dominates their careers is not making money but creating freedom. Fewer people are trying to keep up with the Joneses anymore. At least not in the traditional sense. For Xers, unique experiences are their status symbol, not material possessions.

Depending upon the nature of your company, there may be inexpensive things you can do to enhance their quality of life. We're able to offer free massages for high-performance employees because we operate a spa. One of our company's favorite annual activities is the night we rent a bowling alley and have pizza and beer while the various businesses compete. And not just for the highest score—each hotel or restaurant team comes dressed in their ultimate, custom-made team bowling shirt. This kind of retro fun is a perfect fit for young employees.

RESPECT THEM AS INDIVIDUALS

The proliferation of personal Web pages is a sign that people want to express their individuality. Eclecticism has become an art form among the

HOW TO CREATE A JOINT COMMITMENT

At the end of 1999, we learned a hard lesson about our young managers. Through the grapevine, we'd heard that there was some disillusionment among our junior level of managers (assistant managers, front desk supervisors, etc.). Of course, this was distressing since this group of approximately twenty employees—primarily aged twenty-two to thirty—represented some of Joie de Vivre's future leadership. When we approached them, one of the most common messages we heard was that they felt unappreciated and overworked. Unfortunately, this is quite common for young managers who are trying to satisfy their manager as well as be an ally to their line-level employees. This situation was worsened by the fact that many of these Gen X managers had friends who were making beaucoup bucks at new Internet start-ups that were proliferating throughout the San Francisco Bay Area.

Many of our young managers also thought that the company had implicitly promised them a career growth path that was more accelerated compared to their existing situation. Our Joie de Vivre brain trust realized it was time to make the implicit explicit. We incorporated the following exercise into a Joie de Vivre University class: "The Future Vision of the Company and How It Relates to You." The participants in the class, who were almost exclusively midlevel managers, did a series of exercises that led them to this Joint Commitment statement. The purpose of this statement was to explicitly outline what the managers were looking to accomplish and how their supervisor or mentor could assist them. This exercise helped the young managers realize that (a) they're responsible for managing their own training path, and (b) they need to outline exactly what they're looking for. Try this in your company, for this Joint Commitment is perfectly suited to self-starting, ambitious young managers who will likely seek out other employment if you don't shine a light on some of their implicit career needs and desires.

During the next six months, my goal is to learn more in the following areas: ____. I will obtain this learning by proactively seeking out the following people within the company to help mentor me (include my direct supervisor as one of those people): __________________________. I will commit to meeting with these people on the following schedule in order to accelerate my learning:______________________________________. I am willing to take/teach at least ______JdV University classes in the next six months in order to learn more. If I'm going to teach a class, it will be on the subject of ______________________________________. These goals will be accomplished concurrently with any goals/objectives that my supervisor and I have agreed to (including items on the manager's training checklist). Based upon my commitment to learning, I would like JOIE DE VIVRE to consider the following career path for me:____.

Career advancement depends primarily on two things: my state of preparedness for the new job and the availability of the new job. My responsibility is to become the best-prepared candidate for the position that I aspire to. JOIE DE VIVRE will do its best to try and find positions available that fit what I'm looking for. By six months from now, I would hope that I would have accomplished the following:

____.

During the following month after that time, I will set up a meeting with my supervisor (and my mentor if that's a different person) to review my career progress. The key ways that I'd like to see JOIE DE VIVRE grow are the following:

____.

I am committed to making this happen. I will proactively make sure that JOIE DE VIVRE is committed too.

____

Your Name *Mentor* *Supervisor* *Chip Conley*

young, another way of saying, "Hey, I'm different." Accept that people want to put their individual stamp on their work. Don't patronize them. Respect this as long as it doesn't impact your business negatively.

KEEP EVERYONE INFORMED

As with all of these tips, this applies to everyone in your company. In the Information Age, people expect their company to communicate effectively and freely with them. Xers are especially skeptical of corporate secrets. Make an inventory of what you try to keep secret in your company. Why is this information so clandestine? What would happen if you made it available to everyone? Practicing open-book management (see Chapter 7, "Building Corporate Instinct") will reassure your young stars that you want their input and that they'll be kept informed.

Xers are complex. They want to feel part of a mission-driven tribe, yet they're skeptical of group-think and want to be valued as individuals. They want work to feel like a new extended American family home, yet they're nervous about getting too comfortable or dependent. They're thirsting for wise mentors and workplace heroes, yet they're afraid to put anyone on a pedestal. They want to become masters, but they want it to happen overnight. It's probably futile to try to categorize them as we have in this chapter, but at least you start to understand some of the influences. With this knowledge in hand, you can provide a work environment that allows your young people to flourish. Start today. It's in your best interests.

11. Managing Diversity Like a Potluck

The real challenge facing the world is not geographic distance but cultural distance.

—Ray Bakke

Today's workplace is a potluck. The great human resource challenge for the twenty-first century is enabling people of different ethnicity, religion, gender, sexual orientation, and personality to learn to work together in our multicultural workplace. The Internet has broken down many of the old barriers, but globalization requires even more cultural savvy. Young pop icons like Tiger Woods and Mariah Carey remind us that we don't all fit into simple racial or ethnic boxes. The corridors of power no longer belong exclusively to straight, middle-aged white men.

The argument for welcoming diversity into your company is logical. It has nothing to do with ideology and everything to do with improving your competitive positioning. Rebel employers encourage the whole person to show up at work, not just that part that fits the corporate norm.

Quokka Sports's Al Ramadan explains that the digital world is like living in the fog: it's only your senses that give you direction. Therefore, he wants to ensure that his new employees bring the company two things—diversity and good DNA. Diversity provides radar antennae in all directions so that the company won't be surprised by something coming out of left field. Good DNA is an extension of diversity. It means Al doesn't care what you look like on the outside, he wants to make sure your heart, mind, and soul are carefully aligned with Quokka's high-performance, no-safety-net culture. And, if you bring in good DNA, it will tend to replicate itself in the hiring process.

Before I show how to audit and improve your company's diversity, let me outline some of diversity's tangible and beneficial results:

1. **You better complement your customer base.** Your company's chances of success will improve if your employees are representative of your customers.

2. **You create a more interesting place to work by learning from each other.** Who wants to go to a cocktail party with a bunch of clones just like you? A diverse workplace is more dynamic, and people are more willing to challenge the status quo. This is a place where innovation flourishes. Your blinders come off.

3. **You reap the PR benefits of being a socially conscious and progressive organization.** Whether it's the multicultural faces on your company's annual report or the positive media coverage you receive for sponsoring a community event, your company's reputation can be enhanced through your diversity efforts. You're sending an "open-door" message to the world.

4. **You create a better potluck.** Casting the broadest possible net in the employment marketplace ensures that you'll attract the brightest and let them be their best. No one is benefited when talented employees feel they need to be "under cover" at work.

DIVERSITY GOES BENEATH THE SKIN

When you say "diversity," people often associate it strictly with race or ethnicity. To others it connotes religion, gender, or sexual orientation. Only rarely do we think of diversity as it applies to personality or interests. As the world becomes more of a melting pot, our ethnic and cultural differences actually diminish, but our values and sense of self still define us beneath the skin.

CREATING A DIVERSITY AUDIT (WITHOUT ALERTING THE POLITICALLY CORRECT POLICE)

Recently, I participated in a panel discussion at a nationwide hospitality conference. The head of the conference was welcoming everyone and telling the attendees how important it was that they return next year.

"As a memento and a reminder that we want to see you at this conference annually," he said, "we're giving each of you a pair of customized cuff links and an etched cocktail glass."

From my seat on stage, I scanned the audience and saw 20 percent of the attendees—mostly women—exchange wry glances and knowing nods. Once again a business leader had sent the wrong message to a vital constituency: You're not important. We didn't even think of you.

How can you be sure you're not sending a similar message to people in your company? You may find the following audit enlightening:

1. Is your company holiday event informally called "the Christmas Party"?
   (a) Yes
   (b) No

2. In planning this party, do you consider the entertainment and cuisine based upon the ethnicity of your workers (for example, if Hispanic workers represent 30 percent of the party attendees, do you offer salsa music)?
   (a) No, we don't really think about that
   (b) Yes, we try to include things that will make our various employees culturally comfortable

3. Assuming you offer spousal health benefits to your married employees, do you offer spousal health benefits to the partners of gay or lesbian employees or to heterosexual couples who are unmarried but in a domestic partnership?
   (a) No
   (b) Yes

4. What kind of networking and social events does your company promote?
   (a) *Golf tournaments, classic car concourses, hunting and fishing expeditions*
   (b) *Picnics, hiking and mountain biking, after-work beer busts*

5. Imagine the most eccentric person in your company. Within the company, is this person a
   (a) *Leper and outcast?*
   (b) *Prized asset and role model?*

6. If you listed the ten most powerful people in your organization, how many would be women?
   (a) *Two or less*
   (b) *Three or more*

7. How does your company feel about male secretaries?
   (a) *We never hire them*
   (b) *We hire whoever is best*

8. Are people allowed to decorate their cubicle or office in any way they choose, no matter how outrageous?
   (a) *No, the company sets limits*
   (b) *Yes, we can be as crazy as we want as long as the decoration isn't purposefully offensive*

9. Is there a high-profile gay or lesbian department head within your organization (if so, ask them if they feel comfortable bringing their partner to the company holiday party)?
   (a) *No*
   (b) *Yes*

10. How would your company react if an employee who is an Orthodox Jew asked to switch his holiday days so that he could work on Christmas but take the first day of Chanukah off?
    (a) *The answer would be no, since the company's holiday policy is inflexible*
    (b) *Making the switch would be fine, even if it slightly hinders the business*

11. What percentage of the hires you've made for managerial positions in the past year have been people of color?
    (a) 25 percent or less
    (b) At least 25 percent

12. Do you offer vegetarian alternatives at company-catered lunches or dinners?
    (a) No, we haven't thought about it
    (b) Yes

13. On any forms you ask employees or customers to fill out, when it comes to asking for their racial background, do you offer an alternative called "mixed race"?
    (a) No
    (b) Yes, or something similar to that

14. How would your office react if a secretary began regularly arriving at work in his or her native dress (African dashiki, Indian sari)?
    (a) Our office manager or president would likely convene a secret meeting to discuss it and possibly discreetly tighten the dress code policy
    (b) It would be welcomed as long as it didn't interfere with his or her performance

15. Have you invested in a professional diversity-training program?
    (a) No
    (b) Yes

Now tally your answers, scoring each "a" answer with no points and each "b" answer with one point. How'd you do? If you scored less than a 10, you and your company may need some remedial diversity training.

CREATING A WORK CLIMATE SURVEY

R-E-S-P-E-C-T! Aretha Franklin said it, and that's exactly what we all seek in the workplace, especially if we've experienced discrimination based

★ ★ ★

BUSINESS REBEL HALL OF FAME PROFILE

Oprah Winfrey
(Chairman and CEO of HARPO Entertainment Group)

Against all odds, this woman has become a media icon. To succeed, Oprah had to be a rebel, as she had more than a few strikes against her: coming from outside the media capitals of New York or Los Angeles; being a black woman rather than a white man; lacking the classic beauty of most television celebrities; and being discovered on local, not network, TV.

For those of you who don't know about Oprah's growing empire, you might be surprised to learn that *Fortune* magazine named her the second-most-powerful woman in American business. She has a net worth that is approaching $1 billion and is the highest-ranking woman on the *Forbes* 400 list of wealthiest Americans who didn't inherit at least part of their fortune. *Time* magazine named her one of the hundred most influential people of the twentieth century. All of this for a woman who grew up dirt-poor in Mississippi.

In the past decade, Oprah has rewritten the rules of building a media empire. Instead of purchasing existing assets like most of her competitors, Oprah has used her identity to start up magazines, book clubs, film studios, and Internet ventures like Oxygen Media. The synergy of how these various ventures promote each other is one of the most integrated media universes ever created.

How did Oprah grow into America's most powerful celebrity brand name? Oprah's overarching achievement has been empowering and encouraging diverse and disparate people. She cites her greatest assets as being intention and authenticity, and she represents a powerful rebel role model for anyone who dares to be themselves in business.

upon who we are. The question for the business rebel is "How do we ensure that we're respecting everyone's individuality?"

At Joie de Vivre, we've found that our annual Work Climate Surveys help us to understand whether we're providing a motivating environment in which to work. The information we collect is specific to Joie de Vivre—we want our employees to live our mission statement: "creating opportunities to celebrate the joy of life." But more and more companies of all kinds are taking similar formalized approaches to listening to their employees.

You can create your own Work Climate Survey. Here are four steps to making it happen.

1. Determine the most important issues you want addressed. For Joie de Vivre, those issues revolved around the perception and implementation of the corporate culture, the relationship between managers and subordinates, the workplace morale, the satisfaction with the product we're selling, and the individual's job contentedness. As I'm writing this, I'm realizing that we don't ask enough diversity-oriented questions. Maybe we ought to ask our employees how they feel about statements such as "I have been criticized for expressing my opinion" or "I have seen colleagues mistreated for being different."

2. Determine how you'll administer the survey. If you're not using an outside firm, be careful about how you do this. Do not let the manager administer this to his or her employees. It will skew the results. Be clear when the survey will take place. We believe it's better to complete it all on the same day rather than let employees take it home with them (which means that responses tend to come dribbling back in). Make sure the survey is anonymous and people feel there's no potential for retaliation. Translate it into different languages if necessary. In sum, be sure the process is full of integrity.

3. Tally and analyze the information as quickly as possible. Since we've historically administered this ourselves, let me warn you: it is a mammoth task. Our director of administration, Anne Conley (yes, my sister!) spends a couple of full-time weeks tabulating and formatting the information for all the different businesses. For any mere mortal, it would take nearly a month. Make sure the format you're using to communicate this information to your managers is effective. Do they understand the implications of this data? Our managers know how they did relative to the last survey as well as compared to managers at our other properties. They're able to pick up trends and read uncensored comments from their employees. We ask each of our managers to write an action plan within one week of receiving this information.

4. Communicate with your employees. Our managers are responsible for writing a memo to their staff addressing the results of the survey (we also prefer to have them conduct a meeting with each of the various departments). One of the age-old questions is "Do you share all of the quantifiable results and employee comments with the staff?" The totally transparent company would do this. On the other hand, some of the results (and especially the comments) can be unproductive and potentially hurtful. If you choose to edit comments and then publish the rest, employees will know they're getting a censored list (since some employees' comments won't be listed). One alternative is to write a detailed memo that addresses the biggest successes and problem areas along with survey excerpts and an action plan (and then appoint a team of employees who will tackle certain issues). It is an essential rule that only a short time passes between distribution of the survey and reporting the results (ideally, three weeks or less). Many companies shoot themselves in the foot by asking for employee input with Work Climate Surveys and not following up with results and responses in a timely manner.

DIVERSITY IS CREATED ONE PERSON AT A TIME

Creating a diverse company encourages people to be rebels themselves. It lets them stand and be counted. Here are a few ways to channel your staff's diversity:

Create a "Rebel for a Day" program. Once a month, appoint an employee as the Rebel for a Day. Choose your more off-beat staffers during the first few months to get this program off on the right foot. The only rule of this program is that the rebel is charged with spending all day breaking the rules. The rebel is vested with the responsibility of coming up with at least a dozen radical changes she thinks ought to be implemented at the company. She can either introduce those changes for that one day only (to see how they work) or introduce the ideas at a Rebel Roundtable of fellow employees on their appointed day. The goal is to empower and incite your most diverse employees to act as a force for change in your company.

Let every employee in your department pick a celebration day. Let's assume your department has twenty employees. At the start of each year, each employee picks a special day that represents something meaningful to them: it could be Passover, Canadian Independence Day, or Elvis Presley's birthday. Employees are responsible for highlighting their day with a special culture-specific lunch, educational literature, or anything else that inspires and educates their fellow employees.

Recruit in a diverse fashion. William Steere, the CEO of the large drug company Pfizer, says, "Some people believe that seeking diversity automatically leads to excellence, but I think that focusing on excellence inevitably leads to diversity." This CEO also follows up those words with unique actions such as being the first major drug company to aggressively recruit at traditionally African-American colleges, as well as developing training programs that teach managers how to retain and develop their minority employees.

Let them give you a report card. Ask your employees to create a report card of ten management or leadership characteristics that they'd like to see from you. By letting them create this, you're more likely to tap into the diversity of your workers and get a sense of their ideal manager. Let them rate you twice a year.

Let them tell you how they'll succeed. In many big companies, the manager instructs the employees on the path they have to take to succeed. There's only one path. Diversity, and for that matter ingenuity, is not allowed. Approach this in the exact opposite way. Let your diverse staff dictate the specific path they plan to take. Ask them to finish the sentence, "I am going to succeed because . . ." Coach and instruct them, but let them take the lead, and this approach will ensure that their individual talents percolate to the surface.

Beware of "dominant language." Kathy Levinson, president of E-Trade, says that many companies don't recognize that a dominant paradigm—straight, older, white males—can have a chilling effect on others. As a Jewish lesbian, Kathy is acutely sensitive to whether people have to wear a mask at work. The key solution for dominant language is to be inquisitive and lack presumption. Don't assume that your pregnant sales manager is married. Ask open-ended questions that allow people to self-reveal if they so choose. Taking these cultural blinders off is a healthy practice for any company interested in learning.

"Pass the photos" exercise. Go out and take photos of your frontline service-level employees (in our case, that means front desk staff, bellmen, housekeepers, and the like) doing their job in the workplace. Then assemble your managers around a table (preferably in a retreat location away from the office). Turn on some music. Pass around the photos, asking the managers to look closely at each person. When the music stops, each manager should be holding at least one photo. Ask each manager to identify the person in the photo and consider the following questions from the perspective of that person: (a) On a daily basis, what motivates this person to do a great job? How does she truly feel she makes a difference? (b) Does this person feel listened to? Are her individual needs considered? (c) What are the three biggest complaints this person has about her job? (d) What tools or approach can we immediately implement to make this person more effective? (e) How can we win this person's heart?

ONE LAST STORY

As I've said, diversity doesn't just happen by respecting various groups' needs; it is achieved by learning what turns individual people on. When we took over The Maxwell Hotel, we were faced with a unionized staff that had long been suspicious of management. We were warned about the bell staff, in particular, as they were supposed to be the most resistant to any change. Jack Keating, who'd been with the hotel eighteen years, was supposed to be a real troublemaker.

As we got to know Jack, we found that he was fun and talented. In fact, we learned that he possessed abundant artistic skills. But despite his talent, he'd never sold a piece of art. When we were renovating that hotel, we invited Jack to create some site-specific art to illustrate the individual character of the property.

We were so impressed with his work that we commissioned him to draw portraits of American writers for our conference room at The Rex, our literary hotel. The ten portraits that grace that large room are good enough to have gained attention from local art dealers. And with his art on display, Jack has been commissioned by guests from our hotels. The twinkle in Jack's eyes speaks volumes about his commitment to the company.

A troublemaker? I don't think so. We just needed to respect his individual talents.

V. BUILDING A REBEL REPUTATION IN THE WORLD

12. Customer Service: Employees as Entrepreneurs

Most hotel companies are in the business of "selling sleep" to their customers. I teach our staff that we're in the business of "creating dreams."

—Chip Conley

Just like Hewlett Packard, L.L.Bean uses its founder as an icon for the company's message to its employees. In the case of L.L.Bean, the billion-dollar catalog retailer, the message is "we guarantee customer satisfaction."

In 1912, Leon Leonwood Bean started the company by sending out one hundred pair of his Maine Hunting Shoes, promising to refund customers' money if they weren't satisfied. Company folklore has it that ninety pairs of the shoes came back due to a problem with the product. Mr. Bean made good on his promise, sending refunds by borrowing money from his family. It almost broke his fledgling company, but he made the necessary improvements to the shoes and the rest is history.

Today service is more important than ever, thanks to an explosion of customer choice and a heightened expectation of over-the-top service. Trouble is, most companies still focus more energy on creating the product than on delivering it.

Professors James Heskett, W. Earl Sasser, Jr., and Leonard A. Schlesinger use an exercise with their Harvard M.B.A. students each year to demonstrate the disappointing level of service found in America today.

Each of their students writes and sends two letters resulting from their actual personal service experience, one a complaint letter and the other a complimentary letter. The letters are composed to include a specific reference to what sort of service the customer expected, how it was delivered, as well as some useful suggestions about how the experience could be improved.

Over the next few weeks, the responses start trickling in: some defensive, some apologetic. Thousands of dollars' worth of airline tickets, hotel rooms, and other products are offered to solve the customer's dissatisfaction. Yet when the exercise is complete, more than 50 percent of the students whose letters elicited responses to complaints inevitably feel an even greater dissatisfaction with the company than they did before they wrote the letter. From all of these well-known service organizations, rarely did the students feel their specific letter was answered quickly and sincerely. Instead, more often than not they received a canned response (maybe with typos) and occasionally some compensation just to quiet them.

In the 1990s, the disparity between extraordinary service companies and their ordinary competitors grew. For those few companies that have become service champions, the implications for profitability are astounding. Those same professors, who are also the authors of *The Service Profit Chain,* suggest that a 5-percentage-point increase in customer loyalty produces profit increases from 25 percent (credit insurance) to 85 percent (branch banks) depending upon the industry.

We live in a "concierge culture," in which consumers expect responsive, reliable, and immediate service. With the choices that exist in your marketplace, the discriminating consumer will gladly try your competitors' product if you don't get it right. When customers experience minor problems, 95 percent say they'll repurchase if the complaint is resolved immediately, but this percentage drops to 70 percent if resolution takes even a short time. Imagine how far it drops if the problem isn't resolved at all. The U.S. Office of Consumer Affairs discovered that satisfied customers were likely to tell five other people about their positive experience while unsatisfied customers were likely to tell more than double that number. Does your service model guarantee on-the-spot problem-solving throughout the organization?

EMPOWERING EXTRAORDINARY SERVICE

Your employees' first impressions are an enormous determinant of their future behavior. How high must they jump to meet your company's measure of extraordinary service? What does the company culture tell them about how you respect your customer? How happy are their fellow employees?

At the start of each new employee orientation, I play a game—Name Your Favorite Shop—that reinforces Joie de Vivre's service strategy. As an icebreaker, I ask the new employees to think about a restaurant, clothes store, gift shop, or any other retail establishment that provided service that was memorable enough for them to tell a friend about it. Each person cites an example and tells the group why this place made them so happy. Some of the common responses are, "They always use my name when I enter the restaurant"; "They call me at home when they've got new merchandise that's perfect for me"; and "They love their product and it shows."

After hearing these examples of extraordinary service, I ask the staffers how many people they've told about their favorite establishment. This demonstrates the power of word-of-mouth. Then I ask, "Do you think this business needs to spend much on advertising?" The universal response is no. I continue, "Well, if they don't spend that money on advertising, do you think they can invest it on better training, work conditions, and wages?" People nod enthusiastically. They're starting to get the idea.

"During the last fifteen minutes," I tell them "you've perfectly described the kind of service we want to provide at our hotels, resorts, restaurants, and spas. Those are the kinds of memories we want to create for our customers. That's the kind of word-of-mouth we want to hear on the streets. You are the ones who will determine whether we're the best in our class. And the only way this will happen is if you speak up. In your past jobs, you may have been afraid to open your mouth about a recurring customer problem or something that was bothering your fellow workers. But here at Joie de Vivre, we can't improve without your input."

Then we talk about how they can be involved in running the business. The goal is to create a meaningful first impression that's linked to positive experiences your employees have had as customers. This exercise works across cultural, age, and job classifications—in fact, that's part of the magic. We've all been customers. We've all experienced great and bad service, and the thing we have in common is that we love talking about it. I frequently hear new employees recount extraordinary service memories that are fifteen or twenty years old. Imagine how much word-of-mouth marketing has been created by a firm whose customer vividly remembers such an experience many years later.

One other step we take is to offer each of these new employees a complimentary night in one of our hotels. Make them customers for a day. Why? Many of these folks have rarely spent a night in a hotel—especially the younger ones and immigrants to this country—so how can we expect them to empathize with our guests' experiences? This is an inexpensive treat that educates them at the same time. The better they understand the needs of the guest, the better their performance.

APPRECIATING YOUR FRONTLINE SERVICE PERSONNEL

No matter what industry you're in, there's nobility in providing service. How many CEOs could keep a smile and a positive attitude for eight hours, five days a week, while dealing with the occasional kook, crook, or crank? How many would willingly work nights or weekends while their family is at home or their friends are out playing? How many would be willing to work for wages that require them to take a second part-time job to make ends meet? The first step in creating a rebel service culture is to realize that your service employees bear an enormous emotional load in working with the public.

The service industry is all about empathy.

Customers personalize everything. If the check-in is slow or you've been put in a bad room, subconsciously you assume you're being penalized or that, somehow, the person at the front desk is doling out service according to their perception of how important or worthy you are. While I'll admit that does occasionally happen, the fact is that most service is worthiness-blind. If you're receiving bad or haphazard service, it says more about the system of delivery than anything about you personally. Our staff is trained to anticipate this unfortunate personalization, so they know that each guest must feel they're treated specially. Of course, this same model also applies to the relationship between employer and employee.

The art of extraordinary service is not just about meeting customer expectations but about addressing the customers' *unspoken desires and needs.* Delivering service that speaks to each individual customer's unconscious needs—such as the age-old hotel trick of knowing the guest's name as he arrives at the front desk (this magic act is performed by the bellman, who reads the luggage tag and passes on the name to the desk staff)—should be the aspiration of any professional hotelier and rebel business leaders everywhere. Upgrading the self-esteem of your customers is an audacious goal, but it's one that will provide you lifelong business. It results in a fiercely loyal customer base.

The diagram below outlines the hierarchy of guests' expectations. When extraordinary service is given, an amazing result occurs—the *unexpected,* as opposed to the *desired,* service makes all the difference to that return guest and the success of word-of-mouth promotion. *Expected* service is what every customer anticipates when he checks in.

Xerox discovered that their most satisfied customers (those giving the

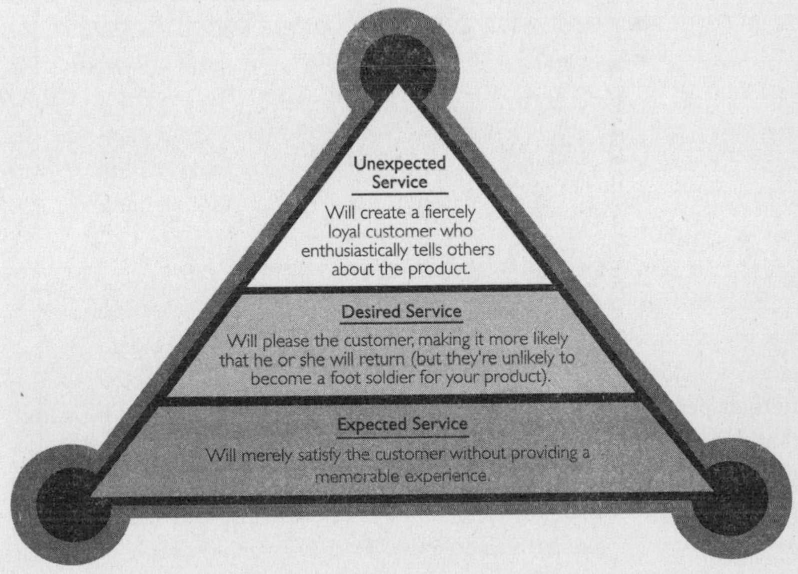

company a score of 5 on a 1-to-5 service scale) were six times more likely to repurchase Xerox equipment than those giving the company a 4 rating. Unexpected service (which would be similar to a 5 rating) elicits rabidly loyal customers, while desired service (similar to a 4 score) may make your customers happy but it doesn't necessarily mean you'll retain them. These results suggest that the best return on investment is hand-holding your customers at the extremes (the 1s and 5s are most liable to spread negative and positive word-of-mouth, while those scoring 2-to-4 don't have a strong opinion). This prompted me to create the Customer Service Smile, a diagram that helps us explain to our staff why the 1s, the "terrorists," and the 5s, the "cheerleaders," are so important to our business. This is why we drop everything to respond to an upset customer. Let a day pass before you respond to an angry letter or e-mail and you can be assured that five to ten more people will have heard what a bad business you're running.

Maybe you need to rethink how you survey your customers. Are you satisfied with just satisfied customers? Or are you attempting to create cus-

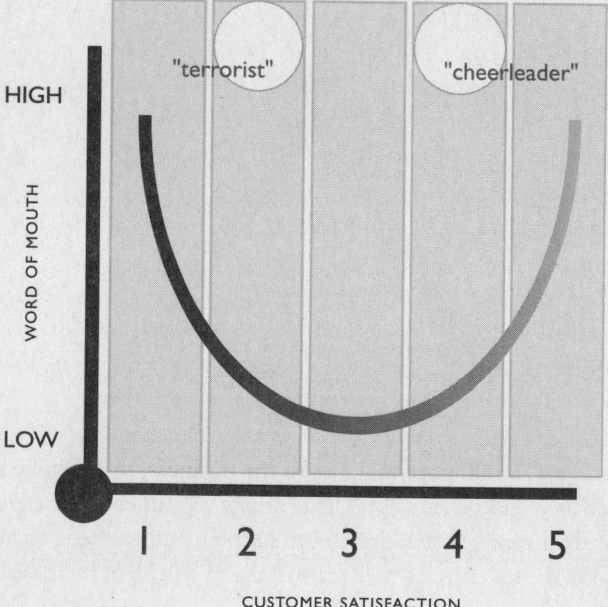

HOW YOUR STAFF CAN CALCULATE THE LIFETIME VALUE OF A CUSTOMER

I remember when I took my first real vacation a couple of years after I started The Phoenix Hotel. I came back to find that one of our most loyal guests had checked out of his suite after the first night of his stay. I asked our general manager about this. All he knew was that one of our new front desk hosts had gotten into a "little argument" with the guest. Knowing that there's no such thing as a little argument with a customer, I called the guest and was appalled to hear that our new desk host (who was soon to become our ex–desk host) had been unwilling to allow the guest's friend to park his Mercedes convertible in our parking lot. You'll remember that The Phoenix is located in a rather rough part of town, so this request by the guest wasn't unreasonable. But, since we expected to be full that night, our host settled the issue by just saying "No." Unfortunately, that's the word our guest used when I asked him if he'd ever be returning to our hotel. And we lost a lifetime of business.

That man traveled to San Francisco four times a year for trade shows and typically spent four nights in the city. These sixteen room nights annually represented approximately $2,000. Additionally, he usually told a few business associates to stay at the hotel during the trade show. These additional guests represented $3,000 annually. Since this guest was in his mid-forties and was likely to continue these visits at least fifteen years, this lost business translated into a minimum of $2,000 times fifteen years, or $30,000, or if you include his associates, you could suggest that this guest represented $75,000 ($5,000 times fifteen years) as a lifetime value to the hotel.

When our staff realized that this two-letter response ("No") represented a $75,000 potential loss to the business, they awoke to the impact they had on our hotel. It is nearly ten times more expensive to attract a new guest than it is to keep the customers we already have. We did an exercise that showed that a 5 percent increase in our repeat guests' likelihood of returning resulted in a 25 percent increase in potential profits, which would allow us to *increase staff wages by at least 10 percent.* Doing this kind of math will get your employees' attention!

tomer elation? The difference will have an enormous impact on your word-of-mouth and the size of your future advertising budgets.

DETERMINING YOUR CUSTOMERS' MOMENTS OF TRUTH

The expression "moment of truth" has caught on in most industries as we're all in the business of providing service to someone. It describes those critical points when a customer comes into contact with some aspect of your service and draws a conclusion about the company's overall service quality. Authors Karl Albrecht and Ron Zemke say that each customer carries around in his or her head an invisible (and likely unconscious) report card about your company. Identifying and scripting the critical points of service increase the likelihood that your staff will receive straight A's.

At a recent Joie de Vivre management retreat, we created a Moments of Truth exercise. We broke up into groups to discuss the four critical stages in our customer's experience: (1) Choosing the Hotel or Restaurant, (2) First Impressions, (3) the Experience, and (4) the Finale. Each group isolated the Moments of Truth within each stage and the specific steps for managing these moments, creating service rules that ensure that a high standard is met every time.

No matter what industry you're in, I highly recommend this exercise. For us it led to a lively debate and some noticeable changes in our service delivery system. Some believed that the Moment of Truth during the First Impressions stage (stage 2) occurred when the "curb appeal" became apparent, while others thought that the greeting at the front door was more important. The dialogue created by this exercise will highlight your employees' perception of the customer experience.

★ ★ ★

BUSINESS REBEL HALL OF FAME PROFILE

George Zimmer
(Founder and CEO of Men's Wearhouse)

I have to admit it. When I first started seeing George on TV, exclaiming, "I guarantee it!," I wasn't impressed. He seemed like a used-car salesman, and the suits looked a little run-of-the-mill. Then I bought a suit there, and my opinion changed. The price and service were incomparable. I filed the thought away: "Maybe George *does* know what he's doing."

Since then, I've become a believer, particularly in George's rebel approach to customer service: a direct-line 800 number to George that customers can call to register service compliments or complaints (he uses these real-life messages—only the compliments—as the foundation of Men's Wearhouse radio advertising). Additionally, George's approach to paying higher sales commissions on larger sales has become the benchmark in his industry. His company has quickly become America's largest discount retailer of men's business attire, with annual sales verging on $1 billion.

When Men's Wearhouse purchased one of the country's largest discount men's tailored apparel companies the *San Francisco Examiner* declared: "Once George Zimmer battled the Establishment; now he dresses the Establishment."

George is a populist and his employees love him. Why shouldn't they? He pays them 15 percent more than competing chains, spends four times as much to train them, and teaches them a blend of New Age and entrepreneurial principles. "Human beings have an innate desire to be both selfish and selfless. Corporate culture and financial incentives must reflect these polarities," he says. This from the man who sells more than one in every ten suits sold in America—a rebel who wore bell-bottom jeans while protesting the Vietnam War.

When you start a company on a shoestring, you rely almost exclusively on word-of-mouth and repeat business to pay the bills. We learned in our early years at Joie de Vivre that the only way our small company could compete against the big boys is by providing service that fostered enormous word-of-mouth. In order to establish that all-important positive reputation, you need to provide service that consistently exceeds expectations.

ENGAGING YOUR CUSTOMERS IN THE SERVICE STRATEGY

I learned a long while ago that the customers can participate in the ongoing evolution of one's business. At our hotels, for example, we're constantly asking our guests about new and unusual services and amenities they'd like to see. In the process, we "co-opt" them, making them part of the process of creating the product. This approach can also be applied to "gatekeepers," those key "influencers" who recommend your business.

At our ten-year-anniversary party for The Phoenix, one of our most important rock-and-roll travel agents took me aside and told me (with a big smile) the only reason that she started booking bands into the hotel was because "you were dumb enough to ask my opinion." She said she feels like part owner of The Phoenix because we've incorporated so many of her ideas into the hotel, such as having massage services on-call or having special guest rooms that were perfectly suited for a tour manager who needed to transact business while acting like housedaddy for his young band-on-the-road.

The successful software company Intuit took this concept of "listening posts" a step further. Intuit set up focus groups with users, actually observing them using the product in their homes, and constantly reworked their well-known product Quicken so that it became more user-friendly. Rather than hire a sales force, Intuit sent out free copies of the software to potential users and offered free technical support for the life of the product. All of this unexpected, spectacular service ended up paying dividends for the company as it built demand through word-of-mouth faster and less expensively than any normal marketing campaign. Microsoft did the same when they beta-tested their Windows 2000 with more than 650,000 customers.

Research has shown that customers can provide service leadership as much as management can. Think about it. Your service staff tends to spend more time with your customers than they do with management. For some employees, the customer can seem more forthright about the quality of the service experience than a manager is about their satisfaction with the employee's job performance. As one of our top service employees says, "You can't fool the customer, but you can distract your manager."

The quality of your employees' relationships with customers may be more relevant to customer satisfaction than is their relationship with their boss. That's a powerful statement. Here are a few tips that will reinforce this critical relationship:

Each month, ask one employee to be the service leader. In this role, the employee goes out of his way to ask customers about their service experience. This frontline employee hears the real-time, unedited version of a customer's disappointment when an expectation hasn't been fulfilled. At the end of the month, the employee produces a memo with her findings and conducts a portion of the staff meeting with recommendations for changes to address the complaints. This employee is also responsible for doing a follow-up call that month to any customers who had a bad experience, just to express your company's interest in having them back (possibly with a special discount offer).

Ask your service staff to call long-term customers whom they haven't seen in a while. There may be a good reason you haven't seen that customer for so long, but they also may have defected. Quite often, that customer may be more likely to spill his guts to their trusted desk-clerk friend than to a manager they've never seen. MBNA, one of the nation's largest credit card issuers, found that with one phone call they regained more than 30 percent of their lost customers by listening attentively to their concerns. If your staff feels uncomfortable calling customers, remind them that Richard Branson calls fifty customers a month when Virgin Atlantic enters a new geographic market.

Personalize the initial encounter between your employee and the customer. We do this by having "Host Profiles" on the front counter that introduce our guests to the employees "onstage" behind the desk. This information—like the host's favorite aspects of San Francisco or the one hidden place they like sending guests—helps break the ice and makes it clear that service is not an anonymous experience.

Ask customers to nominate an employee of the month. There's no better way to build the employee-customer relationship.

Have your employees ask customers about potential referrals. Normally, the sales staff tries to sniff out new customer leads, but your existing customers—who provide you the word-of-mouth—are your best source for new customers. Follow up on the leads.

Your employees will likely have greater job satisfaction when they know they can impact customer satisfaction. The key is to give them the flexibility and clear direction about how far they are permitted to go in satisfying the customer. If you do this and incorporate a bonus plan based upon service scores, you'll see an immediate increase in the number of returning customers.

TREAT 'EM LIKE ROYALTY— YOU'LL BE REWARDED WITH LOYALTY

The rebel company creates a successful customer service process and then constantly tweaks that process with new initiatives. Recently, Joie de Vivre developed the "Dreammaker" program for our front desk hosts in order to institutionalize our aim of providing service that meets the unspoken needs of our guests. We trained our staff to listen for guest preferences that might not have been stated in an inquiry. Each hotel was expected to perform a minimum number of above-the-call-of-duty examples of extraordinary service on a weekly basis and keep track of them in a log.

Let me use one of my favorite examples. A host might know that a VIP was checking into the hotel tomorrow. That host would call the person who made the reservation (often the VIP's secretary) and ask them if the VIP has any favorite snack foods or drinks. We might find out that this VIP loves Kiwi-Strawberry Snapple, cool ranch-style Doritos, and peanut M&M's. When this VIP arrives in his room, he finds this assortment of smile-producing junk food and a note from the staff saying, "We hope you feel at home." Or maybe it's as simple as knowing that you deliver a *New*

York Times to all of your Manhattanite guests each morning without their having to ask for it.

While we have yet to automate these guest preferences, many service leaders like Ritz-Carlton have been able to create a networked database so that a guest who requests a down pillow in Atlanta will also find a down pillow awaiting them in New York.

This Dreammaker program got off to a good start and showed some positive results in our overall companywide customer satisfaction scores (which rose 5 percentage points). After a while, our hosts grew tired of cataloging these service triumphs, and the program started to dissipate (a common problem in many young companies with a short attention span). To give it a boost and help spread the word about great ideas, we created a twenty-eight-page book chronicling the best examples of Dreammakers at each hotel.

SEVEN TIPS THAT WILL MAKE YOUR COMPANY A SERVICE LEADER

Here are a few exercises you might consider to strengthen your company's service culture:

GO ON A SERVICE RETREAT

We expect many of our hotels' front-line staff—in addition to our managers—to attend an annual off-site retreat that focuses on how their business can provide better service. This team-building experience has been a real morale booster, as service providers can easily fall into a rut with their normal day-to-day work existence. It can also be a means of getting cross-functional teams (in a hotel this might mean the bellstaff and the front desk staff) together to talk about how they can collaborate seamlessly for the customer's benefit. Some of the key questions we pose include:

- What do we give our guests that they can't get anywhere else?
- How can I get a guest to remember my name and to build a memory that they can take back home with them?
- What can I give guests that is totally unexpected and absolutely outrageous?

- How do I want people to feel after having contact with me?
- What if we were to charge a $5 admission for guests to enter our hotel lobby? What kind of experience would we have to create to be worthy of that entrance fee? (Obviously, no hotel will do this explicitly, but if our hotel does create a memorable ambience and experience, we're able to charge a higher rate. This question makes our employees realize we're in the entertainment business.)
- How can we build goodwill with our guests and reward our repeat guests?
- What's the most important issue facing the customer standing in front of me right now, and how can I satisfy him?

DEVELOP A MORE SPECIFIC CUSTOMER SURVEY

To simplify tabulation, many customer service surveys are completely numbers-based. They ask for a rating but don't allow the customer to specifically address how things could have been improved. Consider creating a more qualitative survey, in which each time your service quality is rated less than outstanding, your customers are asked to suggest in detail how the experience could have been improved. In essence, ask the customers to assist you in problem-solving.

GIVE YOUR SERVICE STAFF AUTHORITY TO SPEND MONEY

Ritz-Carlton is famous for giving each staff member up to $2,000 to solve any guest complaint. Nordstrom made a name for itself by allowing its sales clerks to accept returned merchandise without a sales slip. Does your frontline staff have any guidance about the limits of how much they can authorize to solve a customer service problem? If your staff has no clue about this, you can assume that your company's customer service will never be extraordinary.

CREATE YOUR OWN "BEN HILL"

Home Depot, one of America's most heralded service companies, came up with a novel approach to dealing with customer complaints. They took an artist's rendering of Pat Farrah, one of Home Depot's founding partners, and created a sign in all their stores saying ARE YOU SATISFIED? IF NOT,

CONTACT THE STORE MANAGER, ___________, OR CALL ME, BEN HILL, DIRECTOR OF CONSUMER AFFAIRS, AT 800-553-3199. That phone number went to the company's main switchboard in Atlanta. So whenever a call came in for Ben Hill, the operators knew it was a customer complaint and routed it accordingly to one of the top problem-solvers in the company. This approach served as sort of a "canary in the coal mine." When customer service was improving at Home Depot, there'd be fewer Ben Hill calls, and vice versa. Additionally, since headquarters tracked these calls, it was imperative for the store managers to solve problems at the store level to make sure that no customer felt they needed to call Ben Hill. By the way, the name Ben Hill came from a small town located near Home Depot's national Store Support Center. Ben Hill sounded like a good old southern guy who wanted to make you happy.

CREATE A POCKET-SIZED SERVICE GUIDE

At Joie de Vivre, we've taken our most important service information—core values, basic service standards, and the mission of our Dreammaker program—and created a small, attractive, laminated guide that all employees are expected to have with them while they're at work.

ADDRESS YOUR CUSTOMERS' TIME ANXIETY

No one likes waiting, but some great service companies like Disney have learned that customers are more satisfied when you give them a fair expectation of how long they'll be waiting in line. The service champions know that it's best to underpromise and overdeliver. For example, the entrance sign notes that the line for Space Mountain will take sixty minutes, but in fact Disney knows it's more likely to take forty-five. Retail guru Paco Underhill, who wrote *Why We Buy,* says this issue becomes even more problematic in traditional retail outlets. He's found that when people wait up to about a minute and a half in line, their sense of how much time has elapsed is fairly accurate. But anything over ninety seconds leads to a distorted sense of time such that customers see the waiting in line as one more activity rather just than being a transitional activity. In our time-starved culture, that's bad news, such that a customer may honestly think she's been in line for twenty minutes when it's only been ten.

REQUIRE THAT YOUR TOP EXECUTIVES LISTEN TO COMPLAINTS OR USE YOUR SERVICE

The large credit card issuer MBNA believed their key executives weren't connected enough to their customers. So they created a program in which each executive spends four hours a month monitoring customer calls at their call center. Another way to get your top dogs into the trenches is to have them use your product or service (in Southwest Airline's case, CEO Herb Kelleher actually helps serve drinks with the flight attendants when he's flying with them). I've heard people complaining in the economy section of a United flight: "If United's CEO flew in a middle seat cross-country on a regular basis, the whole experience of flying would probably improve." In many companies, the top brass that makes the strategic decisions *hasn't* tried its basic service or product in years. Executive sampling of the product is a cornerstone of rebel customer service.

Be a thoughtful and instructive consumer yourself. If you receive remarkable service from a parking valet or a restaurant busboy, tell him how it made you feel, and make sure he knows exactly what he did right. And if possible, let his supervisor know. If you receive poor service, don't create an emotional mess, but offer helpful advice on how things could have been handled differently. Participating in direct and respectful dialogue might actually help the business world at large move beyond its current mediocre standard of service.

13. Creating Brand, Building Buzz

If you're somebody with something to sell and no deep pockets for million-bucks-a-minute advertising blitzes, buzz is for you. Buzz is busy talk, the CNN of the street . . . Buzz needs an igniter—a circumstance, a surprise, a shortage, an inside scoop, a juicy tidbit, a giveaway, even some ambiguity.

—**Author Nancy Austin in *Inc.* magazine**

People don't just buy products. They also buy a representation of themselves. Brands are the mirror we hold up to ourselves, and buzz is the perfume we use to excite and entice.

Paco Underhill underlines this sensual connection: "When does a shopper actually possess something? Technically, of course, it happens at the instant that the item is exchanged for money—at the register. But the register is the least pleasing part of the store; nobody is savoring the joy of possession at that moment . . . Clearly, possession is an emotional and spiritual process, not a technical one. Possession begins when the shopper's senses start to latch onto the object. It begins in the eyes and then in the touch. Once the thing is in your hand, or on your back, or in your mouth, you can be said to have begun the process of taking it. Paying for it is a mere technicality . . ."

MAKING AN EMOTIONAL CONNECTION WITH YOUR CUSTOMERS

Successful brands understand that the purchase decision is emotional, quite often determined by our self-image or aspirations. Your favorite brand flirts with you, but it also represents a promise. Just like a rebel needs to be authentic, so does a brand.

Bob Pittman, president and chief operating officer of America Online, knows a lot about brands. He helped create MTV, revive Century 21 and Six Flags, and now he's the brand steward for America's largest Internet service provider. He says in *Fast Company,* "In the new world of business—a world of overcapacity and sensory overload—brands matter more than ever. Why? Because brands are a form of shorthand." Or Nick Graham from Joe Boxer says, "Brands are great editors. They know what fits and what doesn't."

Buzz starts when an "early adopter" tries the brand and raves about it to friends and associates. The more tightly affiliated the network, the faster the news will spread. The more your business reinforces the specific self-image issues of that network, the more likely you'll find immediate success.

With our rock-and-roll hotel, The Phoenix, the tour managers and band members from various touring groups are all good buddies and stay in constant contact. Back in 1987, this informal network spread the buzz about this new hotel faster than any paid advertising could have done.

After this initial improbable success, I grew Joie de Vivre as a brand based upon a niche strategy, my inspiration and guide often being the magazine-publishing industry. If ever there were a niche industry, this is it. Realizing this helped me create small hotels that found their niche markets just like magazines.

For example, The Phoenix is *Rolling Stone,* a magazine that could be defined by the words "adventurous," "hip," "irreverent," "funky," and "young at heart." Those words are our barometer during the concept-and-development phase, when our architect, contractor, creative services, and operations team ask questions such as, "What style should we create?"; "What services and amenities should we offer?"; or "What should be the profile of our staff?" We've learned that these words create an emotional connection with our guests as they describe the *identity refreshment* the guests are seeking by visiting The Phoenix. By staying at The Phoenix, a guest might feel a little more adventurous or hip, and, to this target market, this is a good thing. People are willing to pay a premium for this experience.

This taught me a lesson. Our target market is not based upon demographics—which describes what you see on the surface—but instead it's based upon *psychographics,* which describes what's going on underneath the surface for each of us—our passions, beliefs and values. Hippie icon Dr. Timothy Leary was one of The Phoenix's most loyal guests before he passed away, God rest his psychedelic soul. While he didn't fit the hotel's demographic profile (twnty-eight-year-old tattooed musicians from L.A.), he certainly fit the psychographic profile, because he would have considered any of those five adjectives a compliment if used to describe him.

Rule number one for brands: the words that a loyal customer uses to describe her dream product tend to be the same words she would use to affectionately describe herself. The rebel entrepreneur can compete with the big guys by amplifying a *psychographic* distinction, or determining what's going on underneath his customer's surface—his passions, beliefs, and values.

What magazine would define Holiday Inn? Who knows? I can name a few words that might describe the chain: "predictable," "modest," "bland," "innocuous," and "convenient." There aren't many people who'd pay for an identity refreshment based upon those five words (that doesn't mean the Holiday Inn chain isn't successful, it's just that they'll never be able to build a rabidly loyal client base or price their product at a premium). So while the rebel can't compete with the sheer size of a corporate giant, he or she can take the risk of tapping into some deeper human instinct of their focused customer base.

Each of my establishments has its own idiosyncratic personality, well suited to the specific market niche to which it appeals. If we do this well, it's like installing a turnstile at the front door and charging an admission price for guests, because your people will pay a premium for an identity refreshment. Just ask Ian Schrager, who's able to charge 25 percent more than his competition at his hotels because he's offering "hip" and "beautiful," and there's no doubt that people are willing to pay for those words.

Historically, most mid-priced hotel chains dared nothing, doing their best to appeal to mainstream tastes, yet creating forgettable products in the process. Times have changed. In the modern age of brand proliferation, the rebel needs to develop a product that dares to have a personality and can manufacture memories.

Steve Pinetti, Senior VP of sales and marketing at the Kimpton Group (the country's biggest boutique hotelier) says that when you're starting any business you ought to ask yourself, "What if it were a brand? What would you do to create a distinct identity?" If you're building a brand, ask yourself the following questions about your target customers:

How can you describe your target market in psychographic terms? For Joie de Vivre, we did this using the magazine analogy.

What lifestyle trends of your target market can you piggy-back on, and how can you repackage your product to take advantage of this? The reintroduction of the VW Beetle was timed perfectly to take advantage of the public's increasing desire for simplicity and our fascination with sixties nostalgia.

Who are the "early adopters," and how do you get your product in front of them? When clothing designer Tommy Hilfiger wanted to displace Calvin Klein as the next thing in fashion, he chose not to take the traditional celebrity route. Hilfiger realized that African-American kids foreshadowed style across the United States as other teens idolized their rebellious style. He targeted rap stars and urban teens as the key taste generators, and today Hilfiger jeans are outselling Calvin Klein in the coveted under-twenties market.

What props can you create to help your fiercely loyal customer base communicate their buzz to others? At The Phoenix, we discovered a little "memory maker" that brought the hotel some worldwide attention. For 6 cents each, we created thousands of removable Phoenix tattoos that bear the hotel name and logo. When guests checked-in or checked-out, they had the opportunity to be tattooed (which can be convenient if you've had a few too many drinks across town and your cabdriver is trying to get you home). I'm sure The Phoenix is the only hotel in the world that tattoos its guests.

How do your customers help proliferate the product? *Forbes* magazine reports that when Red Hat Software asked their customers to check their local stores and e-mail the company when they couldn't find the company's software, they started receiving thirty e-mails a day from fanatical customers who wanted to be foot soldiers for the cause (by the way, this idea was hatched by a twenty-six-year old employee for the company who had a hard time convincing the more mature and experienced marketing leaders at Red Hat that customers could be such a pivotal part of the company's marketing strategy).

PERMISSION MARKETING: GETTING THE GREEN LIGHT FROM YOUR CUSTOMERS

Once you've developed a brand, how do you introduce that identity to new customers without spending a fortune? This is the number-one question on the mind of a rebel company's head of sales. Fortunately, Seth Godin has the answer. Not long ago, he unleashed the best-selling book *Permission Marketing* on the world. The premise is very simple. In this era of advertising clutter, marketers spend too much money interrupting strangers to capture attention for their product, whether it's in the form of television advertising, billboards, or even direct-marketing phone calls during your dinner hour. Consumers have grown tired of this "interruption marketing" and started tuning it out.

Permission marketers attempt to turn strangers into friends by making them an offer they can't refuse. For example, idealab!'s Bill Gross helped create the company Free-PC, which gives away personal computers to users who will divulge personal data and agree to watch targeted advertising. By talking to volunteers, permission marketing guarantees that consumers will pay more attention to their marketing message. It's a long-term, interactive relationship that grows from strangers into friends into customers into loyal advocates.

Permission marketing is not about spamming (junk e-mail). You don't succeed by purchasing mailing lists and blanketing the market with offers. Seth cites an example of how his company, Yoyodyne, created a successful campaign for H&R Block. H&R Block wanted to promote its new Premium Tax Service, which was targeted to an upper-income market that didn't typically think of the company for their tax preparation needs. Yoyodyne created banner advertising on the Net saying, "Play the H&R Block 'We'll Pay Your Taxes' Game." More than 50,000 people enrolled to play the enjoyable ten-week game that simultaneously taught them about the Premium Tax Service and built a relationship with the company. This is a classic form of permission marketing, as the company offered the prospect an incentive to volunteer, and then offered the potential customers a curriculum over time to understand the product. Seth was even able to make learning about taxes fun.

Most companies use a basic form of permission marketing on their Web site. You may ask visitors to your Web site if they'd like additional information about your company or product. When they register their name and e-mail with you, you've gained permission to build a relationship. Unfortunately, most companies only take it one step further. They send a brochure and that's it.

At Joie de Vivre, we've used permission marketing to introduce people to various products in our collection. For example, two of our businesses are the award-winning vegan restaurant Millennium and Kabuki Springs & Spa, the largest Japanese communal bathing facility in the country and Northern California's largest day spa. Millennium and Kabuki attract complementary clienteles—health-minded affluent professionals—yet we'd never tried cross-marketing between the businesses. Millennium had an active e-mail list that was enormously effective in promoting special dinners, so we made an offer to the people on the Millennium list to learn more about Kabuki. A large percentage of the list responded and over time we offered incentives (like a "gourmet bathing" experience or a discount on a new exotic spa treatment) for the Millennium diners to try Kabuki and learn more about its services.

VIRAL MARKETING: TURNING YOUR CUSTOMERS INTO FOOT SOLDIERS

Permission marketing is about getting a friendly foot in the door. Viral marketing takes that a step further. It's about spreading your friendly germs. Successful brands use viral marketing as a means of extending their reach into tightly affiliated networks.

Friends tell friends. And, in the era of the Internet, friends tell strangers. A rumor can now travel the world in a couple of hours flat. But that kind of buzz is best facilitated by people who are already conversing.

When Hotmail's free e-mail product was first launched, the founders had a tiny promotions budget. Instead, they relied on networks of groups who conversed frequently, like university students and professors, to spread the gospel. Within three weeks of the first user sign-ups in India, more than 100,000 additional users came on board. Within the first six months, the subscriber base was over 1 million. Within eighteen months (when the founders cashed out, selling to Microsoft, for $400 million), the subscriber base had grown to 12 million. How in the heck did this happen?

Tim Draper is the founding partner of Draper Fisher Jurvetson, one of Silicon Valley's most successful venture-capital firms. As the lead investor in Hotmail, Tim told me how this experience opened his eyes, "Initially, we were offering free e-mail, but no one knew Hotmail existed. The founding team wanted to put billboards on the highway, but I suggested we write: 'P.S. I love you. Get your free e-mail at Hotmail' at the bottom of every letter sent with Hotmail. They said it would be spamming, but I convinced them it was akin to banner advertising. They finally agreed, but said no to the 'P.S. I love you.'" By putting a hot link next to the message, the message recipient could go immediately to Hotmail's site and sign up for the service. The rest is history, as this example has become the marketing model for new Internet companies.

Tim and his DFJ partners developed a term—"viral marketing"—to describe this new form of chain letter. Like a chain letter or epidemic, the growth is exponential over time. Hotmail's offer was simple. In exchange for free service, current customers sell future customers and, because this all revolves around e-mail, you're spreading the news to the people with whom you most often communicate. The impact is explosive, and DFJ now uses it as virtually a prerequisite part of any new company they plan to fund.

Mary Kay, Herbalife, and Tupperware have used network marketing for decades. Remember MCI's "Friends and Family" marketing program, in which the company gave its customers an incentive to build their own networks of loyal users? MCI offered 20 percent off the phone bill of customers who converted "friends and family" to MCI (you had to convert at least twenty people to qualify). Since MCI is a communications company, it wasn't hard to build some nostalgia around calling friends and family—sort of a counterpunch to AT&T's "Reach Out and Touch Someone."

This successful campaign raised revenue by more than $1.2 billion in its first year and created a "warm and fuzzy" market positioning for MCI. And the beauty of the program was that the incremental costs were a fraction of that revenue increase (the primary costs being the technology necessary to track such a large database of connected customers, although it did require $100 million in advertising to launch the program!).

While network marketing has some historical roots, viral marketing (which costs virtually nothing) is a product of our Internet-crazed time. But, like the telephone or fax machine, it only works better as you have more people in the network (the purchaser of the first fax machine may have been a fool: it cost a fortune, and who were they going to fax?). Companies like America Online become more valuable as they grow their network base. Each new customer brings down their cost to acquire another and makes the service that much more valuable to the users. Costs drop. Values rise.

Are there any risks? Of course. The more your viral campaign looks like advertising, the less effective it will be. The more it looks like a word-of-mouth campaign, the more effective it will be. Giving someone a reward for directing their friends toward your product (as MCI did) can be perceived as mercenary if not handled properly. Also, many companies use deceptive methods to spread network marketing. For example, Hennessey cognac, through their advertising agency, hired some hip, attractive twenty-somethings to hang out in bars and conspicuously order their brand of liquor to build some buzz. This can flop if the world catches on to your little game. Fake word-of-mouth will only lead to bad word-of-mouth.

BUZZ: THE COLLISION OF CULTURE AND COMMERCE

Permission and viral marketing generate buzz, that ultimate form of rebel marketing: contagious, agile, potent, irrepressible, sexy, *and* cheap. Being "in the know" is just plain cool (according to the Yankelovich Report, the number of people who reported this as an important status symbol doubled between 1985 and 1995).

People don't trust advertising anymore. Starbucks's Howard Schultz cites the fact that today only 6 percent of us believe paid advertising, while forty years ago 80 percent trusted the message. But, we do trust the word on the street.

Before we plunge into the world of buzz, let's get our terms straight. Buzz is usually a good thing—authentic and long-lasting. Hype is a bad thing—manufactured and contaminating. A good product can produce buzz without any marketing master plan, but either a good or average product will receive much more attention with a well-conceived buzz-creation plan. Here are the four basic rules that help buzz proliferate:

1. THE SCARCER THE PRODUCT, THE MORE DESIRABLE

That which we believe is disappearing can be most alluring. Try calling any buzz-minded restaurant for a table for two at 8 P.M. and you'll likely get the cold shoulder (even if you're calling six months in advance). The reservations staff is trained to feign an aura of exclusivity. They know we want what we can't have. Ty Inc., the Chicago toy company, is an expert at this rule. The creator of Beanie Babies rode the wave of these popular little dolls during the 1990s. But by 1999, demand was slacking, so Ty Warner (the company's founder) announced that they would be retiring all existing Beanie Babies by year-end. This man knows how to create demand, as doll sales more than doubled overnight after the announcement, and more than 2,000 new Beanie Babies were up for auction on eBay within a couple of days of the announcement. Then, just a week before the end of the year, Ty announced that he would sponsor an Internet consumer election to determine whether the company would phase out the Beanie Babies collection. Of course, the consumers chose to keep the dolls. While this may certainly cross the border of buzz creation to buzz manipulation, the fact is that it's a great example of the value of scarcity.

2. STROKE MY EGO AND I'LL FOLLOW YOU ANYWHERE

Admit it. You like being fawned over. The Mandarin Oriental Hotel in Bangkok knows this. They have gold-embossed hotel stationery waiting in your guest room when you arrive. That gave me a *wow* when I arrived, and dozens of people back home saw the fancy notecards and stationery when I returned. On slow nights in fine restaurants, a waiter will bring you a complimentary appetizer, commenting, "The chef is trying out a few new items for the menu and he wanted your opinion on this dish." Well, who knew? You didn't think you had much of a palate, but the chef wants your opinion so you'll dig in. And, twenty of your friends will likely hear about the restaurant.

3. YOU GOTTA HAVE A STORY

The companies that are able to attach a story or a face to their product will buy more memory time from their customers, which means more word-of-mouth. Ben & Jerry's, The Body Shop, Apple Computers—you know the stories on these products. Herb Kelleher, Oprah Winfrey, Ted Turner—they're great storytellers. Media buzz follows underdog products and iconoclastic rebels. Richard Branson says if you can make your business a crusade, you'll turn your customers into foot soldiers. If you don't have a story, create one. Joe Costello did this when he took over Cad Labs, a small Italian company that was trying to grow in the three-dimensional software market. Joe knew the company needed to define its marketplace more broadly and he wanted to create a community of interested advocates. He created a contest to rename this nineteen-year-old company ("Cad Labs" was too technical). He offered $50,000 (less than he'd likely pay a naming consultant) to the winner. This story got picked up by worldwide media and was one of the hot topics on the Internet. More than 45,000 entries came in from around the world, yet, ironically, the winner ended up coming from a small Italian village just fifty miles from Cad Labs' headquarters. The new name, think3, helped the company be more than just a product—it became a story.

4. KEEP IT STEALTHY

When Linus Torvalds, the Gen X phenom who helped create the hot Linux operating system, joined a new company (Transmeta), it was big news in the digital world. What made it even bigger was the fact that Transmeta was unwilling to announce any product or business plan. In fact, there was an organized "don't talk to the media" policy. And, of course, that stealth campaign helped boil the buzz just a little hotter. Before Bigstep.com, an Internet company that builds and hosts e-commerce sites, unveiled itself to the press in mid-1999, the company's buzzmeisters chose to call the venture "the Springfield project." Prelaunch, the founders purposefully kept the business plan under wraps (with the occasional leak of some intriguing details), so much so that *Red Herring* magazine called it one of the ten private companies to watch in 1999. Ever notice the buzz created just before the Republican or Democratic presidential nominee announces his running mate or just before the Oscar nominees are unveiled? Within forty-eight hours after these announcements, the world has moved on to the next guessing game. Buzz is a little like high-school flirting. The moment you get "on base" it isn't quite as intriguing as it was in your dreams.

THE POWER OF THE MEDIA—BOTH OLD AND NEW

Media create buzz. Media propel buzz. Media feed off buzz. Rebel companies may use viral and permission marketing to promote their message, but the brands that gain widespread consciousness the fastest are incredibly media-savvy. Rebels talk in sound bites, think in photo ops, all while staying true to the product.

Richard Branson has a complete lack of respect for authority figures and decorum, and maybe that's why he scares his competition. Shortly after he launched Virgin Atlantic Airways, he issued an invitation to the British press to meet him at Heathrow Airport, just outside London. He added a hint that it would be wise to bring their photographers. At the appointed time and with a huge press full of anticipation (because they'd seen his antics before), Richard showed up dressed as a pirate and, with remarkably artistic choreography, hoisted himself up next to a full-size model of the Concorde and placed a Virgin logo on top of the British Airways logo that was emblazoned on the plane. Of course, Richard then announced some new initiatives for the airline, but the next day, all the public really noticed was the huge photo of Richard with the Virgin logo.

I guess I'm guilty of being a media rebel too. A few years ago, I won the American Association of Travel Marketing Executives' annual Guerrilla Marketer of the Year award. I was supposed to give a rousing speech at the awards ceremony, but that week I was ready to crawl under a rock because of a souring business venture that was forcing me to beg for money. But, you never would have guessed it at the ceremony. I gave an impassioned speech about creatively partnering with other brands for joint marketing to attract media attention. I cited our widely covered Phoenix Pajama

* * *

BUSINESS REBEL HALL OF FAME PROFILE

Ian Schrager (Founder and CEO of Ian Schrager Hotels)

Nightclubs are the perfect training ground for the buzzmeister since there's a certain illusionary magic that comes with a successful club. No nightclub has ever gained the notoriety of Studio 54. Ian Schrager, now famous for his hotels, was one of the two founders of that landmark hot spot. Ian's first hotel purchase was the Duane Hotel in 1982, a run-down property near Madison Square Garden. He turned it into Morgan's, a 154-room "boutique" hotel (Ian invented the phrase) that catered to the same crowd that used to frequent Studio 54. It was an instant hit, and began a hotel design revolution. Before Ian, hotel industry design was five years behind retail, which was five years behind the fashion industry. Hotels were more focused on functionality and not offending anyone. Hence, hotel design was generic.

Ian changed all that when he realized that hotel design could be the ultimate marketing statement for a property. He admits he's more in the entertainment business than the hotel business. And his focus on design carries through to the staff he hires (he uses a casting agent to pick the model-quality service staff), the uniforms they wear, and the complete ambience that is created. Walking into an Ian Schrager hotel is like being on a movie set. It's a true escape. You feel transported to a strange universe. The experience may be fabricated, but it is engaging. The ultimate payoff for Ian is that you're apt to go back home from his Delano or Mondrian or Royalton Hotel and tell friends about the waterfall hologram in the restaurant or the cryptic technicolor hole in the hallway wall. And now he's taken his buzz-creating machine to London and soon beyond. The Ian Schrager name has become the ultimate brand for the hip world traveler.

Party Package which offered guests free colorful Joe Boxer underwear on their pillow for turndown service as well as a monthly cool poolside slumber party.

And then at the end of the speech, in spite of my Prozac-thirsting depression, I "dropped trow" to reveal yellow happy-face Joe Boxer underwear. With my pants around my ankles and shielding myself from the many camera flashes, I couldn't leave the stage for five minutes because of the standing ovation. Of course, the audience couldn't have been more perfect because these are the people who generate travel press around the world, and all of a sudden, this little San Francisco company with the strange name became part of their language. I still regularly run into marketing executives whom I've never met, who pull out their photos of this classic guerrilla marketing stunt. I've had a few travel writers tell me that the first time they ever heard of me was when someone was describing that evening.

While these examples sound silly, it's really all about understanding that the media want something new that they've never written about or photographed before. One of the smartest moves we ever made was transforming our marketing and PR department into a creative services department. By doing this, we elevated our PR staff from just being responsible for getting press to creatively helping to develop the concepts for new hospitality products. Our creative services department is involved from the beginning of a new idea so that they can mold the business concept into a product that has great potential in the media. And since Creative Services provides art direction, interior design, graphics, and Web design, they can take a spectacular idea and turn it into a real product while constantly thinking how they're going to pitch this new business to the press. This approach dusts off an old management axiom: the people who implement any initiative should be involved as early as possible in the creation of the initiative.

Here are a few rules that will help you or your product become the darling of the media:

KEEP A CLOSE EYE ON WHAT'S HAPPENING IN THE NEWS

The media surf trend waves, so you need to know what's hot and what's not. A couple of young guys, Doug Chu and Scott Samet, own Taste of

Nature, a company that distributes healthy snacks to theaters. They were slowly growing their business in 1995 when, all of a sudden, a study came out suggesting theater popcorn was unhealthy. Doug and Scott dropped everything and started dialing for dollars to the media, making sure that their little company could be the tag line for this growing story. The net result was significant national press, and before they knew it, they were selling in theater chains across the country.

UNDERSTAND THE SEASONALITY OF MEDIA

John Kilcullen, CEO of IDG Books Worldwide, and the creator of the *For Dummies* series (with more than 60 million copies sold), knew that the media was always looking for unique tax stories around April 15. John chose to launch IDG's first book outside computer technology, *Personal Finance for Dummies,* just prior to the April 15 tax deadline. In front of post offices in major media markets, John's enthusiastic staff, dressed up in dummies costumes, handed out a free booklet containing useful tax tips. They were accompanied by representatives from Pepto-Bismol and Tylenol, who were also giving out pain-relief samples—appropriate products for tax time. The net result was national publicity, including a spot on CNBC, that not only helped launch the book but also helped extend the *For Dummies* brand into all categories—from gardening to stock-picking. This is another example of how an unconventional idea can catapult your product, brand, or company into the national spotlight and minds of your customers.

PLAY UP YOUR REBEL OR UNDERDOG ROLE

The media hate Goliath and love David. Richard Branson knows this. While he's now a multinational megamillionaire, he still tries to pick on people bigger than him: British Airways, the British government, Coke and Pepsi. Attacking competitors in dominant positions is a classic rebel role, and you'll virtually always have the media on your side. One hint: look for an industry that has a strong number one, but no recognized number-two company.

Virgin also creates a moral authority when they take on the big guys as if they're the voice of the people. I had an opportunity like this land in my lap a few years ago. At The Phoenix, we'd hired a New York artist, Francis Forlenza, to paint a pop-inspired mural at the bottom of the hotel swimming pool to match the artistic flavor of the hotel. Halfway through the painting process, a stern bureaucrat from the city's health department showed up with a citation and an order to stop work immediately. She informed us that state law mandated that all public pools be painted white (I won't take you through the state's reasoning, but it was illogical for a pool this size). In essence, the bureaucracy was saying if it's art, it can't be a pool, and if it's a pool, it can't be art. With the help of a number of local politicians and arts groups, we rallied against the big, bad government and trumpeted our "free the artist" case to the media (gaining worldwide press) with State Assembly Speaker Willie Brown (now the mayor) introducing a bill in the state legislature making this mural a historic landmark. A victory for the people! And an enormous media windfall for The Phoenix.

CREATE A MEDIA EVENT

The media faces challenges just like you do. They have to fill pages in print publications and time on the airwaves. We hit a home run when we cre-

HOW TO WRITE A KILLER PRESS RELEASE

A good idea won't have journalists rushing to your door. You need to plant a seed in the media, and the old-fashioned press release is just as valuable today as it was twenty years ago.

As I was writing this chapter, I stopped into our creative services office to check in with Rob Delamater, Joie de Vivre's incomparable "media master." He was putting the finishing touches on a press release titled, "San Francisco's Funky Phoenix Hotel Offers Rock 'n' Roll Hairstylist on Call: 'It's like room service for your hair!'" The brief, one-page release captures all of the key elements of a successful release:

1. Use an outrageous title. Most PR writers create their press releases in a style that's sort of like the old-fashioned wire service—dry and fact-filled. Instead, you want to whet the editor's appetite with an improbable title that juxtaposes ideas that haven't been fused together before, like "hair" and "room service."

2. Provide just the right information. A killer press release is well edited. There's no extraneous information, yet there's enough so that a publication could write the story just by reading the release. On the other hand, you don't want to barrage them with too many facts because you want them to call you so that you can romance them further with juicy details.

3. Embed a witty sound bite in the release. Create a quote from the person the media is most interested in hearing from—quite often, this will find its way into the newspaper or magazine when the writer doesn't have time to do an interview.

4. Think in pictures. Make it sexy. Make it visual. If you can include a compelling photo, your chances of getting ink are much better.

5. Understand that timing is everything. Work in the reporter's time frame, not your own. Return phone calls immediately, and give the reporter timely access to the actual decision-makers and key players. You want to be so good at providing information that the writers begin to count on you for future stories.

Finally, a note of caution. The PR business can turn slimy when hyperbole becomes a way of life. Don't oversell. And don't deal with media contacts you can't respect. Ask yourself, "Would I feel comfortable if a fact-checker reviewed every word of this release?" The best people in PR know that integrity goes a long way in this business.

ated the Full Moon Aphrodisiac Night at our Millennium restaurant. When we launched the vegan restaurant in 1994, we wanted to spread the gospel about healthy eating. Stricter than vegetarian, vegan cuisine includes no butter or dairy products and very little oil. For most of the world that sounds like no fun. We thought of our restaurant as stylish and upscale, serving hearty and sexy cuisine, but how could we create an event that spread the word to a diverse audience that Millennium was a fun place? Since many well-known aphrodisiacs are non-animal-based, our remarkable chef, Eric Tucker, developed a special menu each month that included an herbal love potion for two and a three-course feast of love-inducing delicacies. To top it off, we gave the diners on this monthly evening a complimentary room in The Abigail Hotel upstairs. Since these special dinners tended to occur on non–full nights for the hotel, the extra cost to the restaurant was minimal (just the housekeeping cost of cleaning the room) but the media benefit was huge. This sexy bargain gained national media attention by giving a new spin on the health craze, and we launched the idea in January to take advantage of people's New Year's resolutions.

COIN A PHRASE, PREDICT THE FUTURE

Nancy Austin says, "Naming anything assigns it an identity and supplies an easy conversational handle." And, there are all sorts of products with brand names that define their category. FedEx, Kleenex, Xerox . . . In the world of buzz, perception often precedes reality. That's where spin comes in. If people believe your company is hot, it *will* be hot. Describe your ventures as successful and the media might anoint you with a self-fulfilling prophecy. Here's a little tale that shows you how.

Early in The Phoenix Hotel's life, we worked with the well-known local restaurateur Julie Ring and her partner Jeff Gradinger to create a funky Caribbean restaurant and nightclub called Miss Pearl's Jam House. Julie and Jeff created an instant hit that also helped solidify the positioning of the hotel. Unfortunately, a couple of years later, as is often the case with trendy restaurants, the glamour and theme started fading, so the hotel acquired a majority interest in Miss Pearl's and took over management. The product was still good, but the buzz was gone. My friend and PR consultant Susie Biehler mentioned that a local food editor, Michael Bauer, likes to receive columns written by local restaurateurs about the business. The lightbulb turned on. I would write an article about the renaissance of Miss Pearl's and how we'd accomplished it. The only problem was, we hadn't done it yet. I was realistic enough to know I couldn't write just a "puff piece" extolling the virtues of my place. The column had to offer some tangible rules that any entrepreneur could use. Three months after we'd taken over management, I wrote this article in anticipation of our upcoming busy summer season. At that point, it was purely prognostication, though there were some positive signs of business growth. Ironically, Michael Bauer chose to run the article in midsummer, at which point Miss Pearl's revenues had grown by more than 40 percent. When the article did come out, three months after I wrote it, the restaurant was hot again, and the article was perfectly timed to reinforce the new buzz that was building. Sometimes you have to look for the seeds of success, tell the world it's happening, and hope your fearless forecast is correct.

THE MEDIA RECYCLES ITSELF

There are a few publications that want an exclusive story. But, most reporters are rather shameless in using stories that they've seen in other media. They just fashion another spin. When your company or product is featured in the media, make a bunch of copies and send them out, along with a press release, to other media. I once created a "family tree" that visually depicted how one story (the *People* magazine feature on The Phoenix Hotel) led to more than forty additional articles over the next two years. Don't be embarrassed by the attention—it's your most effective and least expensive means of promotion.

GET BUSY BUZZING

Are you buzzed yet? People often ask me, "How do you get in that kind of creative space to come up with these ideas?" The answer is, you need three things.

First, you need to know what activities get your creative juices flowing. For me, the best ideas come while I'm running or taking a shower.

Second, you have to allow some "mental composting" to occur. Creative epiphanies are typically preceded by days or weeks of letting my subconscious take a whack at it.

Third, you need to allow yourself to stub your toe. The most brilliant minds will come up with some of the dumbest ideas. That's okay. It's a numbers game. You can't expect to hit a home run every time you're up to bat. Let it flow. Right behind that stupid idea might be an inspired one.

VI. THE RISKS OF BEING A REBEL

14. The Most Common Challenges Facing Rebel Companies

The difference between a warrior and an ordinary man is that a warrior sees everything as a challenge, while an ordinary man sees everything as a blessing or a curse.

—Carlos Castaneda

The only way most successful rebels recognize their limits is by trespassing beyond them. It's easy to be seduced by success. You look like a genius zigging when everyone else is zagging. Yet your growth can take you in a direction that's exactly the opposite of what made your success possible. The result can be a scary series of speed bumps at 100 miles per hour. One of my business advisers, Dick Bernstein, says that every entrepreneur comes to that day of reckoning when he asks, "Am I controlling my growth, or is it controlling me?"

My entrepreneur-turned-politico friend Gavin Newsom suggests that the two forces driving the rebel are opposites—inspiration and desperation. We're inspired by an idea and desperate to make it work. I've found that with growth come other dualities: "How do I balance efficiency and humanity in our operations?"; "How can I nurture our creative spirit while developing systems that help us mature?"; and "How can I ensure that new and old employees have the same vision?"

Many young companies grow quickly at first based upon the founders' creativity and ingenuity, yet find themselves adrift as they reach the next stage of their growth. Too often, the founder is pressured to give in to the business clichés of the moment: "Grow your company or die"; "Go global"; "Outsource everything." Facing pressures like never before and possibly feeling completely out-of-her-depth, she may allow a newcomer CEO or board member to define a growth path that's at odds with her company's roots.

There are no easy answers. But the first step is to inventory your success story.

A TOOL FOR UNDERSTANDING YOUR "COMPANY DNA"

A couple of years ago, while Joie de Vivre was doubling in size for the third year in a row, I spent an afternoon on the beach and listed the ten elements that had led to our prosperity. I call this list our "Company DNA," and it has helped me maintain my focus as the inevitable capitalist mercenaries (investment bankers, consultants, and "musical chairs" execs) come knocking on my door. Each time one of these people makes an enticing offer or proposes a new strategy for growth, I refer back to our DNA as a checklist to see whether that strategy acknowledges our unique competencies.

Let me share Joie de Vivre's DNA list with you in the hopes that by creating your own you won't get knocked off track by the allure of growth:

- Creating innovative new projects that are handcrafted, not easily replicable, enabling me to pursue a broad range of hospitality deals defined by the idea of creating escapes, not just developing hotels
- Giving management and staff the freedom to break the rules
- Maintaining a roughly equal mix of old and new employees
- Keeping everyone hands-on, either supporting the employees or the customer; no paper-pushers
- Keeping all creative services in-house (PR, marketing, graphics, design) rather than outsourcing.
- Ensuring I meet all new hires within the first month of their employment
- Maintaining geographic proximity, so that senior management can be intimately involved with the properties

- Taking advantage of economies of scale to boost revenue and decrease expenses
- Focusing on "bang-for-the-buck" capital improvements and affordable promotions.
- Using my offbeat persona via speaking opportunities and the media to attract employees and capital

This list saved us from joining forces with inappropriate capital partners. It also assured that we didn't go national too quickly, instead focusing on saturating our regional market. It meant we tried promoting from within as much as possible and remained wary of Johnny-come-lately execs with perfect résumés. And this list allowed us to continue fostering our unique corporate culture and mission statement.

At times, we must have looked like idiots because we passed up some pretty sexy opportunities. But, I was constantly reminded of the business advice of Stewart Brand (founder of the *Whole Earth Catalog*): "Start cheap, small, and local—it will ensure that your initial mistakes are small." As a result, we have experienced growth that has been organic, sustainable, and, most of the time, enjoyable.

What's the consequence of making the wrong decision about growth? Your little rebel company can unravel faster than you can say "Rip Van Rockefeller." Companies that forget their genetic makeup enter a downward spiral: reduced job satisfaction leads to lower customer satisfaction, resulting in declining company profits, leading to lower morale due to training and benefit cutbacks, and so on. You get the idea.

THE TEN PERILS OF REBEL COMPANIES

Rebel companies are built on momentum. Your ability to attract capital, customers, employees, and attention is a function of keeping that sweet smell of success wafting from your business. Here are the ten most common perils you face as you chart your path of growth:

1. YOU OUTGROW YOUR PEOPLE

The skill set of your start-up employees may not fit your company's needs once it has entered corporate adolescence. The founder is often the last to notice that his loyal first staffers aren't keeping up with the growing demands of the company. It's usually the newer employees who recognize this problem first.

What are some of the ways you can minimize this potential peril?

- Provide an aggressive program of learning to keep your staff's skills in step with company growth.
- Engage in frequent informal employee counseling and formal review sessions to communicate the specific necessary improvements.
- Provide a "soft landing" in the form of other career paths within the company for employees who are on a job track that is too fast for them.
- Create mentor programs that help some of the original employees update their skills.
- Do whatever it takes to minimize the threat that your early employees may feel when they see the wave of new faces joining the company.
- If you're a fast-growing company full of young people, bring on an advisory board as quickly as possible because these wise old sages will help mentor your twenty-four-year-old CEO. (And Will Rosenzweig suggests that in these unreal Internet times, young entrepreneurs and managers need a ritual or reminder that connects them to nature because their company's pace of growth can be "unnatural," feeding illusions and egos. Will believes young rebels who forget the cycles of nature will unlikely be able to build anything that's sustainable. How about a company gardening expedition?)

When those solutions fail, you have to consider terminating those employees (including the founder) who can't keep up, distasteful as this may be. Joie de Vivre experienced this painful dilemma firsthand. It was one of the rites of passage from growing a start-up into a mid-sized company.

When our chief operating officer (now president) Jack Kenny joined the company during Joie de Vivre's eleventh year, I found myself making excuses for many of our longtime employees: "She's really very competent, you just have to approach her the right way," or, "Sure he opposes most change, but our customers love him." Jack was more than happy to work with the idiosyncrasies of these loyal employees because, in fact, most of them had been successful over the years.

One day, a friend told me about a painful firing he had to perform, and I realized that Joie de Vivre rarely terminated any key supervisors. In the early days, everyone rose to the level of superstar in their own personal way because our little company couldn't survive without that effort. But as we grew, we began to accept mediocrity because of our family-oriented, collegial work climate. Our managerial standards of performance started to drift downward and the motivation of our superstars declined as they saw that the company accepted underperformers as readily as high-flyers. While Jack never voiced it, I sensed that we were on the verge of malaise just as we were preparing for another spurt of rapid growth.

At the start of the new quarter, I arrived at our weekly meeting with Jack and my partner, Larry Broughton, with a sober but necessary plan. I told them that my cursory review of our hiring and firing practices showed that we'd only terminated one manager in the past year. More often, an unsuccessful manager either left the company on her own or was transferred to another position within the company, sometimes full of resentment and jealousy. In reviewing our top forty managers, I believed there were approximately ten who were "on the bubble"—underperformers or weak links. At many other companies, these managers might have already been terminated for disappointing performance.

I shocked them when I said: "We need to build some new habits. We should set a goal of terminating at least three of these ten managers within the next three months. As difficult as that sounds, setting that goal is the only way we're going to take rapid action to raise the bar of performance for our managers."

We took a four-step approach. First, we made sure that each of those "bubble" managers was confidentially aware of their situation. Second, we provided immediate coaching and training to try to improve their skills. Third, we gave them plentiful, ongoing feedback about their performance. Finally, we made the tough decisions toward the end of the quarter. Of those ten managers, five were terminated, two left on their own, and the remaining three made miraculous recoveries.

Was this difficult? Yes, especially for a warm-and-fuzzy company like Joie de Vivre. Fortunately, we haven't had to repeat it. Was setting a goal of three firings arbitrary or frivolous? The number may have been arbitrary, but the process wasn't frivolous. If one of these managers was on a path of sustained growth, there was no reason for us to let them go. Setting a number forced us to take action in a tangible manner, much the way General Electric's Jack Welch does.

Did it have a negative impact on morale? Initially, yes, as a little fear crept into everyone. During that quarter, it was essential that we gave ample positive feedback to the other managers since, frankly, no one knew there was such a list or whether they were on it. All they knew was that change was afoot. Morale went up quite a bit when we addressed the issue at our midyear manager's retreat at the end of the quarter. The response we got was overwhelmingly positive—the remaining managers felt appreciated and were impressed by the highly qualified and motivated new managers who were joining the company. They also respected our decisive action.

This process doesn't exclude the rebel founder of a fast-growing company. Quite often the company will survive but the founder won't. Recognize that a company's growth demands a constantly changing set of management skills. Do everything you can to make sure you and your employees' skills grow as rapidly as the company.

2. YOU FALL INTO THE EMPOWERMENT TRAP

Rebel companies believe in their people. And, when the company is growing rapidly, the allure of employee empowerment is both practical and inspiring. Professor Haim Mendelson says, "Empowerment has reached the status of motherhood and apple pie." It's often the easy answer for a fast-growing company. Unfortunately, many rebels don't realize that empowerment requires building the "common sense reservoir" within the organization. It doesn't just mean letting your staff do their own thing.

Can you imagine letting your five-year-old ride a bike on a street without supervision or training wheels? That's dangerous. What are the training wheels in your organization that allow empowerment to flourish?

Here are some cautionary rules about empowerment:

Don't assume everyone wants to be empowered. Many employees seek out their place at a lower rung on the entrepreneurial ladder because they want to be sheltered from high-stress decision-making.

Be careful about company secrets. Empowered employees may have access to information that could prove detrimental if in the wrong hands. Also, be cautious in an open-book environment with negative cash-flow information, which can lead to disastrous rumors inside and outside your company.

Recognize that an empowered employee is more likely to make mistakes (since they're not always doing it "by the books"), and this can lead to a demoralized employee if someone has a string of failed judgments because they're "in over their head."

Anarchy and paralysis can be the by-products of empowerment when the decision-making becomes too democratic.

When Robert Knowling, Jr., joined Covad Communications as its CEO, he thought this high-tech upstart was going to shame the bureaucracy he had endured at Ameritech and U S West. What he found was a small company built on consensus decision-making, but the organization rarely made a decision. He immediately implemented a hierarchy that helped to enhance the organization by ensuring accountability and fostering communication.

You *can* have a traditional organizational chart *and* an empowered organization. Implicit in this relationship is trust. Your employees must believe you trust them and won't scold them for making the wrong decision. In turn, they will trust you. Middle managers must see the direct benefit they receive from an empowered workplace; otherwise they'll continue to hoard power.

Finally, senior management needs to create systems that fill the "common sense reservoir." Formal training and informal mentoring can do this. I read a novel approach in Eileen Shapiro's book, *Fad Surfing in the Boardroom,* about Jan Carlzon, formerly CEO of Scandinavian Airlines System. He realized that his employees believed that SAS's highest priority was "delighting the customer," so they did everything in their power to accomplish this, even if it meant holding planes to wait for connecting passengers. Yet Carlzon was surprised to find that SAS's customer satisfaction scores weren't growing. It turns out business passengers were frustrated with late plane arrivals. Carlzon realized he needed to teach some common sense, so he authored the following: "Our first priority is safety, second is punctuality, and third is other services. So, if you risk flight safety by leaving on time, you have acted outside the framework of your authority. The same is true if you don't leave on time (second priority) because you are missing two catering boxes of meat (third priority). That's what I mean by framework, you give people a framework, and within the framework you let people act."

3. YOU SUCCEED TOO QUICKLY

The dream of every entrepreneur is to be an overnight success, yet this is the most common reason why successful entrepreneurs fail. Given the incredible accessibility of capital in the dawning of this Internet age, many ventures that would have been bootstrapped are not. That's too bad, as many old-time start-up junkies will remind you that "necessity is the mother of invention." Because investors are now religious about the "first-mover advantage" (the opportunity for the first company into a market to quickly secure market share), entrepreneurs are shoved out onto the stage like a six-year-old in a tutu. What can be most disastrous is when that young performer gets a standing ovation the first time around. Suddenly, this entrepreneur and the world sense a "Midas touch." Yet, as is true with independent filmmakers and authors, it's hard to follow up on beginner's luck. With the entrepreneur though, the stakes can be in the tens of millions of dollars if the second venture isn't successful. What everyone may have conveniently forgotten is that mistakes create instinct and wisdom. There are dozens of tales of Silicon Valley Internet entrepreneurs who went public or sold their company for quick riches even though the venture had never shown a profit. And then suddenly, millions are thrust in front of their face by investors who want more of the same, yet this entrepreneur has never created a company with sustainable cash flow. Beware of economic periods when profitability isn't the primary measure of success. The skills of the opportunity-driven entrepreneur who can imagine a new product aren't necessarily compatible with the leader who can run a profitable company.

4. YOU AND YOUR BUSINESS ARE PERCEIVED AS ONE

Be careful about letting your organization rely on a single personality. In your company's infancy, the founder must act as the corporate figurehead. Often this is necessary simply to build the required trust with your customers. As your company grows though, it's only natural that other important executives play a pivotal role in your company's operation and strategy. Growth ought to provide opportunities for managers, even if this leads to a dilution of your authority. Although this may seem obvious, many companies have been ruined by a founder who couldn't or wouldn't let go.

Beware of the company built on the cult of personality. We lost a potential hotel management contract a couple of years ago because the owner feared that Joie de Vivre relied too heavily upon me.

If the rebel is larger than life and perceived as running the whole show, all kinds of questions can arise: "What happens if she gets hit by a bus?" (Martha Stewart); "What happens if he decides to go do something else?" (Steve Jobs); "What happens if people don't like her?" (Leona Helmsley).

★ ★ ★

BUSINESS REBEL HALL OF FAME PROFILE

Martha Stewart
(Founder of Martha Stewart Living Omnimedia)

Few rebels possess a brand personality comparable to Martha's. She's successfully transitioned Martha Stewart, the person, into Martha Stewart, the brand. Her brand stands for stylish and traditional American living. She is brilliant at channeling the taste and passion of her customers into new products and media. Her products generate more than $1 billion in revenue annually, and her Web page sees nearly 1 million visitors weekly.

Despite her success, many of us have a confusing, love-hate relationship with Martha Stewart. A hard-charging business rebel, or the model of femininity in the kitchen? An aristocrat? A Kmart shopper? The gracious hostess, or the autocratic taskmaster? Martha Stewart is a rebel because she's been able to fashion a chameleonlike quality to her identity and brand positioning. What gives her some authenticity is the fact that her homespun talents come from her girl-next-door upbringing when cooking and gardening were just a sampling of the basic talents needed in a middle-class family of eight.

I chose Martha as a Hall-of-Famer in this category because she faces some serious rebel challenges. No large American company is more reliant on its founder's image. The public can grow tired of any celebrity. What implication does that have for Stewart's company? While her brand extensions have held up remarkably well, some observers question, "Has the Martha Stewart brand become too unfocused?" If the stock market is the litmus test, the answer seems to be a resounding *no,* as her 1999 initial public offering was an unqualified success. Investors believe that the masterfully agile Ms. Stewart has produced a company identity that lives beyond her personality, standing as an icon for the home as a castle.

Equally important, if your fast-growing company is dominated by you, you diminish your pool of top executives.

5. YOU LOSE YOUR UNDERDOG STATUS

As we discussed in Chapter 13, "Creating Brand, Building Buzz," being the up-and-comer creates a support network that would never rally behind the big boys. Look at Starbucks. In the early nineties, when they were proliferating across America, most people still admired their plucky and quirky ambition. Now they're ubiquitous, and many urban neighborhoods are protesting their entry into the café wars, fearing they'll lose their indigenous, local coffeehouses.

Everybody loves an underdog—until they become arrogant. That's the phenomenon Apple Computer experienced. Back in its heady heyday in the eighties, Apple was easy to fall in love with as they revolutionized our experience with the computer while taking on giants like IBM and Microsoft. But over time, the company's nonlinear approach to management led to prolonged product cycles, terrible internal communications, and an indifferent attitude to their customer base. While Apple was certainly still an underdog, they didn't act like one.

Apple reconnected with its rebel roots and its sense of mission when

Steve Jobs rejoined the company. The ad campaign "Be Different" was designed to reestablish the rebel brand identity that used to define Apple. Closing down Claris and Newton and putting all their "apples" in the Macintosh cart, Steve created a sense of urgency that is emblematic of the underdog. With a small group of dedicated, talented employees, in almost total secrecy, Steve unveiled the new iMac on May 6, 1998, in the same auditorium where the original Mac was unveiled fourteen years earlier. Remarkably, most Apple employees had never even heard of the new computer. In just a few months after his arrival, Steve had helped transform Apple from a rudderless and arrogant also-ran into a sleek and hip underdog once again.

6. YOU PICK THE WRONG PARTNERS

This one probably deserves its own book. The gestation period of baby companies has shrunk, and new companies go public faster than ever. Young entrepreneurs may understand their technology, but there's no rule book for how you pick your financial partners. Consequently, this can be a painful, fateful decision. Marc Canter is one of the fathers of multimedia technology. In 1987, he started the first high-tech firm in what would become San Francisco's Multimedia Gulch (actually, he started it in 1984 and relocated it from Chicago). That company grew into Macromedia, the graphics-oriented software company, but unfortunately for Marc, he was no longer in an operating role when the company went public. Marc comes from the hippie-programmer/alternative-music scene, quite a distance from the buttoned-down venture-capital culture. His vision was "creating really cool products, but all the venture capitalists wanted to do was make money."

Between 1987 and 1991, Marc experienced heartaches and frustration as his venture capital partners rolled up a collection of other companies into Marc's company in order to make Macromedia (which was originally called Macromind) more appealing to the IPO market. In the end, the process was too painful, for his vision and operating strategy weren't in synch with that of his money partners. Someone had to go, and, in cases like these, it's rarely the money that leaves. Marc's lesson was this: venture capitalists have a thirty-six-month cycle when they invest their money. If, at eighteen months, they don't see the possibility of going public soon, they start to meddle and mess with the investment. If you're the founding

CEO, don't be surprised to find yourself out on your ear soon after that (although you may have a fistful of dollars in your pocket).

Will Rosenzweig gives a similar warning from his many start-up experiences. Beware of the angel investor with unfinished business who wants to encroach upon your business but won't commit to an active ongoing role. The best advice is to detail clearly the relationship before you get married.

But for every bad partnership experience, there's probably a good one. Smart money can make you smart if you're willing to learn. Both theglobe.com and Nantucket Nectars were started by an Ivy League entrepreneurial duo. Who knows whether they would have flourished so profoundly if Michael Egan, former Alamo Rent-A-Car chairman, hadn't made an enormous investment of time and money in both fledgling companies? Sabeer Bhatia, who founded Hotmail, might never have risen to such heights without the helpful direction of Tim Draper of Draper Fisher Jurvetson. DFJ, which has done more Internet venture fundings than any other independent venture capitalist, thinks of itself as a service business. DFJ's primary responsibility is to give their entrepreneurs the resources and advice to flourish, and to connect them to their other Internet winners so that a "best practices" community can grow among their businesses.

7. YOU EXPERIENCE THE PERILS OF GOING PUBLIC

Going public isn't all it's cracked up to be. Ask the founders of small companies that went public if they'd do it again; many would likely say no. One friend (who prefers to stay nameless), who made $10 million when his company went public, says, "Of course, there's such an affirmation and bucketloads of money during the first ninety days after the IPO, but I had no idea what it was going to be like shitting in public. Would you take ten million dollars if someone told you that every time you had to use the loo, you'd do it on a Broadway stage with a collection of critics in the audience critiquing your technique? I don't think so."

In the past, the companies that went public were more mature and had a track record. According to Mary Meeker, managing director of Morgan Stanley Dean Witter, "The old rule in the eighties was that a company needed three quarters of profitability and to show a rising trend" before trying a public stock offering. Today, it's more of a crapshoot; thus investors have added skepticism about these new companies' business decisions. In 1997, sixteen Internet companies went public, yet only three of them had created one profitable quarter by 1999. Under such circumstances, it's no surprise that founders are under the watchful eye of the analysts.

Seth Godin suggests that going public can be antithetical to creating a long-term sustainable business. The current IPO craze is based upon (a) raising money from the right people, (b) going public on the right day, and (c) not making a strategic error before your stock options vest. This model naturally diminishes the willingness to take risks, the foundation of any innovative company. Additionally, high stock prices mean high expectations.

Over the next few years, many management teams of new IPO companies will be thrown out the window because they won't be able to hit the unrealistically high growth projections that they sold to Wall Street analysts. The pressure will be on to fabricate earnings growth in short-term ways, typically through acquisitions. Unfortunately, many rebel companies lose their sense of rebellion once they complete their initial public offering.

HOW TO GET RICH QUICK

We live in a funny age. I met David Hayden, a small Berkeley building contractor, in 1994 when we were considering building a day spa next to our Nob Hill Lambourne Hotel. Two years later, I read about David in the newspaper. He and his then wife had founded a company that created the Magellan search engine, and they were selling out to Excite for $18 million. Then, in 1999, I ran into David in the emergency stairwell of a hotel grand opening party, only to find out he'd just raised $280 million going public with the new company he founded, Critical Path. Such is life in the San Francisco Bay Area on the eve of the millennium.

David had an audacious vision for Critical Path. He wanted to be the mailman for the world's e-mail. While you'd think his first hire might have been his chief technology officer and VP of engineering (these were his second hires), David was a little more market-savvy than that. He hired an outside firm, the Addis Group, to help create the brand identity for Critical Path, since the notion of identity on the Internet is so ephemeral. Once the brand identity and vision was set, he built a core engineering team that was second to none.

When Critical Path approached its IPO in March 1999, it didn't have an impressive record of making money. Total revenues for 1998 were less than $1 million, and the company lost $11 million for the year. But, like many other Internet start-ups, Critical Path's valuation shot through the roof: the company was originally valued at $2.5 billion. While the stock price was a roller coaster ride over the next few months, David took it all in stride: "I actually think going public is great, at least for our company. It demands that we perform and mature quickly, and that's a great pressure to have. It's a competitive world, and the capital market valuations, not to mention the capital, give us the leverage we need to achieve our greatest goals. It's all up to us, which is a great position to be in!"

He's right. Five years earlier, who would have imagined so much could happen to a small building contractor? But, David and his team have quite a road ahead, as Critical Path now has to show what it'll do with this IPO money. And, if the market isn't impressed, this post-IPO existence could be a long-drawn-out hangover. But David will still be smiling all the way to the bank.

8. YOU LEARN THE HARD LESSON ABOUT STOCK OPTIONS

Stock options were originally intended to promote loyalty, but the ubiquity of this motivating tool may have had the opposite impact. To a deflated employee with worthless stock options, the meaning of IPO may have shifted from I'm Pretty Optimistic to I'm Pissed Off.

Rebel companies like Microsoft and Starbucks have successfully used stock options to win loyalty from their hardworking employees. Because the stock market was on such a consistent rise during the 1990s, it seemed as if stock options allowed a rebel company to print money. The Internet giant Amazon could offer its lowest-level employees 100 stock options and see a $9-per-hour employee make a paper profit of $7,000 in just one day, based upon upward movement in Amazon's stock price. This allowed the company to attract more upwardly mobile young professionals, yet pay them dirt-cheap wages on their expected path to riches.

Some companies, like E-LOAN, posted continually updated stock prices on their internal computer network, so employees could experience the instant gratification of each moment of their work. For a company like E-Loan, whose stock price jumped from $14 to $74 per share soon after it went public in 1999, this constant reminder of the stock option perk produced a lot of smiles around the office. But, when the shares started to drop a few months later, the stock price was removed from the E-Loan intranet, as it was proving to be too much of a distraction.

Stock options can backfire on companies. Potential new hires may be more focused on being amateur stock analysts than on looking for ways to contribute to the enterprise. One of the worries in Silicon Valley is that managers can become complacent in motivating their staff, as they assume the stock options will do it for them. Or, employees believe they're hot stuff because they're worth a couple million dollars on paper. This arrogance can mask incompetence. Or, everyone gets hyperconservative because, instead of supervising new R&D, all the employees are fixated on the company's stock price. This is what Silicon Valley folks call "*vest* in peace," how an innovative company can lose its edge because its employees become too focused on not making mistakes that might send the stock tumbling.

For IPOs, once the stock does its typical initial soar, it might be difficult to attract new superstars since the stock price won't likely double overnight again. Seth Godin believes this means many of the Internet highflyers risk replacing their superstars (who move on once their options have vested) with mediocre new folks who are impressed they've made it in the gates of the company. Royal Farros of iPrint.com says the only solution for this is to get your superstars on board before you go public so that they can take advantage of the potential meteoric rise.

But this still doesn't address how maturing Internet companies attract new superstars and motivate their vested employees.

And what happens if the stock price goes the opposite direction and the riches don't materialize? This happens to thousands of young companies each year that promise their employees a shot at the IPO lottery. If the company's stock options begin to look devalued, a downward spiral can quickly begin, with mercenary employees jumping ship to another company that looks like it's the next rocket to the moon. Dick Wagner, CEO of Strategic Compensation Research Associates suggests, "Underwater options can be a massive motivator to leave." Even IBM discovered this in 1993 when Lou Gerstner took on the role of CEO. The expensive but necessary solution for the computer giant was to create other compensation incentives that helped restore motivation.

With a business model based upon stock options, the company's ability to make acquisitions or borrow money can evaporate overnight with a Wall Street downturn. Many rebel companies have used this model to accelerate their growth (and thus improve their buzz because of the company's voracious appetite). That appetite turns anorexic when the stock price declines. So this remains a fragile business model, one that a rebel company needs to be cautious of exploiting.

Todd Krizelman of theglobe.com takes a sober stance. If someone joined his company purely for a quick play of the stock options, then they weren't the right kind of employee in the first place. The companies that survive this scenario have ample "cultural glue," and meaningful relationships that can be even more valuable than the short-term riches. The recent option frenzy overstates stock options as an employee motivational tool. The fact is that rebel high-tech companies adopted a "work hard, play hard" mentality long before the current era when secretaries are making millions on an IPO. There's no substitute for the sense of mission and achievement that exist in a rebel company that's on the rise.

9. YOU BELIEVE YOU HAVE TO SPEND MONEY TO MAKE MONEY

Many rebel companies shed their initial bootstrapping strategy once they've gotten a cash infusion from investors. Entrepreneur Paul Hawken believes this is the most perilous period in a company's development. Japanese accountants say that "over is the beginning of under." In essence, be careful when the times are good. I've seen post-IPO Internet companies that had previously been thrifty start-ups making some wild-assed calculations of the lifetime value of a customer. They end up spending tons of money to acquire customers, assuming that they've got them for a lifetime, only to find out that the customers only last until the next new-fangled Internet product comes along. Beware of the lifetime value of the customer value model—it's great for instructing your employees about service, but it can be dangerous as a spending model for how you acquire customers.

I learned early on that expenses were a lot easier to control than revenue in the first three years of a new business. There's so much beyond your control when it comes to sales, but your expenses can typically be predicted with 90 percent accuracy. Since cash-flow surprises are the number-one reason for an early corporate death, I've always been expense-driven.

This is also true with respect to the start-up costs of a business. In our case, since we specialize in cosmetic rehabs of hotels, I have a lot of discretion about how much we invest. My tendency was to initially underrenovate (assuming that the basics of the building—plumbing, electrical, roof—were in good shape) since I couldn't accurately predict our revenue on the front end. Once we were open, we'd typically surpass our revenue projections, allowing us to place additional investment into the building (and taking into account our guests' initial comments about the property). This strategy works only if you are offering a good price-value relationship on the front end.

I call this strategy the "Dominating Denominator." Any return-on-investment (ROI) calculation is based on the unpredictable revenue and net income (in the numerator) and the more controllable costs or investment (in the denominator). Changes in the denominator typically have a more meaningful impact on your ROI than changes in the numerator. Consider the following example.

When we acquired the lease on The Maxwell Hotel, we chose to raise only $800,000 from investors to renovate this 153-room property. Since the hotel hadn't truly been renovated in more than a decade (you should have seen the psychedelic seventies carpet in the hallways!), we could have easily spent three times that amount in cosmetic renovation. But we wanted to test the market first. We assumed that the property would generate about $200,000 net each year to our investors. Two hundred thousand dollars divided by $800,000 equals a 25 percent annual ROI. What impact would a beneficial 30 percent change to the numerator or denominator do to ROI? A 30 percent increase in net income would translate to a 32.5 percent ROI ($260,000 divided by $800,000). A 30 percent decrease in the investment cost (with no change in the original net income) means that the $200,000 is now calculated over a $560,000 investment, which equals a 35.7 percent ROI (more than 3 percentage points higher than a change in the numerator).

As it turns out, The Maxwell's annual distributions to the investors have been more than $400,000, which represents a 50 percent annual return (even after making sizable ongoing renovation investments, since it's clear our customers wanted an even more upscale property). If we'd taken a more aggressive stance toward renovating on the front end, it's unlikely we would have been able to match this 50 percent cash-on-cash return. Keeping the initial investment low enhances your ability to create a solid ROI, regardless of the market conditions that affect the numerator.

Unfortunately, successful rebels can lose sight of this bootstrapping principle because they believe they've become a better controller of the numerator. Or, their ego gets in the way and they decide to build the Taj Mahal, which shoots the denominator to hell. In either case, there's great risk that the successful rebel company will become bloated.

How can you sidestep this peril? First, check your ego at the door. Next, keep an eye on your "burn rate," the rate at which a new company goes through money. (Venture capitalists monitor this in their high-tech startups; a magic number for some investors is to make sure the burn rate doesn't exceed $250,000 monthly or that the company has at least eighteen months' worth of capital to withstand the burn rate.) The higher the burn rate, the faster the company needs to succeed or the bigger the payoff that needs to occur.

Once you're a successful, established company, calculate your burn rate and imagine your revenues being suddenly cut by 25 percent because of market conditions. Do you know where to find the bloat in your company? I used this exercise to create an emergency plan for streamlining our management company in the face of a catastrophic drop in our revenues.

Remember that in our virtual economy intangible assets are more valuable than tangible ones, yet the tangible ones can cost more money. Stay liquid and flexible.

10. YOU LOSE YOUR ESSENCE OR EDGE

Rebel companies tend to have distinct personalities and a strategic focus that are defined by the founder or the initial product. As you grow, there's a risk that your company's personality and focus become diluted or bureaucratized. Additionally, some companies become alliance-reliant and outsource virtually everything but their core competency. While this model may be financially justifiable in the short term, it can beg the questions: How fragile is your business model? What is your in-house expertise? Why can't your competitors just use the same outsourced services?

Most companies fall victim to this loss of essence as they grow from the entrepreneurial to a mid-sized company in their industry. Think Reebok, Laura Ashley, Ben & Jerry's. Some companies, like Southwest Airlines, have proven that their corporate culture can grow stronger as their sales escalate, but it requires a vigilant effort.

Ask yourself the following questions and you'll likely circumvent this peril:

- How does your company hire and motivate great people?
- Who is making sure the original successful culture doesn't die?
- Is your company trying to be all things to all people in the marketplace?
- How many layers of management are you using and how are you compensating your employees?

This last question is particularly important for the fast-growing company. Keep track of compensation in your company, as it can also sabotage morale. Peter Drucker says the ratio of pay between top executives and workers can be no higher than 20 to 1 without injury to company morale. Yet a recent *Business Week* survey found that in the typical large American company this differential (including incentive compensation) stood at 209, rather than 20, to 1 (in fact, a recent *New York Times* survey showed that the CEOs of large companies now make more in a single day than the typical American worker does in a year). In young companies, the top executives are typically sacrificing their compensation package in hopes of the pot of gold. Unfortunately, when the pot of gold arrives, it is often not a shared experience. It's no wonder that an us-versus-them attitude might turn from external to internal under these circumstances.

Vision, passion, instinct, agility—these key aptitudes aren't just important in a start-up. They're vital to the business rebel who's quickly growing his business. But let me add two more aptitudes for the more seasoned rebel: humility and compassion. Without those two traits, the rebel's eyes, heart, gut, and feet will be dwarfed by their rapidly expanding head. And that rebel is bound to fall at some point, much to the delight of those he may have trampled on his way to the top.

15. Being a Rebel in a Big Company

The number one managerial objective in most big firms should be creating a revolution.

—Professor John Kotter, Harvard Business School

Post-it Notes may seem innocuous enough, but they have a rebellious history. Art Fry was working in new product development at 3M, a company that has a history of nurturing its rebels. Art sang in his church choir but was frustrated with the fact that his bookmarkers would fall out of the hymnal while he was singing. In conjunction with a coworker, he created the "repositionable note."

While we now recognize the value of this little invention, Art kept hitting brick walls within 3M as company research suggested that there was only a $1 million market for this new product (maybe they were limiting the market to church choir members). Art knew better, so he began giving samples of his invention to people throughout his company to see how they would use the notes. They became an instant hit, but 3M had to use this same give-away strategy when they began marketing Post-its to the public as initially the advertising was a dud since few could fathom the simple, graceful utility of the product.

In the end, Art created one of 3M's most successful products ever, but only because he championed his innovation when it was constantly threatened with extinction.

One in three Americans dreams of starting his or her own business.

One in five is in the process of doing so. Seventy-one percent of successful new businesses sprout from an idea the entrepreneur encountered while working with a previous employer, proving that the entrepreneurial spirit is alive and well inside America's biggest corporations. Too often though, that impulse is stifled by bureaucracy and rules.

My hat is off to the rebel in a big company. You are the true pioneer, trailblazing in a vast wilderness thirsting for inspiration. If you're too often marginalized in your big company, don't forget that meaningful change always tends to come from the margins. The first part of this chapter is for you. If you're new to a big company, how do your quirky ideas and iconoclastic behaviors survive in a conformist environment? Or if you've been there a while, you should realize that middle-aged workers (thirty-five to fifty-four) were 55 percent more likely to be laid off in the nineties than in the seventies. How can you make your rebellious talent a positive and vital force in your company?

The second part of this chapter speaks to the top executive who realizes that a "sustainable advantage" no longer exists in many industries. Deregulation, technology, and globalization demand resourcefulness from America's corporations as never before. What are you doing to tap into the ingenuity and innovation that exist within the fringes of your company? How do you stop the "brain drain" from *Fortune* 500 companies to America's start-up darlings? You had better act soon or before you know it that start-up will be breathing down your neck.

THE HISTORY OF HERETICS

The counterculture of the 1960s affected corporate America more than most people know. The ideals, the importance of inclusion, the value of teams, the suspicion of authority, the ability to self-express—traces of these once-radical ideas permeate twenty-first century corporate America. Would-be rebels working for large corporations who seek inspiration should pick up a copy of Art Kleiner's book *The Age of Heretics: Heroes, Outlaws, and the Forerunners of Corporate Change.* In it you'll find stories about how brave middle managers stood up to the rules and rigidity that defined most pre–"flower-power" companies.

In rebel companies, heretics are heralded. Hewlett-Packard has a decades-old story that has become folklore within the company. In the company's early days, Dave Packard personally canceled Chuck House's project of creating display monitors for oscilloscopes. In total disagreement, Chuck continued the project undercover, and then persuaded his managers to manufacture it. He sold $35 million of this product before David Packard found out, whereupon David bestowed upon him a medal for "extraordinary contempt and defiance beyond the normal call on engineering duty."

David Packard muses, "How does a company distinguish between insubordination and entrepreneurship? The difference lies in intent." As Chuck put it: "I wasn't trying to be defiant. I just wanted a success for HP. It never occurred to me I might lose my job."

This story sums up what John Kilcullen says is a hallmark of rebel companies. When John launched *DOS for Dummies* in 1991, he added an eleventh value to the company's ten core values: "It's better to ask for forgiveness than permission."

Disturb the peace. That's what a rebel does in a big company. And fortunately, times have changed. Just as Susan B. Anthony inspired and freed women and Rosa Parks African-Americans, countless heroic managers have incrementally transformed our very society. Rebels only rarely must play the martyr, for most CEOs now recognize that "change agents" (an overused but apt expression) are a vital ingredient of the twenty-first century company.

GETTING RID OF FEAR

The common denominator in most big companies is fear. Workers and managers share the fear of being humiliated or fired for telling the truth or breaking the rules. Fear is a crippling emotion that feeds on our imagination. In fact, it is simply impossible to be creative and fearful at the same time. If you are to be a rebel in your company, you have to attack your fears head-on.

I worked for a summer with the venerable investment bank Morgan Stanley in New York City. I felt completely unprepared for the experience: I was twenty-two in a job suited for someone a few years older, I had never lived in New York, and I didn't consider myself a "finance jock." I was mute the first week. My first Saturday, I made a list of the fears that were making me feel like an outcast. These included the fact that I owned only three relatively tacky suits, so I felt costume-challenged; that I had far less experience with computer financial modeling than the typical M.B.A.; that I hated smoking cigars; and that I was just coming to terms with the fact I was gay.

While I expected I would spend a full day compiling the list, it turned out I could only come up with nine specific fears. So I tackled each one in turn, asking myself, "Will I get fired over this?"

When I cast an objective eye on each, I realized that I was wallowing in unfounded fear. In fact, Morgan Stanley spent the summer wining and dining me in order to try to attract me back after I graduated from business school. As conservative as the place was, they seemed to value my oddball, creative perspective and presence.

Don't let your fears paralyze you. It does no one, including your employer, any good.

DEVELOPING A SPONSOR

In Kathleen Ryan and Daniel Oestreich's book *Driving Fear Out of the Workplace,* the authors conclude that the key method of dispelling fear is to build a trusting relationship with your boss. When employees do not have a manager they can trust, they become frustrated and work performance drops. More than 25 percent of the employees they interviewed hesitated to speak up to their direct supervisor for fear of repercussions. The authors estimate that the greatest percentage of intimidating behaviors is committed unconsciously by managers who have no idea how their behavior is being perceived.

Once you've reassured yourself regarding your unfounded fears, take a close look at how you can become an ally of your boss. If you're a rebel, you need the protection of a sponsor. And if you're brimming with ideas, you're likely to make your boss-sponsor look awfully good in the eyes of his or her superiors. Here are a few ways to build such an alliance with your boss (assuming you trust his intentions—if you don't, look for an alternative path for career growth in the company, or another company, under a more sympathetic boss):

- Determine your boss's greatest fears and aspirations. Are there any guiding principles that rule his actions?
- Operate in a manner that makes the fears irrelevant and heightens his aspirations.
- Spend the first three months building trust as a loyalist. This doesn't mean you hold your tongue. It just means you place a priority on being supportive of your boss's objectives.
- Be a source of information. Learn what intrigues your boss and go out and find relevant data that will help him with his cause.
- Start revealing your unique talents in nonconfrontational or nonthreatening ways.
- Be an honest communicator. Vigorously support your boss publicly, but give him private counsel about how his leadership positively or negatively affects his subordinates. Be willing to disagree with him, but practice your arguments. You need to be persuasive.
- Brainstorm with your boss. If you're creative, this is where you'll shine. Since she may not have time for formal brainstorming meetings, take a breakfast or lunch or prework or postwork break with her to introduce your innovations.
- Co-opt your boss. Make her feel like your idea was hers. Let her take the ball and run with it (as long as you're invited along for the ride).
- Identify other work peers who may be threatened by your growing relationship with the boss. Co-opt them too!
- Constantly seek feedback. Don't be a pain in the neck, but at least once a quarter, ask for some specific guidance from your boss about how you're doing.

If you take these steps, you've built an important ally—your boss. If the rest of the company thinks you're the court jester, use these same steps to build credibility throughout your organization. Look for the malcontents in the organization, those mainstream people who recognize that something is wrong with the company but don't know what to do about it. Let them be your voice to some of the more conservative elements of the organization.

★ ★ ★

BUSINESS REBEL HALL OF FAME PROFILE

Charles Schwab (Founder and Co-CEO of Charles Schwab & Co.)

Charles Schwab's company is a big company that acts small. His willingness to bet the company on low-cost Web trading led to the invention of a new kind of brokerage. Big companies aren't expected to move quickly, but Schwab certainly did. In three years' time, they went from $0 to $4 billion worth of securities traded weekly on Schwab's Web site, well over half of the company's total trading volume and roughly equal to its next three biggest online competitors combined.

Just a few years ago, Schwab's research told them that lowering prices to compete on the Web would cost them as much as $125 million annually in forgone revenues. But Charles Schwab's instincts told him that the company would end up on the wrong side of history if it did not take decisive action. So he bet the company and created a secret, nimble team of thirty people to develop a new company strategy that would allow Schwab to compete with the new online brokerages that were opening. When Schwab introduced its new online service in 1996, they reached in two weeks the number of new accounts they'd predicted for the whole first year. In the process, Schwab's Net presence democratized the distribution of investment information.

Chuck Schwab has always been a rebel—from founding his discount brokerage to allowing 40 percent of his company's stock to be owned by his employees (more than 1,000 employees have over $1 million in their accounts from the company's generous stock options). He's proven that becoming big doesn't mean your company has to lose its rebel edge.

HOW BIG COMPANIES CAN ENCOURAGE REBELS

The smart manager in a large corporation will sow the seeds of rebellion among his rank-and-file employees. William Lee, in his book *Mavericks in the Workplace: Harnessing the Genius of American Workers,* suggests that the characteristics that inspired the origins of the United States itself provide guidance for how big corporations can keep their rebel edge:

The Grass Roots. The energy and ideas for the American Revolution came largely from the far-flung populace.

The Threat. What impelled Americans was not an inspired leadership calling them to a new utopia, but the realization that continuing under the status quo would threaten their livelihoods and their personal autonomy.

Sophisticated Communication. Sophisticated and rapid communications were essential to the ability of Americans to act in concert—not only to throw off the status quo, but to devise effective new institutions to replace it.

Does your company use these elements to keep its edge? Here are three examples of how some of the country's biggest companies have used these traditional rebel tools.

Jack Welch at General Electric demonstrates how a big corporation can use its grass roots to keep it on the edge of innovation. He's constantly "pulling the dandelions of bureaucracy" by developing systems that help General Electric reinvent itself. Jack's town meetings, called Work Outs, are an example of this institutionalized internal revolution. These Work Outs involve everyone in the company in smaller meetings with thirty to one hundred people. Everyone has the opportunity to speak. Any subject is fair game. Leaders have to respond to suggestions on the spot. And, if a suggestion needs further review, a decision date goes on the calendar.

Andy Grove's bestseller called *Only the Paranoid Survive* was all about "The Threat." Despite becoming the world's biggest chipmaker under Andy's leadership, Intel constantly improved itself for fear that it would be overtaken by one of its smaller, agile rivals. Grove was able to marshal entrepreneurial energy within his huge company and in so doing armed himself with powerful soldiers to ward off this enemy. Defining the enemy outside the walls of Intel prevented the company from falling into the typical internal bickering that plagues so many *Fortune* 500 companies.

Bill Gates, founder and CEO of Microsoft, espouses the value of sophisticated communication in his book *Business @ the Speed of Thought.* Included in Bill's twelve new rules that define competitive advantage in our digital age are the following:

- Insist that communication flow through e-mail.
- Create a digital feedback loop.
- Use digital systems to route customer complaints immediately.
- Use digital communication to redefine boundaries.

He says: "For a large company to be able to maneuver as well as or better than a smaller competitor is a testament to both the energy of the employees and the use of digital systems. Personal initiative and responsibility are enhanced in an environment that fosters discussion. E-mail, a key component of our digital nervous system, does just that. It helps turn middle managers from information filters into 'doers.' There's no doubt that e-mail flattens the hierarchical structure of an organization. It encourages people to speak up. It encourages managers to listen."

General Electric, Intel, Microsoft. If these big guys can internalize the revolutionary spirit, so can your company.

THINKING LIKE A VENTURE CAPITALIST

The entrepreneurial process is antithetical to the way most big companies operate. It requires room to make mistakes, an incremental process of planning, a willingness to trust intuition, an ability to change direction without full information, and a reverence for the sheer joy of innovation. Most companies are just too slow, too risk-averse, too stuck in the old strategies and products, and too bent on detailed planning to accommodate the entrepreneur. Leaps of faith aren't part of their repertoire.

But times are changing. Many companies now realize that they must review their new ventures like a venture capitalist. They treat their new product teams like a portfolio of investments, investing additional dollars

HOW TO MAKE BIG FEEL SMALL

Bill Gross of idealab! has created a successful model that can help any big company champion its rebels. Idealab! is like the mother ship for a collection of Internet businesses that are in development under one roof. Those that are flightworthy become spin-outs (as opposed to spin-offs, since Bill wants them to stay in the same orbit) and find their own office space and sense of community. He says, "When a company has more than 10 people and fewer than 100, it feels like a tribe—that primordial unit of human organization . . . Within a tribe, people still feel like one clan fighting a common enemy. No one has to be packed off to seminars on team building."

Idealab! tries to limit their seed investing to no more than $250,000 and typically takes no more than a 49 percent equity stake in each spin-out. This way the operation stays in a bootstrapping mode and the initial employees have a sizable equity interest. Compensating employees through equity, as opposed to large salaries, serves as a self-selecting filter. It tends to attract employees whose mind-sets are well suited to high-risk, high-reward endeavors. Idealab! cross-fertilizes its family of companies so they learn from each others' mistakes. Idealab! continues to give the spin-outs administrative assistance in areas like accounting and marketing. The model is working—in its first two years of existence, idealab! generated a 155 percent rate of return.

There's no reason a large company couldn't adopt this same business model. The industrial giant Thermo Electron has been using this approach for decades with its electrical- and chemical-engineering expertise. It may seem counterintuitive, since most big companies tend to spin off their dogs, not their top-performing new units. But since intellectual capital is an information company's most valuable asset, this may be the only way to counteract the upstart start-ups. Bill Gross says, "I believe there's actually a diseconomy of scale when it comes to creativity. It's worse to be bigger." Bottom line: The only way you may be able to keep your creative innovators is to consider spinning out.

in those that show promise and not holding them to the same operating standards as the rest of the company.

Scott Cook, founder and CEO of Intuit, took this approach when he realized that his company had grown to the point that his senior management was becoming a hindrance rather than a facilitator of innovation. He split the company into eight separate, geographically dispersed business units, each about the size of Intuit during its early glory days. Each unit had its own core product, market, and mission statement. The role of headquarters was to foster growth and innovation at each unit while providing certain core services that could better be administered centrally. The net result of this decentralization was a new growth spurt for Intuit.

Richard Branson uses a similar rule of thumb. Once any business gets too big for people to know everyone by their first name, then it is time to break it up. He keeps the different profit centers in different buildings to encourage the informal atmosphere of a start-up. "Usually, there are no more than sixty people in any one building," Branson says.

The irony is that big companies want to think smaller and small companies want to grow into big companies. Herb Kelleher tells his Southwest employees to "think small and act small, and we'll get bigger. Think big, be complacent, be cocky, and we'll get smaller." The big company that thinks small can respond quickly to the market and harness the energy of their people.

The big-company alternative to being a hothouse for little rebel companies is to be a savvy investor. Microsoft is notorious for doing this since it's got such deep pockets. It has invested in Apple, Qwest Communications, Qualcomm, Nextel and many other companies, thus securing its Windows operating system in these high-flying tech companies' future plans. Part of Microsoft's strategy is to get an "early look" at an upstart's development plan, so Microsoft can see where the future of technology is going.

Some companies act as a venture capitalist for their internal superstars. Quantum does this by setting up a small investment fund for their engineering staff. Other companies, like Disney, recognize that these future entrepreneurs will leave the company, so they do their best to stake a claim in the start-up. Top executives of eBay, eToys, Cooking.com, and eStyle have all hatched from Disney in the past couple of years. Michael Eisner finally realized if you can't beat 'em, join 'em. So, when Jake Winebaum, the chairman of Disney's Buena Vista Internet Group, chose to quit his job in favor of his own Internet start-up, Disney signed on as a significant investor in the new venture called eCompanies, which ironically will fund and manage Internet start-ups.

FIVE TIPS FOR INVITING REBEL BEHAVIOR TO THE CORPORATE BOARDROOM

If you're a top exec with a large company, you need to create rule-breaking rules that help foster a little chaos and creativity in your organization. How do you do this? Here are a few steps that will help you increase your company's rebel quotient:

CREATE A REBEL CLUBHOUSE

If you want a new venture or rebel division within your company to flourish, remove them as quickly as possible from your headquarters. In 1999, Hewlett-Packard, which has a history of embracing mavericks, realized it was behind the competition in developing new Internet businesses. It developed a new entity called the e-services.solutions group that is one of only two groups in HP that cut across all of the company's operating units. To give them the autonomy and thrill of a start-up, new CEO Carly Fiorina made sure that this new group had its own building. Disney used a similar approach when they moved Disney Online and Disney.com a few miles from their headquarters. Other traditional companies—from Wal-Mart to Procter & Gamble—have set up their Internet headquarters in the San Francisco Bay Area because of the fertile high-tech community. This isn't about banishment. It's more like creating a cool clubhouse that has its own identity. Make this clubhouse a prized possession of the company. Take field trips there with headquarters staff. Feel the Pavlovian response as you salivate creativity each time you approach the entrance. It's impossible for the innovators to innovate if they're confined to a "corporate" environment. Let them breathe different air. Let them become a cult.

ESTABLISH A BENCHMARK FOR INNOVATION

Create a tough target for the percentage of revenues stemming from new products and services (those introduced in the previous twenty-four months). Hewlett-Packard and 3M have become innovation wizards by using this as a benchmark. Make sure your Rebel Clubhouse takes the lead and is accountable for making the goal.

INVITE ECLECTIC EXPERTS TO THE CLUBHOUSE FOR BRAINSTORMING

While the Clubhouse is the place where your new products are percolating, you can also use this hothouse as a "creative zone." Once a quarter, invite a dozen creative types from various disciplines to your clubhouse to critique your existing products and services. Dissect a recent product failure or analyze the origins of a new success. The more eclectic the group, the better. Try a symphony conductor, a nuclear physicist, a cultural anthropologist, a kindergarten teacher, an advertising guru, and a philosopher. Combine this group with your own creative team and watch the sparks fly. Why should you limit innovation to new ventures?

CREATE HYBRID VIGOR

Paul Hawken points out in *Growing a Business* that when certain strains of plants or animals are crossbred, a superior species is created. Use your Rebel Clubhouse as an "incubator for entrepreneurs." Develop a program that cycles some of your headquarters and other divisional employees through this rebel division so that they can get a taste of the innovation and risk-taking happening within your organization. Hopefully they'll take that experience back to their home workplace and create new habits that help inspire entrepreneurial attitudes. There's no doubt that this kind of "big picture" training helps keep your employees inspired and educated.

CELEBRATE YOUR REBELS

Lynda Clemmons is a twenty-nine-year-old vice president with energy-focused Enron Corporation's capital and resources division. She's also a liberal arts graduate (among technically minded middle-aged men) and a rebel who loves her motorcycle. Most important, she was given free rein to develop a $1 billion business that lets companies buy hedges against weather extremes. Fortunately, the $31-billion-per-year Enron Corporation is run by Jeffrey Skilling, who realizes that he needs to unleash his rebels if Enron is going to compete in this new era of energy deregulation. Lynda's story is a classic success story for a rebel in a big company. At twenty-four, she started in the mergers and acquisitions department of Enron because of her prior experience in M&A. Her mentor was Cliff Baxter, the head of M&A, who went on to become CEO of the Capital and Trade Resources group. She sat in with Cliff on high-level negotiations with companies Enron was acquiring. Soon she became the expert on sulfur dioxides and the emissions credit market. That's where she spotted an opportunity that would allow utilities to buy insurance against the weather. Enron let her start up a one-woman enterprise within the company, and next thing you know, Lynda had a successful venture on her hands. Because of this experience, Enron allows Lynda to be a mentor for other women in the organization and has her speaking internally about how to spot new business opportunities. She's become the lightning rod for many of Enron's rebel entrepreneurs, and she's now a featured orientation speaker during the first week of employment of all new hires at Enron's headquarters.

Each month, figure out a way to publicly honor your innovators and rule-breakers. Take surveys within the company to identify your chief rebels and rabble-rousers. You want to keep these people in your organization even though there are entrepreneurial enticements outside your doors. Consider compensating these rebels in an outrageously lucrative fashion (like an NBA team does for their franchise star) that doesn't conform to your standard executive compensation policies. This may be the only way big companies can compete with their pesky smaller rivals.

16. Rebel Without a Pause

Is your life what is happening while you are making other plans?

—John Lennon

If I had known what it would be like to have it all, I would have settled for less.

—Lily Tomlin

Is your most meaningful relationship that with the Starbucks' counterperson around the corner from work? Do you find yourself sneaking a peek at your work e-mail after putting the kids to bed? Do you answer your cell phone while getting acupuncture? Today's leader recognizes that a balanced life is the best antidote to burnout.

Thoreau wrote, "The cost of something is measured by how much life you have to give for it." In today's world, the cost of work has skyrocketed. We're increasingly intoxicated with the idea of having it all. We seem to be running faster than our legs can take us. The Japanese even have a word for it—*karoshi*—meaning "death by overwork." Fatal exhaustion. For some, death might sound like a welcome break. Dr. Sherman James calls the American version of this sickness "John Henryism," for the American folk hero who outtunneled a steam-powered drill using a hammer. John Henry fell dead upon winning.

This chapter is about creating healthy escapes from your work. While

I'll leave the "why" questions to you and your therapist ("Why are you working so hard?"), I *will* focus on the "how" questions ("How can you 'get a life'?"). There's got to be more to life than just increasing its speed. This chapter is intended to break the dangerous, overwhelming cycle of workaholism to help you get back into your natural, cyclical rhythm.

Rebels are particularly vulnerable to burnout since we have a gargantuan appetite for challenges and a high pain threshold. Most of us don't know the difference between being called and being driven.

ARE YOU ON THE PATH TO BURNOUT?

1. Work consistently precludes me from doing certain important things in my life.
2. I feel competent but not confident at work; therefore I need to work harder than others.
3. I don't laugh much at work.
4. When I get up in the morning, the first thing I think about is work.
5. More than three numbers (phone, fax, etc.) appear on my business card.
6. I find myself using the word "should" a lot more than I used to.
7. When asked the question, "How're things going?" I tend to only talk about work.
8. At home, I'm relying more on "sedatives" (sleeping pills, alcohol, TV) to relax.
9. I feel trapped by my work. If I don't get the work done, it will all come crashing down.
10. I have a low-grade cold more often than I used to.
11. I actively use more than one e-mail address.
12. I feel less motivated to exercise or have sex than I used to. My energy seems flat.
13. If I had just a year to live, I'd change my work life drastically.
14. I can't remember my dreams, or when I do, the dreams are frightening or exhausting.
15. I can't wait for the weekend. It's the time I can catch up at work.

16. Do you live a 24/7 life of work (meaning that you feel you have to be available 24 hours a day, 7 days per week)? Have you ever thought of yourself as a slave?

How'd you do? Have you lost yourself in your work? Five years ago, at least half of those statements applied to me. Fortunately, I've made enough changes in my life so that only a couple still resonate. Before we talk about you, let's talk about how your company can promote a healthier lifestyle for its people.

HOW TO AVERT BURNOUT IN YOUR COMPANY

First, let's dispel a myth. No one can continue to be available twenty-four hours a day, seven days per week, without suffering some negative consequences to their health. I once interviewed a potential restaurant general manager who proudly stated he worked an average one hundred hours per week. I asked him if he was serious. He said yes. I asked him if he meant every week. He said yes, except for those when he took a vacation or was sick. Then, I did the math with him: "That translates to more than fourteen hours per day, seven days per week." He looked a little sheepish and sniffled some (he was coming down with a cold). When I asked about his sick days, I found that he took about three to four days per month due to illness. Even having said all of this, he still wore his hundred hours a week like a badge of courage.

It's time we strip that badge from every victim wearing it before they kill themselves. Absenteeism shot up 25 percent from 1997 to 1998 in the United States. Why? Is our medical system falling apart? No, people are either working themselves to sickness or using unscheduled absences as a method of preserving their sanity. What steps can you take starting tomorrow?

1. Ask your people to identify the three things that most lead to burnout or stress at work.

2. Come up with three solutions for each of the three problems. For example, if commuting traffic is a big one, look at creating flextime hours, satellite offices closer to the suburbs, and sponsoring carpools. Different solutions will satisfy different workers.

3. Develop a wellness program at work, from an on-campus gym to on-demand massages to healthy eating seminars.

4. Champion the employees who have a life outside work. Wild Oats Markets pays one hour of charity time for every forty hours of work. Disney has promised a million hours of voluntary service from its employees. Timberland allows its employees to do forty hours of service a year on company pay and time (check out their Web site, www.Timberland.com, as they have a great section on the value of giving service).

5. Figure out discreet ways to promote workaholism counseling to your people. For more information, including meetings in your area, contact: Workaholics Anonymous World Service Organization, P.O. Box 289, Menlo Park, California 94026-0289, or call 510-273-9253.

"MY LIFE IS MY MESSAGE"

Mahatma Gandhi said, "My life is my message." Put those words on your computer screen saver. Rebels are authentic and courageous. Their lives are consistent with their mission and message. They live their lives as if there's one resonant theme that makes their life a wonderful story. What's the theme of your life?

Make a list of Twenty Things You Want to Do (or People You Want to Be) Before You Die. This exercise will help you get off that producing-consuming treadmill to discover what's truly important to you. If you're looking for balance in your life, make sure at least half of the list has nothing to do with your career. What steps are you taking to accomplish these twenty things? I did this exercise four years ago and then lost the piece of paper. Recently, I found the list and was pleased to see that I'd accomplished seven of the twenty things on the list without even consciously pursuing them. I also realized that I'd replace at least five or six of the things if I were to re-create the list today. There's no reason you can't change this list over time.

HOW TO SUCCEED IN BUSINESS WITHOUT REALLY FRYING

"Get a life." I doubt that phrase existed during Thoreau's time. It shouldn't require the threat of death or a reunion for you to get off your butt and rethink your life. It doesn't require trekking off to India to find a guru. What it does take is some attention. While there's no secret formula for creating a blissful life, here are four things you can do that will help balance the frenzy that keeps trying to sweep you away.

1. GETTING BACK TO BASICS

This section could be called "Cutting Out the Clutter," or "Living Beneath Your Means." Whole religions and ancient spiritual practices have their origins in certain of these ideas. During the nineties, a simplicity movement (led by author Elaine St. James) sprouted across America, founded on the idea that happiness is inversely proportional to how full your calendar is.

Getting back to basics means cutting out the pretensions and being who you really are. One method people use to simplify their life is to take up a contemplative practice. No, I don't mean watching TV—that fills your brain with more clutter. I mean prayer, meditation, yoga, tai chi. These ancient practices help bring us into the present rather than keep us dwelling on the past or looking into the future too much—the latter of which seems to be a special problem in our overly cerebral lives. For some of us, sitting still is excruciating, so your contemplative practice might be walking on a beach, running in a forest, or gardening in the yard. The point of all this is to stop "being occupied," a phenomenon that's a tragedy if you're a foreign country but it's a way of life in modern America. Your imagination can't accumulate strength if you're always occupied. Contemplation allows you to connect with deeper inspiration and intuition.

Sometimes visualization can be beneficial. At the risk of losing a few of you, let's try an exercise that will make you feel better (if you don't want to feel better, that's your prerogative!). Close your eyes and imagine going into a beautiful expanse of a room that is partly indoors and partly outdoors. Imagine all of your concerns packaged in two suitcases, one marked "past" and one marked "future." Set both suitcases down on the floor next to the door. Walk inside the room and close the door behind you. Take one deep breath and just savor the moment. Imagine the fragrance of the freshly cut grass and blossoming flowers. Keep following each breath until you have a nice slow rhythm, feeling each muscle of your lungs, chest, neck, and nose. Free your mind of any baggage that wants to enter this beautiful room. Imagine that the gravity in this room lifts suitcases and ushers them out onto the horizon. Keep breathing and sensing for five minutes. You can't help but feel a little freer after this exercise.

Let me tell you about one of my weirder methods of getting back to basics. Once a quarter, I do a three-and-a-half-day fast with two of my best friends, Jon Staub and Jeff Finney, and Jon's father at their ranch in the wine country. We drink organic grape juice, herbal tea, and bottled water for nearly ninety hours. Throw in a couple of hikes, a few naps, a nightly steam bath, and some great "how to change the world" bull sessions, and you've got a pleasant retreat. During certain crazy times, it takes a "fast" to slow me down. By the end of the weekend, I'm feeling like I could continue for days. My skin feels cleaner, my energy purer, and my thoughts are crystal-clear. Compulsion seems to melt away. In its place is an appreciation for the simpler things, like taking fifteen minutes to eat a small cucumber salad (the first meal at the end of the fast). Sometimes you have to give up something to realize what a gift it was in the first place. You also come to appreciate how little you need to survive.

There are other steps you can take to clean up the clutter: Don't read or watch the news. Don't get caught up in purchasing items that wreak of snobbery. Throw away everything in your closet that hasn't been worn in the past year. Don't get caught up in gossip. Don't volunteer for activities that you don't enjoy with people you don't want to see.

2. DEALING WITH STRESS

Americans cited the nineties as twice as stressful as the average twentieth-century decade. The percentage of Americans who believe life is too complicated has also grown in the past decade from 58 percent to 73 percent. While we're gravitating to alternative health therapies from massage to herbal medicine to cope with the stress, the fact remains that stress is the number-one cited work-related illness in most American industries today. Here are some tools you can use:

- Discover your limitations and live realistically within them. Stress often comes when we're stretching what we can realistically accomplish. Rebels have a voracious appetite for challenges. The message in their heads is often "Through sheer willpower, I can conquer anything." Most rebels would do well to learn the serenity prayer: "Grant me the serenity to accept the things I cannot change, the courage to change the things I can, and the wisdom to know the difference."
- Stressed spelled backward is "desserts." When you've experienced a particularly challenging time, reward yourself. Give yourself a little dessert. Search out "deep play" experiences, activities that help you completely lose track of time: the endorphins that kick in on a run, the feeling of rapture when you're singing from your heart, the joy of playing with an infant. Plato said you can discover more about a person in an hour of play than you can in a year of conversation. Create healthy rituals that you don't deviate from, no matter how busy you are.
- Monitor your internal dialogue. Studies have shown there's a clear correlation between managing your thoughts and managing stress. By a two-to-one margin, those who can manage their mind experience low levels of stress relative to those who aren't adept at managing their mind or emotions. Use humor, irony, and a little detached philosophy to lighten up a difficult situation. Imagine how you'd try to coach someone else who needed support, and apply that same strategy to yourself.
- Know your downtime. What are your high-energy and low-energy times of the day? How can you schedule your day appropriately given this knowledge? Be aware of the times of the year that trouble you. I find the dead of dark winter depressing, along with the first two weeks of April. No, it's not just because of property and income taxes. It also represents the end of our slow season in San Francisco, so it's typically when our cash flow is at its lowest. Knowing this means that I alter our purchases accordingly and am mentally prepared for what comes. I manage my expectations.

- Find "magic in traffic." Whether I'm stuck on the freeway, in a supermarket checkout line, or waiting for a teller at the bank, the stress-producing situation can be turned around into a meditative dessert. Focus on your breath, remembering that breathing is a window to your emotions. If you're standing, bend your knees slightly and act as if you're sitting on air. Take a little one-minute vacation and imagine your favorite paradise. A beach in Hawaii. A country village in England. A lake in Chile.

3. TAKING A SABBATICAL

Life isn't as linear as it used to be. Our parents' idea of a vacation was a couple of weeks during the summer so that they could take the kids on a family station-wagon trip with their AAA guide in hand. That was also an era when Dad got home from work at six and Mom had dinner ready for the family by six-thirty. Each year that family lived that same pattern. We don't live in that era anymore. Both parents, assuming they're together, now often work. We work more hours. We commute more hours. The solution for burnout isn't yesterday's vacation. Instead, it's total immersion, taking a long enough break to truly escape from your stressful work existence.

Sabbaticals allow you to ponder deep questions. One that I find provocative for the success-driven rebel is "Are you being driven by your ego or your soul?" This isn't a question that you can deeply consider when you're in the midst of deadlines and crises. But, it is a very relevant question for anyone who has been on the success treadmill for very long. Success can breed ego and ego's wishes can supersede your soul's desires. How do you know if your soul has taken a backseat to your ego? Ask yourself the following questions while on your sabbatical: (a) How would you feel if you got no credit for the most successful project you're currently working on (a rebel without *applause*)? (b) Would you still pursue your current career if you were only half as successful in this line of work? (c) When was the last time you felt truly enthused and inspired by the work you do on a day-to-day basis?

Joie de Vivre developed a sabbatical program that offers any salaried employee a one-month paid vacation (in addition to their regular paid time off) for every three years of continuous employment. We sweetened this by taking on the North American sales and marketing duties for two small Balinese resorts, which enables us to offer complimentary or reduced-price accommodations to our employees on sabbatical in a paradise on earth. Our base line of business is hospitality, so why not give deserving employees an opportunity to experience the legendary graciousness of the island of Bali?

4. BECOMING SOMEONE'S HERO: THE NEW PHILANTHROPY

Too many rebels choose hobbies or extracurricular activities that are a repeat of their work life. I learned this in my early years as an entrepreneur. Just after my thirtieth birthday, I found myself on the board of directors of five different nonprofit organizations. While I believed strongly in the missions of each of these organizations, I came to realize that my two primary board roles were raising money and sitting in meetings. Sound familiar? I was already doing too much of those two activities in my work life.

Within a few months, I'd resigned from four of the boards and instead put my time into project roles for some of those organizations. For example, I started tutoring inner city kids at the YMCA rather than being involved as a leader in their capital-raising campaign. My job was progressively becoming more managerial; I didn't want my volunteer work to be redundant.

Other successful entrepreneurs want to get their hands dirty. Paul Brainerd, who sold his software company, Aldus, to Adobe, founded a group of 135 members called Social Venture Partners that gives $1 million each year to youth causes in the Seattle area. Individuals or couples who are members donate at least $5,000 a year. Allen Myerson of the *New York Times* calls this "venture philanthropy," as Social Venture's intent is to apply to the charities the same skills that these rebels applied to their companies.

Brainerd says: "It has to do with a generational shift. These are people in their thirties and forties who have more to give than just their money. They have their intellects, their minds. Their idea is more than just charity. It's investing."

The generational shift is apparent. It's not surprising that these younger rebels eschew the old hierarchical charity pomp and circumstance. They're not pouring their time into the Masons, Shriners, or Ki-

★ ★ ★

BUSINESS REBEL HALL OF FAME PROFILE

Ted Turner (Media and Sports Mogul and Philanthropist)

Ted Turner has the worst and the best qualities of the rebel all wrapped up in one good ol' southern boy. He was called "Terrible Ted" at the military school he attended in Tennessee because of his odd habits: practicing actual taxidermy and growing lawn grass in his room. Maybe this was a precursor to his love of the outdoors—he owns a 107,000-acre Montana ranch where he's helped in the rescuing of the endangered bison. He won the America's Cup in 1977 with his yacht *Courageous* and then showed up drunk to collect the prize. He has worn a Confederate officer's uniform, complete with sword, to corporate negotiations. And he even challenged his archenemy, Rupert Murdoch, to a televised boxing match in Las Vegas.

Yet, despite this image as a "loose cannon," Ted has been a visionary, dreaming up CNN, buying libraries of old movies from MGM before cable sent their value soaring, and inventing the superstation TNN.

More recently, after his company's purchase by Time Warner, Ted has focused on giving back. In 1997, he once again proved himself a rebel by announcing a $1 billion gift, up to that time the largest single donation by a private individual in history, to the United Nations (roughly equal to the U.N.'s annual budget). Many felt it was a typical grandstanding measure by Ted, but his intent was clear. He wanted to engage America's aristocracy in a new measurement of success. Even in his philanthropic life, Ted is always trying to change the rules. Whether it's politics or sailing, fly fishing or speaking at the U.N. headquarters in New York, he's a Renaissance man who is passionate in everything he does.

wanis as a charitable affinity group. The leaders of the new economy are more savvy and selfish in their philanthropic goals. They want to make an impact in people's lives. They want to focus only on those issues that interest them. They want to hold the charities accountable for using their "investment" wisely. They don't want to be bothered with the traditional social benefits (the cocktail parties and the plaques) of giving.

MY CURE FOR BURNOUT

Fate acts in funny ways. As I mentioned earlier, I began tutoring YMCA kids as one of my outlets from work. There I met thirteen-year-old Damien Hall, a cocky kid completely uninterested in my social studies and English tutoring. While he didn't reveal much, I understood he was proud of his car-thieving prowess. After a few months, he stopped coming in.

Almost two years later, I got a call from the YMCA's youth director who told me that Damien was living in a group youth home because his parents were homeless. Damien wanted to see me. That was a surprise. When I visited Damien, he was in a very different place. Scared and humbled, he wasn't the arrogant teenager I once knew.

Then, one rainy January afternoon, Damien called our home looking for a place to stay. It seems that "the system" had been moving him from one group youth home to another, and now he had fallen through the cracks in that system. Damien spent the night at our house. And then a few more. A bond began to develop between us. It wasn't until he'd been gone for a week that his counselor even realized he was missing. When she did, she warned me it was against the law for me to continue to house him.

I was faced with a dilemma and an opportunity. Damien had potential. He certainly had street smarts, yet he also seemed to have a conscience. "The system" saw him as just a number—a kid they'd take care of until he was eighteen, when his next station in life would probably be jail. I asked Damien what he wanted. He said he wanted to stay. I told his counselor I would start the process of applying to be his foster parent. Amazingly, she consented, even though it was against the rules.

So here I was with the opportunity any self-respecting, liberal-minded rebel might appreciate: the chance to have a huge impact in one person's life. Forget all the politically correct organizations I'd joined. No more words—it was time for deeds. Here was my opportunity to mentor and influence someone truly in need. Little did I know that I was going to learn more about myself than I'd ever imagined.

I'm not sure I can suggest that having kids will avert burnout. Raising children is a full-time job. But while it did complicate my life, it also enriched it in a multitude of ways. I got in touch with my memories of what it was like being a teenager. I focused less on my own selfish interests and instead worked on the needs of someone else. I was called to task for my inconsistent behavior. I came to appreciate my parents even more. I gained a confidant who, at times, was like the kid brother I was always hoping for. I felt more human.

The path wasn't easy. We dealt with teen pregnancies (yes, I'm a grandpa twice over and recently babysat these little gremlins for four days), drug and alcohol abuse, the accidental death of Damien's mother, and a whole range of emotions that had been bottled up in that young man since his early childhood.

It was difficult. It almost ended my own relationship. It demanded my attention late in the night. It forced me to direct my attention away from Joie de Vivre. But you know, that was a godsend. Raising Damien actually extricated me from the vice grip of entrepreneurial burnout. And it wasn't a moment too soon.

Most important, this experience taught me to use new muscles—less from my head, more from my heart. For the first couple of years, I had thought of him as a project I wanted to complete. Fortunately, I no longer look at Damien from an ROI (return-on-investment) perspective. I treasure the Father's Day cards Damien gives me each year and the deep friendship we've created.

Being the proud papa, I have to report that Damien has blossomed. He's still struggling with his emotions and occasional depression, but he's got an unmatched gift of intuition and sensitivity. He can "read" people incredibly well. Damien is making a remarkable contribution as a nurse's assistant, and at age twenty-three he is already earning more money than I was making at his age.

We live in an exhausted and exhausting culture. Too often, our work and extracurricular activities don't feel meaningful, so we become complacent. Recharge your batteries by fighting for something you believe in. Find *joie de vivre* in who you are and what you do. Rarely do we look back on life and say, "I was too adventurous and fun seeking." More often, we say the opposite. This last little story might help you put it all in perspective.

A businessman was at the pier of a small coastal village when a small boat with one fisherman docked. Inside the small boat were several large yellowfin tuna. The businessman complimented the fisherman on the quality of his fish and asked how long it took to catch them. The fisherman replied that it took only a little while. The businessman then asked why he didn't stay out longer and catch more fish. The fisherman said he had enough to support his family's immediate needs. The businessman then asked, "But what do you do with the rest of your time?"

The fisherman said, "I sleep late, fish a little, play with my children, take a nap with my wife, stroll into the village each evening where I sip wine and play guitar with my friends. I have a full and busy life."

The businessman scoffed, "I have an M.B.A. and I can help you. You should spend more time fishing and with the proceeds, buy a bigger boat. With the proceeds from the bigger boat, you could buy several boats. Eventually, you would have a fleet of fishing boats. Instead of selling your catch to middlemen, you could sell directly to the processor, and, someday you could own your own cannery. You would control the product, processing, and distribution. You would need to leave this small coastal village and move to the big city to be closer to your financial sources.

The fisherman asked, "But, how long will all this take?"

The businessman replied, "Probably fifteen or twenty years."

The fisherman looked puzzled, "But what then?"

The businessman laughed and said, "That's the best part. When the time is right, you would announce an IPO and sell your company stock to the public and become very rich. You would make millions."

The fisherman still looked puzzled, "Millions? Then what?"

The businessman said, "Then you would retire. Move to a small coastal fishing village where you would sleep late, fish a little, play with your grandkids, take naps with your wife, stroll to the village in the evenings where you could sip wine and play your guitar with your friends."

Work Climate Survey (Sample)

The purpose of this survey is for Joie de Vivre to understand whether we are providing a motivating environment in which to work. Joie de Vivre's mission statement of "creating opportunities to celebrate the joy of life" is just as relevant to our employees as it is to our customers, so we're particularly interested in your feedback since you're on the front lines of service. Please fill out the following survey, not based upon how you specifically feel just today, but based upon your general feeling during the past few months.

Your answers will be confidential. Next to each statement, place the appropriate number based upon the following answers:

1 = Agree Strongly
2 = Agree Partially
3 = Neutral
4 = Disagree Partially
5 = Disagree Strongly
NA = Not Applicable

Statement	Answer
1. Relative to other jobs I've had in this industry, I like this job more.	_____
2. Relative to other jobs I've had outside this field, I like this job more.	_____
3. Compared to the first three months on this job, I currently like this job more than I did then.	_____

4. I feel I have good job security. _____
5. I feel my compensation package is fair and reasonable. _____
6. I feel I have opportunities to advance within this company. _____
7. I respect my direct supervisor and feel that he or she is a good role model. _____
8. I respect my general manager and feel that he or she is a good role model. _____
9. I regard my direct supervisor as someone with whom I can talk openly and freely. _____
10. I regard my general manager as someone with whom I can talk openly and freely. _____
11. I feel my direct supervisor treats me fairly relative to other employees. _____
12. I feel my general manager treats me fairly relative to other employees. _____
13. There is a comfortable familylike atmosphere at my job. _____
14. The managers of this property encourage people to listen to each other. _____
15. The managers of this property have provided to me the training and development necessary to do my job properly. _____
16. I have a high level of morale for my work. _____
17. My fellow employees have a high level of morale for their work. _____
18. We regularly have fun events at work or as a part of Joie de Vivre that I can participate in. _____
19. I understand what is expected of me from my supervisor. _____

20. I have a good sense of whether I'm meeting my supervisor's expectations. _____

21. I am satisfied with the performance review process. _____

22. I feel very committed to my job. _____

23. I have high energy for my job, always searching for ways to improve and serve our guests better. _____

24. I rarely feel burned out with my job. _____

25. I feel my work environment is healthy and comfortable. _____

26. I respect my direct supervisor's ethical approach to our business. _____

27. I respect my general manager's ethical approach to our business. _____

28. I believe that my direct supervisor represents Joie de Vivre ideals well. _____

29. I believe that my general manager represents Joie de Vivre ideals well. _____

30. I am recognized for the contributions I make to my property. _____

31. My direct supervisor uses positive reinforcement more than negative reinforcement, encouragement rather than fear, in managing me. _____

32. My general manager uses positive reinforcement more than negative reinforcement, encouragement rather than fear, in managing me. _____

33. I understand Joie de Vivre's role as the management company and the specific ways it helps our hotel serve our guests. _____

34. I take great pride in my work. _____

35. I take great pride in our property (the product and services we offer). ____

36. I believe our work environment fosters creativity and new ways to do things and my input is welcomed. ____

37. I'm excited about the growth of Joie de Vivre and the opportunities this presents for me. ____

38. The management staff at my property keeps me informed of upcoming Joie de Vivre University classes and company events. ____

Please Answer the Following Questions:

39. If I want to talk about how to advance my career, transfer to another property, or opportunities that are available to me within Joie de Vivre, I know whom to speak with. Yes/No (circle one). That person is:

____

____

40. The words that best describe our workplace quality of life, morale, and energy level include:

____

____

____

41. If I were the boss, I would make the following changes to my business, my workplace, or Joie de Vivre:

____

____

42. What classes would you like to see offered in Joie de Vivre University?

____

____

43. What fun employee events would you like to see Joie de Vivre sponsor?

____

____

44. What is the thing that most frustrates you about your job?

____

____

____

Additional Comments:

____

____

____

(NOTE TO READER: As your company gets larger, you may find that you want to use an outside company to create and administer your work climate survey. We now use Market Metrix, which is able to benchmark our scores versus other hospitality companies. They can be reached at 800-239-7515.)

Rebels' Results and Relationships Grid Prescriptions

(See page 151 for grid illustration)

QUADRANT ONE: HIGH RESULTS/HIGH RELATIONSHIPS (BOXES 1–4)

The long-term success of the company is based upon attracting and cultivating managers who score in one of these boxes. The company's goal is to assist all managers so that they can be in this high-scoring quadrant. Managers who score in Quadrant One have a much greater likelihood of career growth with the company.

BOX 1
We can't ask for anything better—the rare marriage of spectacular performance and great relationships. It is likely your business or department is performing at the highest levels, since you've learned how to create a synergistic environment where strong values support strong performance, and vice versa. You are a role model in the company! Help us figure out how we can clone you.

BOX 2
You are a positive-minded cheerleader in the organization to whom people tend to gravitate. People trust and believe in you. They want you and your endeavors to succeed. Keep focused on positive relationships, but put a little more energy into achieving better tangible results. If you're unclear, ask your superior what specific and measurable results they're looking for. Is your superior realistic? If not, have a good heart-to-heart (you're

a master at that kind of thing) to make sure you have parallel expectations with your boss. The same goes with your staff—if you're unclear with your boss, you're likely unclear with your key subordinates. Hold your people accountable, but coach them to success. Do this well and you'll be in Box 1 very soon.

BOX 3
You are driven and can be your own harshest critic. Your results are spectacular, but some of your internal high standards may lead to less than stellar employee relations. How do you express your disappointment with your staff's performance? Is it constructive? Does it lead them to want to be more effective? Do they think you want them to succeed? Are they clear about your expectations? Ask for some guidance (even from your staff and peers) about how you can be a better role model for your company's values. Look for a high-profile company activity that can demonstrate you know how to live your values at work.

BOX 4
You're the strong, silent type. This is the most prevalent kind of manager in Joie de Vivre. You've exhibited solid results and you've built a reputation for being a fair manager. Yet, you're not a superstar in either area. Would you like to change that? Identify the category (results or relationships) that comes most naturally to you and develop an action plan for becoming a superstar within the next three months. Managers who tend to fall into this box can easily be forgotten by their superiors because they're not causing problems and they're not flashy. Make sure you demand a little more attention with some specific suggestions from your supervisor for career growth.

QUADRANT TWO: LOW RESULTS/HIGH RELATIONSHIPS (BOXES 5–8)

The goal is to get you into the first quadrant. The trick is to figure out if your low results are reparable. Do you have the capacity to grow? Have you been given the proper attention and tools? Are you saddled with a position that has defeated prior managers consistently? Is success achievable in this position? Typically, this quadrant is preferable to its inverse, Quadrant Three, since new habits that create positive results are easier to learn than new relationship habits.

BOX 5

You may be inexperienced in this job. Clearly, you have strong skills in building relationships and the kind of attitude that personifies the company's values. But, you aren't succeeding in the tangible areas of your job. Do you need some mentoring? Are you clear on what's expected of you? You can't do it on personality alone. Talk with another manager who's consistently meeting her goals and get some advice. It's easy to move from Box 5 to Box 2 if you develop a game plan for meeting your benchmarks.

BOX 6

This is an unusual box—very low results with great relationship skills. Sometimes it means you've inherited a bad situation, but if you keep up the positive attitude, it may turn around soon. If you've been in this job awhile, maybe you're a slacker. Maybe everyone loves you because you're so easy on them. Or maybe you just have an engaging personality. Or maybe you're just good at faking the company's core values. This won't last, as bad results will become a cancer for the whole team. Is the poor performance fixable? If not, you may need to look for another management position that can highlight your ability to create positive results. Immediately find small successes that provide everyone some confidence that the results will improve—if you don't do this, your great attitude is likely to disappear quickly.

BOX 7

You need a confidence-booster. Your results have been disappointing, but you're doing a successful job articulating the company's values. Keep focusing on building relationships and make sure everyone on your team understands your tangible goals. You may have a blind spot: a lack of technical know-how, a supporting cast that isn't being held accountable, unclear expectations from your supervisor. Your job may be in a fragile place, so use your strengths to start improving your department's performance. Make things measurable. Make it clear to your supervisors that you know what needs to be done.

BOX 8
This is not a good box to be in, as you're likely on your way to Box 14, exhibiting subpar attitude. You have talents in the relationship area—are these being used enough to improve performance? Since you're not likely to stay in this box long, immediately develop an action plan with your superior that focuses on how short-term results can improve.

QUADRANT THREE: HIGH RESULTS/LOW RELATIONSHIPS (BOXES 9–12)

This is the most confounding and challenging quadrant, as you tend to fall into one of three categories: (a) highly authoritarian taskmasters or entrepreneurs who tend to rule through intimidation; (b) effective managers who've become disillusioned with the company for some reason (often due to a dispute with their boss or their lead subordinate); or (c) ineffective managers who are fortunate enough to be running businesses that are doing well (and whose strong performance won't last forever).

BOX 9
Can you be won over? Can you effectively live the values of the company? You know how to run a business or your department, yet you're considered a "black sheep" in the company. That's okay if you just have a unique personality, but if employees are scared to work for you or other managers find you to be difficult, your path of career growth may become stunted because no one is rooting for you. Go back and read your company's mission statement and core values. You may have been too focused on the bottom-line results and have forgotten the softer people issues. You are a performance-driven person, so come up with some relationship or values goals to help you redirect the focus. All you need to do is alter some of your habits.

BOX 10
Which direction are you moving in? Toward Box 4 or Box 13? This will determine whether you'll succeed. You're a stellar performer, but are you irritated with your superior or with the company? What steps can you take to rebuild some relationships that aren't working like they should? Do you have the support of your people? If not, how can you turn that around? Get

some candid feedback from a company peer who knows your strengths and weaknesses.

BOX 11
Like Box 6 at the opposite end of the spectrum, this is not a viable long-term place for any manager. You need help to fix this quickly because your staff or peers may think you take too much credit for your department's success. In the process, you're alienating people. People feel you don't care about them, or when you do, it's a manipulation to get what you want. Beware of a mutiny.

BOX 12
Unlike Box 11, which is more likely to contain a new manager, Box 12 is where some long-term managers find themselves. You may have performed adequately enough to keep your job, but you seem to bear little goodwill toward the company or your staff. It's unusual to find a manager in the hospitality business in this box as it's more appropriate for some industrial/manufacturing companies that are purely bottom line–driven. If you've given up hope, it's time to leave the company. Otherwise, let's infuse a little positive idealism into your work life so you can climb out of this box.

QUADRANT FOUR: LOW RESULTS/LOW RELATIONSHIPS (BOXES 13–16)

A manager who finds himself in this quadrant ought to be looking for a new job, because he's not doing himself or the company much good. It may not be his fault—it's just the reality of the situation.

BOX 13
This is the only salvageable box in this quadrant, but the manager must be making rapid progress toward one of the other three quadrants. The best strategy is to focus on getting the manager to Box 7, since better alignment with company values should help rally her troops and ultimately lead to a performance improvement that puts the manager in Box 4. If you are such a manager, work with your superior on steps you can take to be more of a

positive-minded leader. Magic may strike if you become a role model for the company's core values.

BOX 14

How do you feel you're doing? If you're in this box, it's likely that you're sinking. What's the trend line? Were you doing better before and then things just started falling apart? If there's any good news, it's that you didn't score a 4 for relationships, so put some energy into rebuilding your leadership role. We need to get you to Boxes 7, 8, or 13 immediately or you'll lose your job.

BOX 15

Maybe you're not a good fit for the company. You've scored a 4 on relationships and a 3 on results. You're probably not a lot of fun to be around these days, as your department's substandard performance may be feeding a negative attitude that's pervasive in your workplace. You've likely got a foot out the door, so I'm not sure there's any good advice for you. But, if you want to turn it around, you have to make major changes in your attitude ASAP.

BOX 16

This is an extremely rare box for anyone to be in. If you're in it, it would be best to create an exit plan for you today because you're not doing yourself or the company any favors sticking around. As you move on to your next job, make sure you understand what didn't work in this job, because you don't want to repeat this experience.

Bibliography

BIOGRAPHIES

Beatty, Jack. *The World According to Peter Drucker.* New York: Free Press, 1998.

Branson, Richard. *Losing My Virginity: How I've Survived, Had Fun, and Made a Fortune Doing Business My Way.* New York: Random House, 1998.

Dearlove, Des, and Stuart Crainer. *Business the Richard Branson Way: 10 Secrets of the World's Greatest Brand-Builder.* New York: AMACOM, 1999.

DeGeorge, Gail. *The Making of a Blockbuster: How Wayne Huizenga Built a Sports and Entertainment Empire from Trash, Grit, and Videotape.* New York: Wiley, 1996.

Drucker, Peter Ferdinand. *The Effective Executive.* New York: HarperBusiness, 1993.

Freiberg, Kevin, and Jackie Freiberg. *Nuts! Southwest Airlines' Crazy Recipe for Business and Personal Success.* Austin, Tex.: Bard Press, 1996.

Iverson, Ken. *Plain Talk: Lessons from a Business Maverick.* New York: Wiley, 1998.

Jackson, Tim. *Richard Branson: Virgin King.* Rocklin, Calif.: Prima Publishing, 1996.

Kelly, Patrick. *Faster Company: Building the World's Nuttiest Turn-on-a-Dime Home-Grown Billion-Dollar Business.* New York: Wiley, 1998.

Monette, Paul. *Becoming a Man: Half a Life Story.* San Francisco: Harper, 1993.

Schultz, Howard. *Pour Your Heart into It: How Starbucks Built a Company One Cup at a Time.* New York: Hyperion, 1997.

Semler, Ricardo. *Maverick: The Success Story Behind the World's Most Unusual Workplace.* New York: Warner, 1993.

Tobias, Andrew. *The Best Little Boy in the World Grows Up.* New York: Random House, 1998.

CAREER AND PERSONAL GROWTH PATH

Anderson, Walter. *The Confidence Course: Seven Steps to Self-Fulfillment.* New York: HarperCollins, 1997.

Bolles, Richard Nelson. *What Color Is Your Parachute?* New York: Ten Speed Press, 1991.

Kotter, P. John. *The New Rules: Eight Business Breakthroughs to Career Success in the 21st Century.* New York: Free Press Paperbacks, 1995.

Miller, Alice. *The Drama of the Gifted Child: The Search for the True Self.* New York: HarperPerennial, 1997.

Ziegler, Mel; Will Rosenzweig; and Patricia Ziegler. *The Republic of Tea: Letters to a Young Zentrepeneur.* New York: Currency/Doubleday, 1992.

CREATIVE, ARTISTIC, AND INSPIRATIONAL

Cameron, Julia. *The Artist's Way: A Spiritual Path to Higher Creativity.* New York: Putnam, 1992.

Goldberg, Natalie, and Judith Guest. *Writing Down the Bones: Freeing the Writer Within.* Boston: Shambhala, 1986.

Shekerjian, Denise, *Uncommon Genius: How Great Ideas Are Born.* New York: Penguin, 1990.

Sinetar, Marsha. *Do What You Love, the Money Will Follow.* New York: Paulist Press, 1987.

Stone, Richard. *The Healing Art of Storytelling.* New York: Hyperion, 1996.

Ueland, Brenda, *If You Want to Write: A Book About Art, Independence, and Spirit.* New York: Greywolf Press, 1997.

Whyte, David. *The Heart Aroused: Poetry and the Preservation of the Soul in Corporate America.* New York: Bantam Doubleday Dell, 1996.

CUSTOMER SERVICE

Albrecht, Karl, and Ron Zemke. *Service America!* New York: Warner, 1985.

Heskett, James L.; Earl W. Sasser, Jr.; and Leonard A. Schlesinger. *The Service Profit Chain: How Leading Companies Link Profit and Growth to Loyalty, Satisfaction, and Value.* New York: Free Press, 1997.

Schneider, Benjamin, and David E. Bowen. *Winning the Service Game.* Boston: Harvard Business School Press, 1995.

EMPOWERMENT

Barrett, Richard. *Liberating the Corporate Soul: Building a Visionary Organization.* New York: Butterworth-Heinemann, 1998.

Bradford, David I., and Allan R. Cohen. *Power Up: Transforming Organizations Through Shared Leadership.* New York: Wiley, 1998.

Byham, C. William, and Jeff Cox. *Zapp! The Lightning of Empowerment.* New York: Development Dimensions International, 1988.

Case, John. *Open-Book Management: The Coming Business Revolution.* New York: HarperBusiness, 1996.

———. *The Open-Book Experience: Lessons from Over 100 Companies Who Successfully Transformed Themselves.* Reading, Mass.: Addison-Wesley, 1998.

James, Geoffrey. *Success Secrets from Silicon Valley: How to Make Your Teams More Effective (No Matter What Business You're In).* New York: Times Business, 1998.

Nelson, Bob. *1001 Ways to Reward Employees.* New York: Workman Publishing Co., 1994.

Ryan, Kathleen, and Daniel Oestreich. K. *Driving Fear Out of the Workplace: Creating the High-Trust, High-Performance Organization* (Jossey-Bass Business and Management Series). New York: Jossey-Bass Publishers, 1998.

Stack, Jack. *The Great Game of Business.* New York: Currency/Doubleday, 1992.

HOW TO START AND GROW A BUSINESS

Belasco, James. A., and Ralph C. Stayer. *Flight of the Buffalo.* New York: Warner, 1993.

Gerber, Michael. *The E Myth Revisited: Why Most Small Businesses Don't Work and What to Do About It.* New York: HarperCollins, 1995.

Godin, Seth. *The Bootstrapper's Bible: How to Start and Build a Business with a Great Idea and (Almost) No Money.* Chicago: Dearborn Financial Publishing, 1998.

Godin, Seth, and Chip Conley. *Business Rules of Thumb.* New York: Warner Books, 1985.

Hawken, Paul. *Growing a Business.* New York: Fireside, 1987.

MANAGEMENT AND LEADERSHIP

Bennis, Warren, and Joan Goldsmith. *Learning to Lead.* Reading, Mass.: Addison-Wesley, 1997.

Bennis, Warren G., and Robert Townsend. *Reinventing Leadership: Strategies to Empower the Organization.* New York: Morrow, 1995.

Boyett, Joseph H., and Jimmie T. Boyett. *The Guru Guide: The Best Ideas of the Top Management Thinkers.* New York: Wiley, 1998.

Collins, James C., and Jerry I. Porras. *Built to Last: Successful Habits of Visionary Companies.* New York: HarperCollins, 1994.

DePree, Max. *Leadership Is an Art.* New York: Dell, 1989.

Fox, Jeffrey J. *How to Be a CEO: The Rules for Rising to the Top of Any Organization.* New York: Hyperion, 1998.

Gardner, John W. *On Leadership.* New York: Free Press, 1990.

Goleman, Daniel. *Working with Emotional Intelligence.* New York: Bantam, 1998.

Heifetz, Ronald A. *Leadership Without Easy Answers.* Cambridge, Mass.: Belknap Press of Harvard University, 1994.

Patler, Louis, *Don't Compete . . . Tilt the Field!* Oxford, U.K.: Capstone Publishing, 1999.

Pfeffer, Jeffrey. *The Human Equation: Building Profits by Putting People First.* Boston: Harvard Business School Press, 1998.

Pitino, Rick, with Bill Reynolds. *Success Is a Choice: Ten Steps to Overachieving in Business and Life.* New York: Broadway Books, 1997.

Senge, Peter. M., et al. *The Dance of Change.* New York: Currency/Doubleday, 1999.

Tichy, Noel. M. *The Leadership Engine: How Winning Companies Build Leaders at Every Level.* New York: HarperBusiness, 1997.

Wind, Jerry Yoram, and Jeremy Main. *Driving Change: The Wharton School's Groundbreaking Research on the Future of Management.* New York: Free Press, 1998.

MARKETING AND TRENDS

Brooks, David. *BOBOS in Paradise: The New Upper Class and How They Got There.* New York: Simon & Schuster, 2000.

Godin, Seth. *Permission Marketing.* New York: Simon & Schuster, 1999.

Meehan, Mary; Larry Samuel; and Vickie Abrahamson. *The Future Ain't What It Used to Be: The 40 Cultural Trends Transforming Your Job, Your Life, Your World.* New York: Riverhead Books, 1997.

Naisbitt, John, and Patricia Aburdene. *Megatrends 2000.* New York: Morrow, 1990.

Pine, Joseph B. *The Experience Economy: Work Is Theatre & Every Business a Stage.* Boston: Harvard Business School Press, 1999.

Popcorn, Faith. *The Popcorn Report.* New York: HarperCollins, 1992.

Ritchie, Karen. *Marketing to Generation X.* New York: Lexington Books, 1995.

Smith, J. Walker, and Ann Clurman. *Rocking the Ages.* New York: HarperBusiness, 1997.

Underhill, Paco. *Why We Buy: The Science of Shopping.* New York: Simon & Schuster, 1999.

Wolf, Michael J. *The Entertainment Economy: How Mega-Media Forces Are Transforming Our Lives.* New York: Times Books, 1999.

NEW ECONOMY

Bridges, William. *Job Shift.* Reading, Mass.: Addison-Wesley, 1994.

Bronson, Po. *Nudist on the Late Shift: And Other True Tales of Silicon Valley.* New York: Random House, 1999.

Brown, Shona L. and Kathleen M. Eisenhardt. *Competing on the Edge: Strategy as Structured Chaos.* Boston: Harvard Business School Press, 1998.

Christensen, Clayton. *The Innovator's Dilemma: When New Technologies Cause Great Companies to Fail.* Boston: Harvard Business School Press, 1997.

Davis, Stan, and Christopher Meyer. *Blur: The Speed of Change in the Connected Economy.* Reading Mass.: Addison-Wesley, 1998.

Fine, Charles. H. *Clock Speed: Winning Industry Control in the Age of Temporary Advantage.* Reading, Mass.: Perseus Books, 1998.

Grove, Andrew S. *Only the Paranoid Survive.* New York: Currency/Doubleday, 1996.

Kawasaki, Guy. *Rules for Revolutionaries.* New York: HarperCollins, 1999.

Levine, Rick, et al. *The Cluetrain Manifesto: The End of Business As Usual.* Cambridge, Mass.: Perseus Books, 2000.

Mendelson, Haim, and Johannes Ziegler. *Survival of the Smartest.* New York: Wiley, 1999.

Oliver, W. Richard. *The Shape of Things to Come: Seven Imperatives for Winning in the New World of Business.* New York: McGraw-Hill, 1999.

Peters, Tom. *The Circle of Innovation.* New York: Knopf, 1997.

———. *Thriving on Chaos.* New York: Harper & Row, 1987.

Petzinger, Jr., Thomas. *The New Pioneers: The Men and Women Who Are Transforming the Workplace and Marketplace.* New York: Simon & Schuster, 1999.

Shapiro, Eileen C., *Fad Surfing in the Boardroom.* Reading, Mass.: Addison-Wesley, 1995.

Southwick, Karen. *Silicon Gold Rush: The Next Generation of High-Tech Stars Rewrites the Rules of Business.* New York: Wiley, 1999.

REBEL IN A BIG COMPANY

Kleiner, Art. *The Age of Heretics: Heroes, Outlaws, and the Forerunners of Corporate Change.* New York: Currency/Doubleday, 1996.

Lee, William G. *Mavericks in the Workplace.* New York: Oxford University Press, 1998.

STRESS REDUCTION AND EXTRACURRICULAR ACTIVITIES

Ackerman, Diane, and Peter Sis. *Deep Play.* New York: Random House, 1999.

Buford, Bob. *Half Time: Changing Your Game Plan from Success to Significance.* Grand Rapids: Zondervan, 1994.

McDonald, Bob. D, and Don Hutcheson. *Lemming Conspiracy: How to Redirect Your Life from Stress to Balance.* Marietta, Ga.: Longstreet Press, 1997.

McLaughlin, Peter. *Catch Fire: A Seven-Step Program to Ignite Energy, Defuse Stress, and Power Boost Your Career.* New York: Ballatine, 1998.

Pearsall, Paul. *The Pleasure Principle: Discovering a New Way to Health.* New York: Simon & Schuster, 1995.

Weinstein, Matt. *Managing to Have Fun: How Fun at Work Can Motivate Your Employees, Inspire Your Coworkers, Boost Your Bottom Line.* New York: Simon & Schuster, 1997.

YOUNGER EMPLOYEES

Coupland, Douglas. *Generation X: Tales for an Accelerated Culture.* New York: St. Martin's, 1991.

McCall, Morgan W., Jr. *High Flyers: Developing the Next Generation of Leaders.* Boston: Harvard Business School Press, 1998.

Rushkoff, Douglas. *Playing the Future: How Kids' Culture Can Teach Us to Thrive in an Age of Chaos.* New York: HarperCollins, 1996.

Tulgan, Bruce. *Managing Generation X: How to Bring Out the Best.* Santa Monica, Calif.: Merritt Publishing, 1995.

Index

About the Author

Chip Conley founded Joie de Vivre Hospitality in 1987 at the age of twenty-six, buying a rundown ghetto motel and turning it into a landmark rock 'n' roll hotel with an impressive celebrity guest list. Since then, Chip has created nearly two dozen innovative hospitality businesses, which has earned him feature stories in *The Wall Street Journal, The New York Times, USA Today,* and *Time* and *People* magazines. Chip combines his Stanford M.B.A. degree with a rebellious artistic spirit to create some of the country's most unique businesses, from urban boutique hotels to Japanese-style serenity spas to luxury campgrounds. He has been awarded "Entrepreneur of the Year" in the real estate category for the San Francisco Bay Area as well as "Guerrilla Marketer of the Year" by the American travel industry.

For more information on the growing business rebel movement, check out the Web site www.rebelsrule.com.